THE NEW SYNTHESIS
OF PUBLIC ADMINISTRATION FIELDBOOK

JOCELYNE BOURGON

THE NEW SYNTHESIS
OF PUBLIC ADMINISTRATION FIELDBOOK

DANSK PSYKOLOGISK FORLAG

Jocelyne Bourgon
THE NEW SYNTHESIS OF PUBLIC ADMINISTRATION FIELDBOOK
© 2017 Jocelyne Bourgon

First published in Denmark 2017 by Dansk Psykologisk Forlag A/S

Publishing editor: Signe Lindskov Hansen. Script editor: Inger Lomholdt Vange.
Design and layout: Mette Schou/Gipsy Graphics. Cover design: Lea Rathnov / Helle Jensen.

The cover of A New Synthesis of Public Administration – Serving in the 21ˢᵗ Century reproduced
on the jacket of this book: Ahmad Akkaoui "The Centennial Flame at Parliament Hill, Ottawa,
Canada"

First Edition 2017
ISBN 978-87-7158-582-7

BoD – Books on Demand / IngramSpark
Printed in Denmark 2017 / Worldwide (Print on Demand)

This book was produced with the assistance of Public Governance International (PGI).

Dansk Psykologisk Forlag A/S
Knabrostræde 3, 1., DK-1210 København K, Denmark
www.dpf.dk

Library and Archives Canada Cataloguing in Publication
Bourgon, Jocelyne, 1950-, author
    The new synthesis of public administration fieldbook / Jocelyne
Bourgon. -- First edition.

Includes bibliographical references and index.
ISBN 978-8-7715-8582-7 (softcover).--ISBN 978-8-7715-8583-4 (PDF)

    1. Public administration--Philosophy. 2. Public administration--
Case studies. I. Dansk psykologisk forlag, issuing body II. Public
Governance International, issuing body III. Title.
JF1351.B65 2017   351.01   C2017-902668-2
                                             C2017-902669-0

Also published by PGI

For Public Servants

TABLE OF CONTENTS

ACKNOWLEDGEMENTS

The New Synthesis of Public Administration Fieldbook is written based on my experience in conducting New Synthesis (NS) workshops and labs across the world. The NS Initiative owes a debt of gratitude to the participants of these events, including senior public servants at all levels of government. Their devotion and tireless work to generate their own "New Synthesis" to address the complex challenges they face informed the NS Initiative over the years. While drawn from the insights of practitioners, the interpretation of their ideas and the findings of this Fieldbook are my own. I take full responsibility for any errors or omissions in capturing their narratives.

It would not have been possible to publish this volume without the contributions of many. The appendix of this Fieldbook is a collection of case studies written on innovative public sector practices. Lena Leong and Civil Service College of Singapore generously granted me permission to republish the Singapore Prison Service case study in this volume. Michel Bilodeau held a pen to recollect his memory on how he initiated the Champlain Complex Care Program in Canada as the Chief Executive Officer of the Children's Hospital of Eastern Ontario. Christian Bason, Jesper Christiansen, Kristian Dahl, Karen Heebøll and Helene Bækmark were kind enough to review the draft of the Elder Care case in Denmark. Similarly, Sirpa Kekkonen offered help in finding resources related to the Helsinki Cleaning Day case study. I am grateful for their contribution.

The NS Initiative has been blessed by incredible individuals whose intelligence and devotion to the work I will never forget. I thank Peter Milley, Patrick Boisvert, Geoffrey Dinsdale and Rachael Calleja for providing leadership for the NS research agenda in their role as Director of Research over the years. Their guidance has elevated the NS thinking process.

I would also like to acknowledge many individuals for their significant contribution to the NS Initiative as team members. Ahmed Akkaoui, Andree Larose, Anju Kandathil, Ashley Pereira, Blair Parson, Brian Johnson,

Farzana Jiwani, Gar Lam, Harold Jalkema, Henri Kuschkowitz, Jacqueline Stesco, Jason Minor, Jennifer Macdowell, Jocelyne Comeau, Kaylan Brunet, Kofi Kobia, Marian Gure, Patrick Wilson, Uri Marantz and Yulia Minaeva have dedicated their time to the NS Initiative in different roles during the past.

I am indebted to Michel Bilodeau for his continuous support for the NS Initiative. The NS Fieldbook was enriched by his judicious comments as well as his intelligence and practitioner's perspective.

Most recently, the current members of the NS Team have been committed to publishing this volume. Rishanthi Pattiarachchi managed and coordinated the project by enlisting the support of many stakeholders. She also assisted with research and editing. Ian Allan was a great help and assisted with writing and editing the text. Rachael Calleja supported with writing and reviewing. Queena Li designed figures in this book and assisted with writing the cases at the end of this book. With a sense of pride, I thank the NS Team who helped me immensely to achieve an ambitious goal within a short period of time.

INTRODUCTION
AN IMPROBABLE JOURNEY

The New Synthesis (NS) Initiative is an unusual project. It started inadvertently. It grew because of the commitment of those who joined in. It was supposed to end several years ago, but instead continues to evolve as people in various countries take hold of its key findings and adapt them to meet their needs. The common denominator among the people involved in the NS adventure is that they share an interest in preparing government for the challenges of serving in the 21st century.

In many ways, the NS Initiative is an *improbable project* that aims to modernise public administration. Research work in public administration is typically conducted by scholars in an academic environment. These research projects are funded by universities and frequently benefit from the support of research granting organisations or policy research institutes. Some organisations such as the Organisation for Economic Co-operation and Development (OECD), the United Nations Secretariat, the World Bank, the European Commission, the Commonwealth Secretariat and regional development banks periodically conduct research to encourage their members to adopt good governance practices. None of these factors apply to the NS Initiative.

AN IMPROBABLE BEGINNING

The NS Initiative was borne out of a shared concern among some senior practitioners over the growing disconnect between the reality of practice and the concepts and principles that have shaped the functioning of the public sector up to now.[1]

Although public administrations come in many different shapes and sizes, they play similar roles. They give form to concepts and values pertaining to the exercise of power in society. They are the instruments used to transform governments' ideas into reality. They embody concepts, principles and values about what it means to govern, the role of government in society and the relationship between the State and citizens. Periodically, profound changes occur that transform the world we live in, the role of government and the relationship between government and citizens. The recent past has been marked by deep changes that were signs of further changes to come.

The people who launched the NS Initiative were at the helm of important public organisations. They had experienced first-hand the difficulties that governments face when looking for solutions to issues of increasing complexity in a hyperconnected and sometimes polarised world. They had seen their respective governments struggle to adapt to a fast-changing landscape and a disorderly global environment prone to volatility and uncertainty. The policies and solutions that had been used successfully in the past were no longer producing the desired results. Inventing solutions to emerging problems required a *different mental map* than the one civil servants had been using for the past 50 years. The NS Initiative was borne out of the need of senior public sector leaders to discuss the changes at play to gain a better understanding of how these changes might transform the role of government in the future. By the end of 2009, there had been sufficient discussion between several senior leaders in a number of countries to determine there was a strong demand to launch exploratory conversations about what it may mean to serve in the 21st century.

AN IMPROBABLE APPROACH

The NS Initiative has been self-organised and self-funded from the start. No one owns the NS Initiative. It is not the project of a particular government or organisation. It is a collective effort that brings together people from various countries, domains of practice and disciplines. Public sector leaders participating in the NS Initiative share their practical knowledge and experience, not as official government representatives but as individuals. The purpose of exploratory conversations is to share and learn from one another, not to defend past actions and decisions or to justify a government's position.

This approach provided participants with much needed freedom to challenge conventional ideas, re-think issues and re-conceive public administration from a broader perspective. The collective effort was largely shaped around the topics of interest to the group. The role of the NS Project Leader and NS Team was to set the table for ambitious exploratory conversations, undertake literature reviews to document what was already known about a topic, and bring together lead thinkers and master practitioners to explore the implications for government and its relationship with citizens. The conversations that took place between 2008 and 2010 were deliberately future-oriented and looked at the world from a public sector perspective. The following question was at the heart of all exploratory conversations: *What do we need to do to ensure that the capacity of government to invent solutions to the problems facing society keeps pace with the increasing complexity of the world we live in?*[2]

Participants shared responsibility for the project from the beginning to the end. They contributed to and benefited from the findings that emerged along the way. Participating organisations led on some aspects of the research and contributed to the work of others in other areas. They produced case studies to learn from and deepen their understanding of approaches used in other countries.

This model of international collaboration engendered a deep sense of commitment among participants. Along the way, the project benefited from the professional and financial support of an academic and a corporate partner. Their contribution enriched the collective effort.

The NS Initiative used an unusual approach to conduct research in a field like public administration. It worked because the participants shared the view that important ongoing changes were altering the way modern societies would be governed in the future. Shared purpose, shared responsibility and skilful network management sustained the collective effort through five international conferences spread over more than two years. By the end of 2010, more than two hundred people had participated in the effort.[3]

One of the factors that contributed to the success of the NS Initiative was a shared commitment to a diversity of perspectives and a blending of new knowledge drawn from multiple academic disciplines as well as practical experiments. This became known as the "blended approach" and it remains a trade mark of the NS Initiative.

The commitment to diversity was reflected in the initial mix of participating countries, the design of events and the efforts made to reach beyond the traditional domains of public administration. During the initial phase, six countries joined the network: Australia, Brazil, Canada, the Netherlands, Singapore and the United Kingdom (UK). No one was under the illusion that this constituted a sufficiently diverse group of countries to adequately reflect the circumstances faced by governments around the world. The group was deliberately kept small; participation was limited to a handful of developed countries, or rapidly developing in the case of Brazil, where the system of government is based on democratic principles, even if a dominant party is in charge. The goal was to bring together a group of countries diverse enough to have a meaningful conversation, but not so diverse as to stall a process based on co-creation and self-organisation. These six countries brought a diversity of perspectives to the conversation. The group included participants from unitary states and federations, from parliamentary government and presidential systems as well as states with highly centralised and decentralised approaches to governing. It brought together people from countries with different cultures, political philosophies and approaches to economic, social and democratic development. There were two countries from the Americas (Canada and Brazil), two from Europe (the UK and the Netherlands), one from South East Asia (Singapore) and one from the Pacific region (Australia).

The lead partner in each participating country created a coalition of interested organisations. For example, the Ministry of the Interior, the lead partner in the Netherlands, enrolled scholars from the University of Rotterdam and Leiden University. The lead partner in Brazil, the National School of Public Administration (ENAP), recruited the Ministry of Finance, the Office of the President, the Getúlio Vargas Foundation and others. This expanded the reach of the NS Initiative and brought new perspectives to the table. The fact that the lead partners in the six countries worked closely together also served to strengthen the NS network.

Each participating country hosted an international roundtable on a selected theme and played a key role in sustaining the efforts of the group. The roundtables were used to integrate research and insights from practice through a process of co-creation enriched by the participation of thought leaders and master practitioners. The participants shared the responsibility of supporting a small secretariat to coordinate the network.

Efforts were made not only to bring diverse perspectives to the table but also to explore issues using ideas from a variety of disciplines not traditionally associated with public administration. Concepts related to complexity theory, networks, resilience, emergence, adaptive systems, collective intelligence, psychology and many others figured prominently in discussions. These concepts challenged participants to think beyond the models and theories that have emanated from the more usual fields of political science, public and constitutional law and public administration that have shaped public administration in the 20th century.

The network performed beyond expectations. Much of the credit for the results achieved during the early phase of the NS Initiative goes to the members of the NS network.

AN IMPROBABLE CONSENSUS

Several factors contributed to the success of the NS Initiative in the early stages. Perhaps the most important one was the group's decision not to strive for consensus. Efforts to reach consensus can lead at times to the adoption of the lowest common denominator and to a negotiated position that, in the end, satisfies no one. Instead, the group committed to exploring issues and to learning from one another. If a consensus happened to emerge, it was acknowledged by the group and used as the basis for ensuing conversations. This approach proved to be immensely useful. It gave everyone the freedom to advance creative ideas and the option to agree or disagree with others' views.

The crafting of an *evolving narrative* at the end of each roundtable was also key to the success of the NS Initiative. As mentioned earlier, five international roundtables were held over a fifteen-month period. Each one lasted two to three days. They required a considerable amount of advance work. The NS Project Leader provided a synthesis of key findings at the end of each roundtable. The summary was circulated to participants and used as the starting point for discussion at the following roundtable.

By the third session, *the improbable happened*. What had started as an exploratory conversation about various aspects of the challenges of serving in the 21st century with no commitment to forge a consensus was moving towards a conceptual framework of public administration substantially different from any prevailing at the time. A view emerged that did not reflect industrial age concepts with a heavy reliance on division of labour, clear delineation of responsibility, delegated authority and control mechanisms, while still making use of all these capabilities. A distinctively public sector narrative was giving shape to a conceptual framework that was weaving together the role of government, the contribution of multiple agents in society and the contribution of citizens as public value creators.

Despite the diverse nature of the network – or perhaps because of it – a consensus started to form around the fundamental elements of public administration: serving a public purpose, promoting the collective interest, generating results of increasing value to society, using the authority of the State as a lever to propel society forward, and contributing to civic results by enlisting the contribution of citizens and others. What emerged was not a model but a set of interacting elements where governments, citizens and multiple other actors transform the environment in which they operate through their actions and are themselves transformed by the changes in the environment their actions provoke. The individual elements of the conceptual framework that the network came up with were not particularly new or noteworthy. What was new was the way in which the various elements came together to form a coherent framework that opened up a vast range of choices to government in its search for solutions to real life challenges.

This development came as a welcome surprise but there was no expectation that the emerging conceptual framework would survive more in-depth scrutiny during the remaining two international roundtables. As it turned out, discussions at the fourth and fifth sessions deepened the consensus. By the end of the last session in November 2010, the group was in high spirits. Participants felt that they had made a modest but useful contribution to the study and practice of public administration and generated ideas that they could put to use in their respective environments.

Some members of the group wanted to immediately launch a new phase of collaboration. They were eager to disseminate the results across their governments and present the conceptual framework to schools of public administration. Others felt that a pause was needed. While a great deal of work had been done, most of the information gathered was not in a usable form. Documenting key findings and writing up some of the case studies used along the way would require a significant investment of time and effort. In the end, it was decided that a book chronicling the NS journey up to that point should be written. There was some concern that a long hiatus would bring the NS Initiative to an end. Participants would move on and assume new responsibilities, and reactivating the network would be difficult. The publication of a book was a natural and logical end point. And so, a book entitled *A New Synthesis of Public Administration: Serving in the 21st Century* was published in the fall of 2011, ten months after the last roundtable.

AN IMPROBABLE EVOLUTION

As the leader of the NS Initiative, the first phase of the project left me with a number of lingering questions. What difference would such a conceptual framework make in practice? Would it improve the likelihood of success for governments looking to invent solutions to issues of public concern in areas as vast and varied as law and order, social security, climate change and income inequality? The only way to find out was to test the framework in practice. NS fieldwork would be the litmus test of the NS Initiative.

The first opportunity to test the concepts of the NS Framework came from the Singapore Civil Service College (CSC). The idea was to design a master class for senior practitioners. Fifteen senior leaders from fifteen different ministries enrolled in a programme designed to introduce them to the NS Framework. The programme ran for a full day every other week over a twelve-week period. Participants were required to identify a real challenge they faced and were committed to addressing in their current position. They returned to their challenge or 'live case' after each session to apply the concepts discussed during the master class and explore avenues to achieve the desired public outcome they had identified. Participants learned from one another during exploratory conversations, helped their colleagues improve the likelihood of success of their respective strategies and used the time between sessions to test ideas in their respective work environments.

The NS Master Class was designed to test whether the NS Framework was relevant to ministries with very different missions, and whether practitioners who had no prior exposure to the NS Initiative could use its concepts to craft a strategy with the potential to generate their desired outcome. In many cases, this meant fashioning an approach that would not only garner the support of their colleagues, employees, superiors and minister but be worthy of public support as well. This was a bold move on the part of the Singapore Civil Service College and the Head of the Singapore Civil Service, particularly given the considerable commitment of time and resources the project required.

The results of the master class programme and some of the most powerful live cases discussed during the programme have been published by the Singapore Civil Service College.[4] The NS Framework proved to be robust and relevant to all ministries involved, irrespective of their mission. The participants quickly became masterful at exploring the multiple permutations that the concepts of the NS Framework offers. The work done in the ensuing years revealed that many of the participants were able to bring their ideas to fruition.

One of the most important findings of the NS Master Class was that the NS Framework could be used by practitioners as a tool to reframe public policy issues from a broader perspective. It could be used to position the contribution of public agencies in the broader context of government-wide or system-wide efforts. It helped improve the overall societal impact of government initiatives and bring a citizen-centric perspective to public policy issues.

This insight influenced the design of all subsequent NS Master Classes, workshops and labs that were conducted in various countries between 2012 and 2015. Each event was designed for a specific purpose and with a particular group in mind. NS workshops and labs were attended by ministers and officials alike. They were used in different situations to re-think the role of the centre of government, bring a citizen-centric perspective to government priority setting, lead public sector transformation and develop law enforcement strategies.

Sessions were held in Australia, Canada, Denmark, Finland, Singapore and Malaysia.[5] By the end of 2015, 1,000 practitioners had been exposed to and had used the NS Framework in some way. The results were consistent: NS is *a conceptual framework* that resonates with practitioners, but it is also a *tool* that can be used to expand the range of options open to government and bring coherence to problem solving and decision making. In the hands of practitioners, NS was becoming a *process of discovery* to create solutions to problems of concern to society and produce results of increasing public value.

During the period between 2012 and 2015, the NS Team's time was spent learning from practitioners using NS concepts and documenting their discovery processes. This book is the result of that work. It picks up where *A New Synthesis of Public Administration* left off in the fall of 2011. Chapter 1 explores what is different about serving in the 21st century compared to the previous century. Periodically, changes come about that transform the world we live in, and in the process, transform the role of government. This chapter argues that we live in such a time. Chapter 2 posits that conventional thinking about public administration and current practices are insufficient to guide the actions and decisions of government in a world characterized by deep uncertainty. Chapter 3 introduces the NS Framework and its concepts. The framework brings together the role played by government, multiple agents in society and citizens in a way that opens up a vast range of choices to government in its search for solutions to real life challenges.

The framework offers a dynamic perspective of public administration where governments are able to learn, adapt to changing needs and circumstances, and co-evolve with society. Part II is an introduction to NS *as an applied process of discovery*. It describes the steps that public sector leaders have found most useful for discovering pathways to a better future. Chapter 4, 5, 6 and 7 present what has been learned from the practitioners who have used the NS Framework to lead public sector transformation initiatives. The NS Framework does not provide answers; it opens up new lines of inquiry and integrates findings in ways that generate coherent narratives of change.

A number of consequences flow from a dynamic view of the role of government in society. This includes an adaptive view of the interaction between the public, private and civic spheres of life in society, a deeper appreciation of the importance of civic results and the role of citizens in building governable societies.

The way we think about government or democratic governance influences the actions that will be taken for their improvement, and what results will be achieved. Part III poses difficult yet fundamental questions concerning how to re-conceptualise the responsibilities of the State in the 21st century. Chapter 8 broadens the conversation about public innovation. Chapter 9 reframes the discussion on public sector leadership, and Chapter 10 opens a conversation on the need to re-think, re-frame and re-invent the functioning of modern democratic societies.

In preparing this Fieldbook, the NS Team made particular use of live cases discussed by practitioners in NS labs and workshops. The book includes four case studies from four different countries that exemplify NS concepts in practice. Each of the cases highlights a dynamic process of discovery focussing on public purpose, building on the strength of others and empowering citizens as problem solvers.

Appendix A examines the transformation of Singapore's prisons from correctional facilities to centres contributing to the successful reintegration of ex-offenders. Appendix B provides an example of leveraging to improve care to children with complex diseases in Canada. Appendix C explores how co-creation and co-production were used to respond to challenges facing elder care in Fredericia, Denmark. Appendix D provides an account of the Helsinki Cleaning Day initiative and how self-organisation with support from other actors, including the public sector, can spark new ways of doing things.

The NS Initiative had an unusual start. It generated a consensus that no one expected. It was supposed to end with the release of a book in 2011 but kept going. It took on a new life and brought us to unexpected places.

There is a thirst for conversations to figure out what it takes to peacefully resolve some of the most complex and intricate problems of our time. There is a search for ideas to bring coherence to public administration and provide guidance to government actions. There is a craving for a public sector narrative about the role of government and public institutions in society crafted from a public perspective and reflecting public values.

The NS Initiative is part of an effort to craft such a narrative: one powerful enough to transform the way we think about the role of government in society, coherent enough to guide public sector leaders' actions and decisions, flexible enough to be useful in a diversity of contexts and circumstances, and inventive enough to build the capacity of government to face the challenges of serving in the 21ˢᵗ century.

The New Synthesis is an *improbable initiative* supported by people committed to building the capacity of governments and public institutions to meet the challenges of our times. Governments fit for these times must find ways to reduce frictions and steer their societies peacefully through an unprecedented process of change. This is the main driver behind the NS Initiative, and the most important chapters remain to be written.

PART I

DIFFERENT TIMES, DIFFERENT IDEAS, DIFFERENT WAYS

When writing a book, it is always a genuine question to ask why is this book necessary? A straightforward answer is that the NS Initiative has continued past the initial publication of its findings in 2011. Between 2012 and 2015, fieldwork tested the NS Framework by putting it directly in the hands of practitioners. This book documents the key findings and insights gleaned from practitioners using the NS concepts.

A less straightforward answer concerns the contemporary situation of public servants and public sector leaders. In NS labs and workshops, when asked to discuss the problems or challenges they face, public servants frequently made use of a narrow perspective that rarely goes beyond the boundary of their respective units. This is perhaps not surprising given the legal, administrative and financial constraints on public organisations, and the burdens of compliance and departmental reporting that individual agencies and public servants operate under. Recent reforms have encouraged a drive for efficiency and productivity and generated a narrow and sometimes distorted view of the role of government in society.

This book challenges this perception in two ways. First and foremost, it attempts to reconnect public servants with the fundamental principles of public administration. Public organisations serve a public purpose and promote the collective interests of society. These are the principles that make the public sector uniquely valuable to society.

For the participants in NS workshops, this recognition has been liberating, in part because it provides a unique public service perspective by grounding the actions of public servants within a valuable pursuit. As important, it is liberating because it greatly opens up the range of options available to solve the problems we are facing collectively.

The recognition of a public purpose alone is not sufficient. It is also necessary to uncover how government actions can be used to generate results of increasing value for society. The original NS Framework provided public servants with a way to integrate their practice within a guiding frame of reference. This book provides public servants with a systematic approach to articulate and fulfil their public purpose. Concepts and ideas matter, and there are a number of implications to be drawn from the NS Framework concerning the role of government in contemporary society. These are the focus of Part III of the book.

This first part reflects on the conditions of contemporary public administration that make a New Synthesis of public administration necessary to serve in the 21st century. Chapter 1 explores what is different about serving in the 21st century. It describes some of the changes and their implications in preparing government for the challenge of serving in the post-industrial era. Chapter 2 argues that public administration as a discipline has been unable to guide practitioners' actions and decisions. Chapter 3 introduces the NS Framework and describes how a dynamic concept that binds government, citizens and society together is better adapted to the challenges of serving in a global, interdependent and hyperconnected world.

CHAPTER 1

SERVING IN THE 21ST CENTURY

Every society needs a State apparatus able to ensure peace and order, regulate the exercise of power, serve the needs of the broader community and peacefully resolve conflicts that inevitably emerge in societies.

The State apparatus includes the public institutions used to govern with legitimacy and to steer society through an ongoing process of change to secure a better future for its citizens. There is no well performing society without well performing public institutions.[1] The State is the source of legitimacy of the actions and decisions of government; the governing body of a country.

While there is much debate over the extent to which government should intervene in society, no matter the choices that are made, government must be able to govern and the State must be able to get things done. The sustainability of a governing system depends on its capacity to adapt to changing needs and circumstances. Herein lies one of the most important challenges faced by those in government today.

THE MODERN STATE

The Modern State has taken form over a long period of time and through a number of successive transformations. Modern States are supported by an elaborate state apparatus; they are governed by the rule of law and use a variety of mechanisms, including elections, to encourage public accountability and the responsiveness of government to the collective interests of society.

Francis Fukuyama argues that state apparatus, the rule of law and accountability to citizens may appear at different times and in different orders, but that the sequencing of their occurrence is critical to the efficacy of the State.[2] These elements shape the way a society governs itself. They exist in different combinations in various countries. For instance, China has an elaborate state apparatus but weak rule of law. Russia has elections but a weak capacity to provide public services. Some countries suffer from a deficit in all three dimensions, weak state, weak laws and little public accountability. Typically, liberal democracies rely on all three pillars to govern their societies.

Public institutions matter. Policies may change, governing parties may come and go, but public institutions endure. They conserve established practices that contribute to the continuity of the State and provide a reliable basis for life in society.[3] They codify the rules, norms and principles that govern social behaviours and by which societies organise themselves.[4] By nature, public institutions are conservative and resist change; this is a strength and a source of vulnerability.

The State is an institution like no other. It possesses a monopoly over the legitimate use of force and coercive measures to keep peace and enforce laws over a territory.[5] The Modern State is an administrative state.[6] Public institutions and organisations are expected to treat all citizens in an impartial way. The relationship between citizens and the people who govern is not dependent on family, tribal or personal ties; it is based on their status as citizens. People's loyalty is owed to the institutions rather than the incumbents.[7] This separation ensures that public institutions persist beyond the tenure of individual leaders.[8] The transition from loyalty to a ruler to loyalty to the institution ensures the continuity of the State and is an essential characteristic of a modern society.

The State and the Citizen

A society governed by the rule of law essentially adheres to standards of behaviour that apply to all members of society, even its most powerful actors. This acts as a constraint on the behaviour of those who govern and on the exercise of power in society. While some parts of the world did not make the transition from feudal or tribal regimes to state-run societies, others operate without the benefit of the rule of law and are thus vulnerable to arbitrary decisions.

Public administrations reflect the nature of the relationship between *the State and its citizens*. In authoritative, military or autocratic regimes, order is maintained by the use of force and through coercive measures. In modern liberal societies, order is sustained through a combination of top-down and bottom-up forces. The State and communities share an understanding of how to live as a society. Such an arrangement reflects a special bond between the State and the citizen. Citizens recognise the authority of the State to make and enforce rules, and voluntarily comply with laws as part of their responsibility as members of a broader community. Many factors can cause an erosion of this bond based on trust. When this happens, it becomes increasingly difficult for the State to exercise its authority with legitimacy without relying on the use of force. This may lead to civil unrest and increasing disorder.[9] Ultimately the capacity to maintain order without the use of force is the main difference between a modern liberal state and an autocratic or military regime.

Liberal democracies have integrated a strong state apparatus, the rule of law and democratic principles in various ways. This model of government has contributed to the success of some of the most developed countries in the world and most OECD nations. In these countries, the State must be able to balance a market economy and democratic principles to engender economic prosperity and improve the standard of living for its citizens. This model of government was particularly well adapted to the challenges of countries undergoing a fast process of change due to the rapid industrialisation of their economies. These countries enjoyed an extended period of growth and prosperity as the governing model was fit for the time. But, that was then and this is now, and a very different landscape is emerging.

Fit for the Times?

No institution or governing system is fit for all times. Some will fail to adapt. Some will adapt with great difficulty and will go from crisis to crisis at a great cost to society. Others will be unable to contain the pressures exerted by interest groups or other powerful elites whose voices come to dominate and undermine the capacity of the State to serve the collective interest. However, some will invent new ways to govern that are better aligned with the reality of the 21st century. They will re-define the role of the State; the values, rules and norms that provide a normative basis for the functioning of society; and the relationship between State and citizens from a contemporary perspective.

Liberal democracies have existed for approximately 200 years, a relatively short period of time in historical terms. This is not the only way to govern a society and no one knows if it will be the ultimate way of governing in the future.[10] Countries are experimenting with a broad range of approaches to governing society. In the process, they are changing the rules of engagement and redefining what it means to be a member of a broader community.

Over time, some of these practices will come to dominate and replace those that existed before because they will be better suited to the challenge of governing through a period of profound technological, environmental, socio-economic and political transformation.

The enduring value of a governance system depends on its capacity to adapt to new circumstances, respond to changing needs and co-evolve with society. The countries that benefited the most from a governing model adapted to the industrial age may find it especially difficult to challenge the conventional ideas and practices that served them well in the past.

One of the challenges faced by people in government today is to build public institutions able to steer society through a transformation process that may be as deep and steep as the one experienced during the industrial revolution. This may be their most difficult challenge and their most lasting contribution to the well-being of their country. This begs the question, what is different about serving in this early part of the 21st century?

A CHANGING LANDSCAPE

What is so different about the 21st century? Surely there were challenging times before. Previous generations of public sector leaders served through a great depression, two world wars, and post-war reconstruction. They have put an end to colonialism and expanded civil rights. They built an elaborate social safety net that pulled people out of poverty and contributed to increasing social and economic prosperity. Every generation of public sector leaders is confronted with a unique set of challenges and must chart an original course because we have not been there before. What is different about serving in the 21st century that warrants changing the way we think about the role of government in society or the approaches used for collective problem solving?

The *New Synthesis of Public Administration* published in 2011 argued that serving in a post-industrial era has a number of distinct characteristics compared to prior times.[11] Governments are confronted with issues of increasing complexity. People in government today are the first generation of leaders to serve in an environment where social media transform the issues and context within which solutions must be found. They serve in an environment characterised by a high level of uncertainty, volatility and unpredictability. This diagnosis remains relevant today. However, five years after the release of the *New Synthesis of Public Administration*, a somewhat modified description is needed to set the context for the forthcoming chapters.

Difficult, Complicated, Complex

It is interesting to note that there is a much better appreciation today of the differences between difficult decisions, complicated undertakings and complex issues than was the case in 2011. At that time, it was necessary to argue that these differences were worthy of attention by public sector leaders and that complex issues could not be addressed in the usual way.

It is always *difficult to* make choices and set priorities. Some decisions are heart-wrenching, in particular when making choices between issues equally deserving of attention. Some are difficult because they entail ethical and moral dilemmas. Government will always be called upon to make difficult decisions.

The public sector of modern societies is well equipped to lead, initiate and manage *complicated* undertakings of all kinds. Sending a man to the moon was complicated, but so are the negotiations of multilateral agreements that involve numerous parties with conflicting views, or the management of vast social programmes that must reach millions of people without a glitch. Public organisations have uneven capabilities but, by and large, governments know how to deal with complicated issues and run complicated operations.

Complex issues are different. They are multidimensional and respect no boundaries. They are made of multiple elements interacting with one another and, as a result, they display dynamic characteristics. A change in some parts of the system produces changes in other parts that cannot be predicted with accuracy.[12] For instance, the decision to initiate a military operation to topple a dictator is difficult. A successful military operation is a complicated enterprise requiring careful planning, coordination, and sophisticated intelligence gathering. The operation, once launched, unleashes a complex set of events that no one entirely controls or can predict. The situation can evolve in any number of directions. A new situation will emerge out of the actions, reactions and interactions among multiple agents responding to each other and their changing environments.

Finding solutions to climate change, mitigating the impact of rising income inequalities, and stemming a flow of refugees seeking safety and a better future for their children are complex problems. These problems cannot be solved by gathering more information or by analysing their component parts. A different way of thinking, a holistic approach and openness to different ways of generating solutions is needed. A collaborative effort that cuts across multiple boundaries and involves numerous parties is necessary to generate a viable solution where there was no prior agreement on the mechanisms for problem solving.

In our global and interdependent world, governments are facing an increasing number of complex issues. As the world is more tightly connected, events are accelerating and interacting with each other. This world is prone to volatility and unpredictable cascading effects as manifested in the cases of the real estate crisis, the crisis in the financial sector and the great recession that started in 2008. It is also manifest in the effects of climate change, other human changes to the biosphere, and in the difficulties faced in developing a concerted approach to address these common challenges.

There is every reason to believe that the pace, scale and frequency of shocks and disturbances will continue to increase in the future. This is putting pressure on all countries and may lead to the undoing of some.

Governments are too often left in a reactive position, unable to anticipate and introduce corrective actions in a timely fashion to mitigate the impact for the most vulnerable in society. Serving in a context of high uncertainty requires a different way of thinking and a different approach to problem solving and decision making.

A Hyperconnected World

In the early phase of the NS Initiative, it was argued that the hyperconnectivity of society was a distinguishing feature of contemporary times. The argument was that people in government today are the first generation of leaders to serve in a world where a high degree of connectivity transforms public policy issues and the contexts in which solutions must be found. For instance, social media can be used to encourage mobilisation but also for misinformation. Modern information and communication technologies are compressing the time available for deliberation and for shaping solutions that would respond to the needs of the larger community.

Five years after the publication of *A New Synthesis of Public Administration,* we see more clearly some of the new dimensions of the present wave of technological innovation and their implications for government. Technological innovations have periodically transformed the world we live in and have played a key role in human history. The effects of technological innovations are cumulative and transformative. There is often a long lead time between discovery, early implementation and the moment when their full impact is revealed. Farming and agricultural technologies ensured an abundant food supply that enabled settlements and eventually the development of cities. Population density encouraged innovation and the accumulation of wealth. Military technologies allowed cities and well-endowed communities to expand their dominance over vast territories. For thousands of years, human development followed a progressive trajectory. This pattern changed 200 years ago when the Industrial Revolution "bent the curve of human history".[13]

The Industrial Revolution was the result of several nearly simultaneous innovations across a number of disciplines including mechanical engineering, chemistry and metallurgy. Of central importance was the development of the steam engine, and other technological innovations that gave rise to the mass production of goods, the industrialisation of the economy and the modern way of life. The Industrial Revolution took shape over several decades. It started relatively slowly and gained momentum until reaching a point of inflexion that deeply transformed the economic, social and political world orders.[14] Some countries navigated through this transition successfully, some could not keep up with the pace of change, and others have not yet fully recovered from the consequences of not undergoing an industrial transition in a timely way.

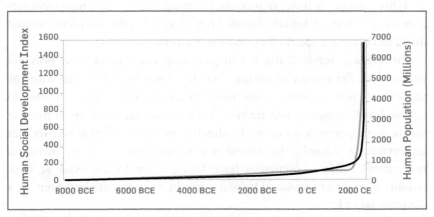

Figure 1.1: What Bent the Curve of Human History?[15]
(Data from Morris (2010), 89-92. Adapted from Brynjolfsson and Mcafee (2014), 4.)

Today, we are witnessing the early signs of another technological revolution. Countries are navigating through a period of transformation that will be as deep and steep as what was experienced during the Industrial Revolution.

The digital revolution is the result of the coming together of multiple related technologies.[16] The engine of change this time around is fuelled by the exponential growth in computing power, storage capacity, networking and interoperability that gather and process massive amounts of data at a previously unknown speed. Technological revolution is once again changing the economic, social and political orders. It is challenging conventional ideas that were taken as immutable truths and that until recently went unchallenged. The digital revolution is generating unparalleled opportunities and unprecedented risks. It is unleashing deep emotions: excitement for some about the unprecedented potential, fear for others about the capacity to absorb the dislocation associated with this transformation, and even anger for those who are losing hope that they may benefit from the new emerging economy in spite of their best efforts.

A Changing Policy Landscape

The digital revolution is making apparent the weaknesses of the policy prescriptions inherited from a prior time. The policy landscape is changing faster than the capacity of government to invent solutions to the emerging challenges. This is illustrated most prominently by the growing disconnect between wealth creation and job creation.

Fifteen people at Instagram created software that 130 million customers have used to share 16 billion photos. After 18 months, the company was sold for $1 billion to Facebook; they became multi-millionaires.[17]

TurboTax automated the job of preparing tax reports. This provides people with the option of having their tax done free of charge with the support of their algorithms. As Tom Goodwin writes, "Uber, the world largest Taxi Company, owns no vehicle. Facebook, the world most popular media owner, creates no content. Alibaba, the most valuable retailer, has no inventory. Airbnb, the largest accommodation provider, owns no real estate".[18] These companies have found ways to monetise services nobody thought of providing before: a seat in a car, a spare bedroom, or a commercial link.

In these examples, workers are not displaced by cheap labour in other countries. In fact, the same phenomenon is occurring in China and other Asian countries. Manufacturing in China has fallen by 25 percent since 1996.[19] Rather than an issue of displaced labour, technology allows companies to produce more output with less labour.

For years, one of the working assumptions of public policy makers was that people could get ahead and achieve a middle-class status by working hard, getting the right skills and playing by the rules. A good education was the key for their children to do better than themselves. Quoting Thomas Friedman, "this is just not true anymore".[20] Income and wealth inequality in many developed countries has soared in recent years, even in some of the most egalitarian countries like Germany, Sweden and Denmark, and even more rapidly since the 2008 recession.[21]

During and following the Industrial Revolution, a conventional idea was that technological advances worked alongside wage increases. Recently, median wages have stopped matching productivity gains. A small fraction of people captures an increasing portion of the benefits of growth.

Many public policies are based on the assumption that income distribution follows a normal curve, where the largest proportion of the population is found in the middle. Moving away from the centre, the number of people in higher and lower income brackets drops rapidly. An "average" person is conceptualised as one in the middle of a normal distribution. If this was still the case, the median income over the last 10 years would have risen with the average income.[22] However, this has not been the case.[23] This assumption, like others, needs to be revisited. There is a need to challenge conventional ideas and re-frame issues from a different perspective to invent solutions adapted to the changing policy landscape of the post-industrial era.

A world where the unimpeded functioning of the economic sphere would be heading towards a "power law distribution" of income and economic opportunities would give rise to a very different set of challenges than previously experienced. This would mean that a small group of people would reap a disproportionate share of the benefits of growth and wealth creation. Most people would end up below the average income, yet Gross Domestic Production (GDP) would continue to rise without an appreciable income increase for the vast majority of people. The tide would not lift all the boats. Rising inequality has a corrosive effect on the governance of a country.[24] Public sector leaders need to figure out what can be done to encourage shared prosperity, and what society is willing to do to help fellow citizens through an unprecedented period of adjustment.

The key point is not so much to debate the merit of various policy prescriptions but to recognise the fact that these problems do not solve themselves. They require deliberate government actions and a robust mix of public policies to ensure that the pace of disruptive technological change does not outpace the absorptive capacity of society.[25]

Competing policy choices will set countries on different trajectories with various degrees of success. The difference in the performance of countries will largely depend on the capacity of government to challenge conventional ideas, re-frame issues from different perspectives as well as their willingness to explore new ways of generating results of value for society as a whole.

A Changing Political Landscape

Citizens are political beings. This has always been the case, but the concept is taking on new meaning in this early part of the 21st century.

The State plays a key role in transforming people into citizens who accept the constraints and responsibilities that stem from living in a society.[26] As citizens, people must reconcile the pursuit of their individual interests with their interests as members of a broader human community. The State plays an essential role in building a governable society by creating shared mechanisms to reconcile differences, make choices and set priorities. Governments have a special responsibility to nurture a civic spirit conducive to collective action and to build the civic capacity for collective problem solving. A governable and well performing society needs people willing and able to share and build a better future together. In this day and age, governments are facing new and unprecedented challenges in this regard.

The capacity to gather large crowds does not guarantee societal or democratic progress. There is ample evidence that vast mobilisations that require much courage and sacrifice can be co-opted by groups pursuing a very different agenda but with some organisational capacity on the ground.

The rise of the angry hashtag activists may be a force for change but it does not necessarily contribute to civic results. It operates as a network where outrage and anger are the currency used to galvanise people.[27] This may be used to advance a cause but it also leads to a hardening of positions that make it more difficult to search for solutions acceptable to the broader community.[28] Moral outrage is rarely a source of inspired solutions, and compromises are more difficult to achieve when people with opposing views are portrayed as the enemy. In a hyperconnected world, politics and the political landscape are changing.

A Disorderly World

In an increasingly disorderly world, government must find new ways to reduce frictions. This world displays a reduced level of consensus over how countries can work together to address issues of global or international concern. This is what Thomas Friedman calls the "world of disorder".[29] Disorder takes on different forms and manifestations.

Every day, there are people fleeing the world of disorder at great risk to their life, only to find that the doors to the "world of order" are closed to them. There are more displaced people today than at any time during World War II.[30] By comparison, the Cold War era was relatively orderly. There were two dominant views competing to extend their influence and ensure their ascent. There were coalitions of countries willing to act in concert and international institutions to bridge divides and set the general rules of engagement. Today, the situation is all at once more difficult, complicated and complex – no one knows how best to govern in an increasingly disorderly world, and the solidarity among modern countries is increasingly fragile.

There are other dimensions to an increasingly disorderly world. In societies that have benefitted from a stable state and rule of law, one can find enclaves of disorder where exclusion has created a fertile ground for radicalisation. Unequal societies are more difficult to govern, and they are spawning anger and unpredictable developments. There are people born in a world of order and economic prosperity who choose a radical path because somehow the modern world, in spite of the wealth and freedoms it offers, does not fulfil their aspirations. This reveals a yearning that modern society has problems satisfying.[31]

* * *

In summary, there are significant differences to serving in the 21st century as compared to any time prior. The factors mentioned so far, and others, are interacting and transforming one another. In a hyperconnected society, people are experiencing the plight of others in direct and visceral ways; this builds pressure on government to "do something" and to do it quickly, even though complex issues require a diversity of actions by a number of actors working in a synergistic way to bring about viable solutions.

The growing gap between the complexity of issues and the capacity of government to invent solutions erodes public confidence in the capacity of governments to defend and promote the collective interest. Some leaders are tapping into emerging public fears and concerns about the future. This is on display in Denmark, France, Hungary, the Philippines, the UK and the United States of America (USA), to name a few. The political landscape is shifting and policy solutions are in a state of flux.

NOT ENTIRELY OF THE PAST AND NOT YET OF THE FUTURE

Governing in the 21st century may not be more difficult in absolute terms than what was faced by previous generations of public sector leaders, but it is different. Serving in government today means serving in a world undergoing deep socio-economic, geo-political, technological and environmental transformations. *This is a different world.*

The sustainability of a governance model depends on its capacity to adapt to changing needs and circumstances. Different times require different ideas than the ones that gave rise to some of the problems we are now facing.[32] Governments all over the world are struggling to adapt to a fast-changing landscape, and the signs of malaise are manifest.

We are witnessing a number of weaknesses in the institutional arrangements that have contributed to the success of modern states. We are witnessing *institutional deficits,* where public institutions are lacking or where their capacity is not commensurate to the scale of the challenges at hand. For instance, the European project is running into difficulties because of a lack of common institutions to support it and its weak link with citizens.[33]

We are witnessing *institutional breakdowns* when public institutions designed for deliberation, consensus building and collective decision making are paralysed and unable to make timely decisions due to entrenched positions. The USA is facing a crisis of authority because the mechanisms created to enforce the will of the majority are weak and the power of interest groups has been institutionalised.

Recent events around the world have been a powerful reminder of the devastating consequences of *a lack of public institutions*. The Arab world is in crisis because hegemonic systems prevented the creation of strong public, private and civic institutions. This leads to a high risk of chaos when such regimes eventually collapse.

Concurrently, and a contributing factor, has been a *deficit of political leadership*. While an institutional breakdown signals that public leaders lack the *means* to achieve desirable public outcomes, a breakdown of political leadership indicates political leaders prioritize other concerns over the collective interest. In part because democratic governance has become entwined with a "permanent campaign" where office holders must keep a constant eye on future electoral chances and place their political party's needs ahead of those of society.[34]

Public institutions matter and, in a period of rapid transformation, they play a role of critical importance. The irony is that they are showing signs of weakness and some governments display a lack of confidence in their ability to steer society through an important period of transformation at the very moment that they are most needed. Many factors described have contributed to this lack of confidence.

Fifteen years of crises have eroded public confidence in the capacity of government to anticipate, prevent and pre-empt events with deleterious consequences for the collective interest. For instance, the 2007 real estate crisis in the USA that led to the collapse of the American financial sector or the 2009 sovereign debt crisis in Greece, Spain and Italy raised concerns about the capacity of government to defend the collective interest, particularly when policy decisions have transferred the risks of private actions to society as a whole.

Thirty years of public sector reforms in many of the most developed countries have focused on the inner workings of government. While some reforms have improved the efficiency of government programmes or the quality of government services, most have given insufficient attention to the importance of the role of the State for a well performing economy and society. Reducing public spending has dominated the public discourse in recent years in a number of countries and overshadowed other considerations including the importance of an abundant supply of public goods. These are the goods that we consume collectively or that benefit society as a whole, including a well-educated population, public health, clean air and the preservation of water resources. Not everything can be monetised or managed as a commodity.

Over time, a government-centric focus to public sector reforms has generated a narrow and distorted view of the role of the State. As a result, we are at risk of losing sight of what makes the public sector unique and its contribution most valuable for society. This is a challenging time but it provides an opportunity to re-think the relationship between the public, private and civic spheres in modern terms. Preparing government for the challenges that lay ahead will require more than a frame of reference inherited from the industrial age and reliance on past practices. *Where will the ideas come from to guide the actions and decisions of public sector leaders facing the challenge of serving in a post-industrial era?*

This is an opportune time to renew the field of public administration as a discipline and a domain of practice. This is the subject of the next chapter.

CHAPTER 2

IS PUBLIC ADMINISTRATION FIT FOR THE TIME?

The previous chapter mentioned some of the distinctive characteristics of the 21st century that transform the role of government. Public sector leaders are facing issues of increasing complexity in a number of realms that affect life in society, such as climate change, population growth, new technologies and new public threats.[1] Public expectations of government are changing. This world displays a high degree of interconnectedness. The actions of governments and other actors interact with each other in ways that are not entirely predictable and that unleash dynamic consequences on a large scale. This is a different world from the one faced by prior generations of public sector leaders and decision-makers.

Governing in conditions of high uncertainty requires a different approach to problem solving and public policy making. There is a need to craft public policies that are "flexible enough to accommodate change and robust enough to withstand multiple scenarios for the future".[2] Ongoing adjustments are needed to ensure that existing policies and programmes respond to fast changing circumstances. This places a premium on the capacity of government to capture new knowledge gained from experience on the ground.

There is a need for frequent course corrections to generate desired societal outcomes. This requires a heightened capacity to detect emerging issues and introduce corrective actions in a timely way. In practice, this means uncovering how to use the levers of the State to unleash a sequence of events that propels society towards a more desirable future. From this perspective, government intervention is not the end of a change process, but part of a long chain of interrelated actions used to influence behaviours and transform society.

Every government intervention is deliberately intended to transform society in some ways. These interventions must fit within a vast ecosystem of interrelated activities in the public, private and civic spheres of our lives. Governments must be able to draw insights from the best available intelligence about a context that is continuously changing, and at the same time take account of emerging risks and opportunities.

People in government today are inventing the public administration of the 21st century and shaping how their countries will be governed in the future. They are devising new ways for putting the levers of the State to productive use and are drawing lessons from the successes and failures of reforms conducted before them.

Countries with public institutions and organisations fit for this time will have a greater capacity to adapt to changing circumstances and prosper even in conditions of high uncertainty. They will have a heightened capacity to influence the course of events in their favour. Public sector leaders are struggling to ensure that their countries will be among those that will successfully navigate through such a transition. The stakes are high and the demand for change has not been this strong in a long time.

But where will the ideas come from to guide the actions and decisions of public sector leaders and decision makers? What principles can they rely on to bring about viable solutions to the complex problems of society and the intractable problems of this time?

PUBLIC ADMINISTRATION

The fundamental purpose of public administration is to govern.[3] Public administration transforms political will into public results or, to put it differently, public administration translates politics into a reality experienced by citizens.[4] The levers of the State are used to transform ideas into a reality considered desirable for society.

Public administration is both a domain of practice and a field of study. A theory of public administration that does not keep up with the time but continues to be held as the gold standard would be a barrier to renewal. A lack of a theoretical frame of reference would be equally damaging, and lead to fragmentation.

The past century has seen much progress in various public policy areas by breaking down issues into their elementary parts. Governing in the 21st century will instead require a capacity *to integrate and synthesise* knowledge and insights from a diversity of sources to understand the behaviour of complex systems and influence them to yield more desirable outcomes for society.

Public administration is an applied domain.[5] Practitioners in other applied domains like engineering, medicine or law rely on their respective academic disciplines to capture new knowledge and integrate discoveries from a diversity of related fields. For instance, new discoveries in material science transform engineering, breakthroughs in biotechnology or genetics open up new avenues in medicine, and novel jurisprudence transforms the practice of law. The systematic integration of new knowledge ensures that practice evolves and that practitioners remain at the leading edge of available knowledge in their respective domains of practice.

In the case of public administration, the situation has been different. Public administration has struggled to generate ideas to guide the task of making government work in a changing world environment. It has had great difficulty guiding the actions and decisions of government in recent times and as a result, the intellectual influence it once had has declined compared to other disciplines.[6] In the recent past, public administration as a discipline did not provide a compelling view of the unique and irreplaceable contribution of the State. It did not put forward a comprehensive set of ideas about what needs to be done for forging governable societies.

The field of public administration must find its voice if it is to play a much needed role in framing conversations about how to govern societies in a post-industrial era. There is a need to bring coherence to new knowledge from a diversity of disciplines such as systems thinking, complexity theory and psychology, as well as practical insights from issues as divisive as the impact of the digital revolution, mass migrations and new security risks.

Renewing the discipline and rethinking the practice will need to take place in tandem to find answers to some of the "big questions" societies are facing. How to govern our hyperconnected global and interdependent societies? Will politics in the 21st century be the instrument that it once was; that is to peacefully resolve conflicting views and interests? Are we witnessing an erosion of some of the conditions necessary for the functioning of "governable" societies including civility, a civic capacity for problem solving and civic will to act collectively?

Renewing the Discipline

Public administrations have existed since time immemorial. An elaborate state apparatus and a meritorious public service existed in China thousands of years ago. The public administration that emerged in the "modern world" is not the only one that warrants attention nor the only one from which important lessons can be drawn.

That said, the public administration that took shape in the North Atlantic axis is the one referred to in this chapter. Public administration as a field of study is relatively young. Its origin can be traced to Western Europe in the late 19th Century and the USA during the early 20th century. The discipline bears many characteristics of the thinking prevailing in these societies at that time. This model of government contributed immensely to the success of countries that underwent an accelerated process of change resulting from the industrialisation of their economies and the democratisation of their societies. Ironically, the countries that benefited most from a model of government adapted to the industrial age may also be the ones that will experience the greatest difficulties to adapt to the challenges of governing in a post-industrial era.

Many have noted the declining influence of public administration in guiding public sector leaders and the increasing influence of other disciplines since the late 1970s.[7] Disciplines such as economics and business administration as well as finance, audit and communication specialists have exercised a significant influence in shaping public sector reform agendas around the world since the early 1970s. These disciplines owe their influence to their ability to articulate and put forward a comprehensive set of ideas about the role and the functioning of government in a timely way.

The influence of economics and business administration in particular grew significantly when some governments faced difficult fiscal and economic conditions in the late 1970s. The UK had to appeal for assistance from the International Monetary Fund in 1976. A tax revolt was raging in California in 1978. Western economies were confronted with stagflation – a combination of low economic growth and high price inflation during most of the 1980s.[8]

Some scholars and thought leaders from economics faculties and businesses were able to bring forward a comprehensive blueprint for change. The general approach encouraged a business perspective of the role of government in society and gave priority attention to expenditure reductions. There was a strong demand for new ideas, but little else was on offer to assist government facing unprecedented conditions.

The point is that a public administration perspective about the changing role of the State and making government work in changing circumstances has been lacking for some time. Christopher Pollitt famously said that public administration suffers from "multiple personality disorder".[9] This may be so. In academic circles, the debate continues about the focus and relevance of the field. Should public administration be supported by a grand design theory, a unified theory or a theoretical framework of public administration? What should be the relationship between public policy and public administration? Does public administration offer something unique and distinctive?

These debates provide little comfort to those who are shouldering the responsibility of guiding their countries through a rapid process of transformation. It does little to build public decision makers' confidence in the capacity of the discipline to guide their actions to uncover solutions to the challenges governments are facing in real time.

From a practitioner's perspective, public administration *lacks focus* and this lack of focus has serious consequences. It damages the reputation and influence of the discipline in government circles, and leads to increasing fragmentation within the field.

Finding Its Voice

During the late 1990s and early 2000s, the study of public administration has become increasingly disaggregated. This makes it even more difficult to integrate knowledge across many subfields of study ranging from entrepreneurship, innovation, value for money, outcomes–based approaches, deliverology, behavioural incentives and networks. As subfields become disjointed, the internal coherence of public administration suffers. This further impoverishes the domain.[10]

One of the most serious consequences of this lack of focus and internal coherence is that, without the benefits of some common principles, it becomes impossible to prepare future public sector leaders and ensure that their practice is grounded in what makes the public sector unique and most valuable to society.[11] Unless the field has a distinctive personality and a unique contribution to make to the task of governing, there are no compelling reasons why public servants could not get their core training from schools of business management, economics departments or any other academic faculties. If there are differences between leading public organisations and leading private ones, then it should be possible to explain what these differences are, and one would expect these singularities to be reflected in the curriculum of schools of public administration. As things stand, there are limited similarities in the curriculum provided by schools of public administration around the world and even in the same country.[12]

And yet, one would expect public servants to master the art and craft of their field and to be knowledgeable about the role of public institutions, the constitution, constitutional conventions as well as democratic and civic principles. Governments benefit from public servants experienced in law making, public problem solving and decision making in a democratic system. Some countries are trying to provide public servants, public sector leaders and elected officials with some support by funding development programmes and operating leadership development centres. This is done with varying degrees of success. Several of these programmes have been the first targets of expenditure reductions when stringent fiscal conditions prevailed.[13]

The field of public administration *must find its voice* and articulate what it stands for and has to offer to the task of governing. Its role is to contribute to the tasks of building States with the authority and the legitimacy to get things done, governments able to govern and public institutions able to co-evolve with society.

RE-THINKING THE PRACTICE

Public sector leaders do not have the luxury of standing still; they have no other option than to move boldly ahead with or without guidance. But is it reasonable to assume that the best way to prepare government and public institutions for the challenges of the 21st century is to leave this ambitious task entirely to practitioners? Is it likely that such an approach will yield timely solutions to the complex problems we are facing as a society?

The reforms introduced since the early 1980s provide a useful perspective on the likelihood of such an outcome. Since then, the world has witnessed a flurry of reforms, new tools and experimentations of all kinds. Reforms do not necessarily transform the governing system or the core functioning of public administrations. In fact, reforms often contribute to preserving conventional approaches by introducing adjustments at the margin. New initiatives add layers of complexity as they accumulate without giving much attention to re-thinking the administrative systems in place. There is no evidence that recent reforms have improved the capacity of government to detect and prevent emerging and preventable crises, that they improved public trust in government or built a greater capacity for collective problem solving.

Some of the problems faced by contemporary practitioners bear resemblance to the challenges faced by the academic field. Public sector leaders are at risk of losing sight of the big picture as they initiate multiple reforms to respond to the pressing calls for change. Without a compass and *clarity of purpose*, reform efforts move in all directions with few durable effects. New initiatives, even when successful, last for a time, but eventually conventional approaches reaffirm themselves.

Public Purpose First

A revolution has taken place in the instruments for public action over the last fifty years. There has been a massive proliferation of the tools available for government action and the instruments used to address public problems. The possible choice of instruments embraces an expanding array of taxes, vouchers, bonds, grants, loan guarantees and contracts. Each instrument has its own set of operating requirements, and brings about different impacts for society.

The choice of instruments is not merely a technical decision. The decision transforms the nature of the good being produced and the risks that will be borne by society. It also transforms the role of government and the relationship between government and citizens. Should a good be available to all in likewise circumstances or to some under certain conditions? Is it a public good that we consume collectively or a private good available to those who can afford it? Is the role of government limited to protecting the most vulnerable in society? What guiding principles could help public sector leaders think their way through the consequences that such choices entail?

When the consideration of the means, tools and techniques supersedes the consideration of the public purpose served and desired societal outcomes, then public organisations become prone to adopting the 'fashion of the day'. Yesterday the focus was on lean techniques, today it may be design thinking and behavioural economics, tomorrow it may be big data or data analytics.

Practitioners are charging ahead without the benefit of a frame of reference to guide their search for solutions or a set of guiding principles to help them bring coherence to an expanding mix of possible choices.

A proliferation of delivery channels also transforms the relationship between government and citizens. Public services are provided through a vast array of "third parties." Commercial banks, private universities, private hospitals, public-private partnerships, and other levels of government deliver publicly funded services and pursue publicly authorised purposes. These measures transform the nature of the good produced from a public good provided with the usual requirements for accountability, transparency and neutrality, to goods that defy conventional concepts of ministerial duty and public accountability. In a very real sense, "the public administration problem has leaped beyond the borders of public agencies".[14]

In most spheres of public policy, public agencies are introducing new initiatives in a dense web of existing measures and in a complex ecosystem of interdependent relationships involving a host of other organisations and partners. These relationships are not self-governing and self-regulating. Without clarity of purpose and an articulation of the desired societal outcomes, it is difficult to ensure that these relationships serve the collective interest.

RE-CLAIMING PUBLIC ADMINISTRATION

Preparing public institutions and governments for the challenges of serving in the 21st century will require re-thinking the practice and renewing the discipline of public administration. It will require a better alignment between theory and practice to extract meaning about the use of an expanding range of tools and instruments, and to reveal the consequences that various choices or combination of choices entail for society.

This will require overcoming a reluctance to theorise about the dynamic interrelations between the public, private and civic spheres to generate desired societal results. Theorising does not provide definitive answers but a coherent approach to testing ideas and discovering what may work in practice in a given set of circumstances.

Every year, a vast amount of literature on public administration is published with limited discernible impact on the decisions of government. Some publications focus on the study and analysis of what has already been done, and while these articles provide a critical perspective on past government activities, few extrapolate about the potential of applying lessons learned beyond the initial context where these initiatives have taken place. These articles typically start with a look at the past and end with a call for more research. Most have limited credibility with practitioners and little influence in shaping the realities of practice.

Other articles are generated by practitioners to explain government initiatives. They frequently present an overly optimistic view of what was accomplished and the results that were achieved. They have limited credibility in academia and a limited influence on the research agenda. On occasion, an idea takes hold and becomes the new "in thing" that governments try to emulate. Without a frame of reference, any technique is potentially as relevant as another. As a result, public administrations are vulnerable to embracing new practices with limited consideration for how these reforms will fit in their governance ecosystem.

Neither approach does much to modernise public administration, bridge the gaps between theory and practice or encourage collaborative efforts between academia and practitioners. Better alignment between theory and practice would improve the credibility and influence of the field.

A stronger synergy could be achieved by focussing on ideas that match the needs of governments struggling to adapt to the challenges of serving in a post-industrial era. For instance, the discipline is still debating how best to reconcile a strong reliance on hierarchy as a tenet of public administration with the inescapable reality of mobilising resources and capabilities across government, across systems and across sectors. The practice has crossed that bridge years ago but the systemic transformation needed to facilitate the co-existence of hierarchical organisations and collaborative networks is still lacking. Hierarchical organisations are needed to build deep expertise and ensure the efficient management of resources. Collaborative arrangements are needed to ensure effectiveness across vast systems and to pool knowledge, know-how and capability across multiple boundaries. The difficulty resides in inventing the ramps and building the capabilities for both to operate synergistically.

Similarly, the concept of a policy-administration dichotomy is increasingly disconnected from the reality of practice. Policy formulation and implementation are iterative phases of a much broader dynamic system aimed at generating ideas that work in practice.[15] In reality, policy decisions do not emerge fully formed, and in many cases there is no consensus on how best to frame an issue. The policy formulation process is akin to an experiment in progress: where the framing and reframing of an issue will go through several iterations; where a solution will require a mix of concurrent actions, some by governments and many more by others; where citizens are likely to play a key role in generating a viable solution; and where the most important ideas will be co-created along the way. This is quite far from the view that public problem solving comes from all-knowing people at the top of vast organisations.

A concept of public administration based on a dichotomous or binary view of public policy decision making and administration is incompatible with a concept of government able to detect early signs of change, co-create solutions and co-evolve with society. A mechanistic view of public administration where there is one right place for everyone and one right way for everything is antithetic to building public institutions fit for the challenges of serving in the 21st century.

A dynamic and synergistic view of public administration is needed to improve the likelihood of uncovering answers to pressing challenges for which there are few comprehensive ideas.

The Return of "Big" Questions

At the end of the day, public administration is about converting political choices into reality to build a better future and improve human conditions.

In many ways, public management has run its course and it is time to re-discover and re-claim public administration. Public management is useful for what it does, but it is primarily concerned with the performance, efficiency and productivity of public organisations. The focus is on managerial issues.

A public administration perspective is needed to confront some of the big questions about how to build the capacity and legitimacy of the State to govern increasingly complex societies in a period of unprecedented changes.[16] The bigger questions entail a need to re-think the role of the State in contemporary terms and reflect on what can be expected of government in a global, uncertain, hyperconnected and interdependent world.

Some big questions have been overshadowed by small ones concerning systems, structures and the functioning of public organisations.[17] Instead, institutional and civic capacity building should be the primary focus of attention in this period of change. This means to build the State capacity to deal with unfamiliar challenges, such as terrorist attacks, financial breakdowns, migration flows, and growth without jobs. These challenges test the capacity of the State to fulfil its core mission to protect citizens and promote the collective interest in all circumstances.[18]

Civic capacity building recognises the central role of citizens in well performing societies. Governable societies depend on governable subjects. A civic capacity for collective problem solving and a civic will to put this capacity to productive use are the main ingredients of governable societies able to adopt and prosper in changing circumstances.

Public management and business administration have little to offer on how to build governable societies.[19] The efforts of the past 30 years at increasing efficiency in public agencies will come to nothing if public institutions do not have the capacity to govern with legitimacy and if societies become less governable.

As Alasdair Roberts points out, "the broad aim of public administration is the construction and renovation of public institutions to fit the needs of the moment".[20] On that basis, there must be a way to renew the discipline and guide the practice. There is no shortage of work to be done if there is a will to bring discipline and practice together.

* * *

Public administrations exist to make the governance of society possible. They reflect concepts, principles, conventions and values about the exercise of power in society. They give meaning to life as members of a broader human community and embody a concept of the relationship between people and government.[21]

Periodically, profound changes emerge in society that transform the role of government and the practice of public administration. We live in such a time; a period characterised by uncertainty, volatility, complexity and hyperconnectivity.[22] As a result, public administrations are under stress and governments are struggling to adapt.

Preparing public institutions for the challenges of serving in the 21st century requires re-thinking the practice and renewing the discipline of public administration. The discipline needs *greater focus*, and the practice needs *clarity of purpose*. This period of rapid transformation provides an opportunity for the discipline to renew itself and play a much needed role in framing the conversation about the task of *making government work.*

There is a need for a public administration discipline with standing, legitimacy, prescriptive and theorising capacity that welcomes the contribution of other disciplines. There is a need for a domain of practice with a distinctive personality aimed at uncovering ways to improve the likelihood of success of government interventions in order to build a better future and improve human conditions.

People in government need and deserve all the help that can be marshalled in support of their efforts as they are facing the task of once again re-thinking and re-calibrating the role of government in society. It is with this in mind that the NS Initiative was launched in 2009.

CHAPTER 3
A NEW SYNTHESIS OF PUBLIC ADMINISTRATION

Public administration has been operating without the benefit of a guiding frame of reference for quite some time, a situation that is particularly precarious in periods of rapid change, as is the case in this early part of the 21st century. Don Kettl succinctly summarized the situation when he wrote, "public administration without a guiding theory is risky; administrative theory without connection to action is meaningless. That dilemma is the foundation of a genuine crisis in public administration".[1]

The NS Initiative was launched with the explicit purpose of "exploring the new frontiers of public administration in the hope of providing practitioners with a narrative that would better equip them to face the challenges of serving in the 21st century".[2] The core idea is that public administration is lacking a *New Synthesis* to coherently integrate past theories, conventions, principles and practices of enduring value with new ones better aligned to today's reality of practice and future challenges.[3]

The early NS work led to proposing a conceptual framework of public administration that is substantially different from conventional thinking. It brings together the role of government, people and society in a co-dependent and dynamic governing system. Between 2012-2015, the NS Framework was used to conduct exploratory conversations with senior public sector leaders in a number of countries. During this period, the NS Framework continued to evolve as new layers of exploration were progressively added. This chapter briefly describes the latest iteration of the NS Framework as it stood at the end of 2015, complementing and expanding on the more detailed presentation published in 2011.

SERVING A PUBLIC PURPOSE

There is more to the role of the State than to make laws and enforce them through coercive measures. There is more to the role of government than to collect taxes, spend and go to war. And there is more to the role of public servants than to manage publicly funded programmes and provide public services. Public institutions, public organisations and public servants serve a public purpose.[4] At the most fundamental level, this is what makes the public sector unique and most valuable for society and what gives meaning to government decisions and actions.

The articulation of the broad public purpose changes over time and takes on different meanings depending on the mission, the desired public outcomes and the context prevailing at the time. At the most macro level, the role of public institutions and government is to steer society towards a better future and improve human conditions in a manner that accounts for the interests of present and future generations.

The public sector is exclusively dedicated to serving the collective interest. This provides *a distinctively public sector perspective* to the role of public institutions, public organisations and public servants.[5] This has a number of implications, including the fact that governments bear the ultimate responsibility for ensuring that the interrelationships between the public, private and civic spheres serve the overall interest of society.

The private sector contributes to advancing society, but does not bear the responsibility for ensuring the overall well-being of society or improving human conditions. The primary responsibility of the private sector lays elsewhere. It plays an essential role in generating growth and contributing to the economic prosperity of society. Companies and enterprises are expected to act legally and responsibly in pursuing growth opportunities and generating profits. Many enterprises take their social responsibilities seriously and act as good corporate citizens. That said, the market may be a source of wealth creation and innovation but it is not self-regulating. Government is responsible for regulating and setting the conditions to ensure that the pursuit of individual interests is not detrimental to the overall interests of society.

In the same vein, civil society plays an essential role in building vibrant, resilient and innovative societies by encouraging solidarity and community actions. Civil society is a source of renewal and social innovation. That said, civil society does not bear the responsibility for generating public goods that benefit society as a whole or that we consume collectively. Nor is it accountable for generating the conditions for the functioning of modern societies. This responsibility rests with government.

The private, public and civic sectors are unique and irreplaceable, each one in its own way. It is this uniqueness that makes them valuable for society. Serving a public purpose and steering society through an ongoing process of transformation that will ultimately serve the overall interest of society is the fundamental role of public institutions, public organisations and government. This role can be fulfilled in many different ways but it *cannot be surrendered nor delegated*. The State must be able to get things done and government must be able to govern in the interest of society as a whole. This is the starting point of the NS Framework.

The NS Initiative has put forward a conceptual framework of public administration that is the result of the contribution of thought leaders and senior practitioners over several years. The NS Framework is not a model that generates an easily replicable set of answers. In fact, it does not provide answers but helps practitioners challenge underlying assumptions and bring coherence to a diversity of ideas, perspectives, actions and possible government interventions.

The NS fieldwork conducted between 2012 and 2015, involved 1,000 practitioners from different countries. In the laboratories and workshops conducted over that period, practitioners used the NS Framework to frame issues and explore possibilities to generate more desirable outcomes for society.[6] The decisions about what to do and how to proceed are contextual and can only be made in practice.

One of the key findings of the fieldwork to date is that in spite of diversity of missions, contexts, cultures, governance systems or circumstances, the *same lines of inquiries* proved relevant to guide practitioners' search for solutions to the issues they were facing.

A BROADER MENTAL MAP

The NS Framework provides a dynamic view of the role of government, standing in sharp contrast to a more conventional view of public administration that encourages a government-centric perspective focussing primarily on public agency results and the inner-workings of government.

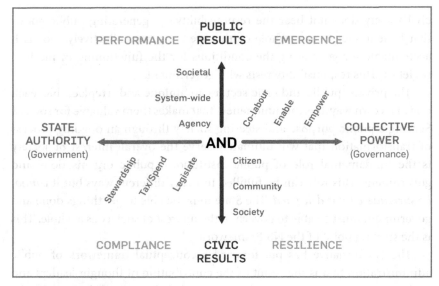

Figure 3.1: The New Synthesis Framework

The NS Framework is depicted in Figure 3.1. It is framed around four vectors that interact dynamically with each other.

Serving a public purpose is realised by generating *public and civic results*. Governments must generate results of value for society but they must also find ways to fulfil their public mission in a manner that builds the capacity of society to solve problems and generate better public results over time. The public sector has a special responsibility for building the *civic capacity* for collective problem solving.

Traditionally, public and civic results were seen as one and the same. In fact, they are quite different and there are significant trade-offs involved in balancing a drive for achieving better public results with a commitment to building the capacity of society to play a greater role in solving problems of public interest. Exploring the tensions and trade-offs between achieving better public results and improving civic results helps reconcile the need to make progress in the short term with the need to build the collective capacity for generating viable solutions over time. It reveals how a different sharing of responsibility between government, citizens and communities may eventually yield better results at a lower overall cost for society.

Public results provide a sense of direction, and *civic results* contribute to collective capacity building. Together, they provide a foundation of trust and build the resilience of society to absorb shocks and disturbances, and invent solutions to emerging challenges.[7]

Public Results

Public results provide a measure of society's overall progress.[8] These results run through a continuum from agency results, toward system-wide outcomes and societal impacts.

Conventional public administration focuses on the performance of individual programmes and services provided by particular public entities. These entities may be a division, branch, agency, department or large ministry, as the case may be. The results generated are monitored along hierarchical chains of delegated authority. This provides a basis for accountability for the use of taxpayers' money and the exercise of delegated authority, but it also encourages an *agency-centric* focus. Public policies and programmes are instruments used to serve a broader public purpose and generate desirable societal results. Agency or programme results are important in so far as they contribute to generating better societal results, but they only tell part of the story.

Framing an issue in societal terms has a direct and sometimes dramatic impact on the approach that will be selected and the solutions that will be found. A focus on societal results makes it possible to explore the interrelationships between agency, government-wide, system-wide and societal results. It helps gain an appreciation of the ripple effects of government actions across vast systems. It reveals the multidimensional nature of complex issues and the need for co-operation across multiple agencies, with other governments, the private sector and civil society. Public organisations must position their contribution in the broader context of government-wide actions to optimise the production of societal results. A focus on agency results leads to sub-optimal results.

A broader mental map helps to reveal the deficiencies of existing practices such as agency-centric performance measurement systems, the lack of accounting systems to encourage collaboration across agencies, the absence of accountability systems for shared responsibility across vast networks and the weaknesses of systems used to monitor the societal impact of government actions. A focus on agency results obscures the results that matter most for society. At the most macro level, societal results include economic prosperity, well-being, improved human conditions and intergenerational fairness. A focus on societal results encourages greater *clarity of purpose* and improves the coherence of government actions.

Civic Results

Civic results provide the foundation of a society where people are able and willing to share and build a better future together. Public administration is not separate from people, communities and society. Civic results bring together the role of government, its relationship with citizens and the contribution of people as public value creators.

Civic results include but are not limited to an active citizenry, resilient communities, civic capacity for problem solving and a civic spirit that infuses every aspect of life in society by encouraging collective action.[9]

Civic capacity endows a society with the energy and capabilities needed to address complex issues and adapt to unforeseen circumstances.[10] Civic results emerge when there is a will to deploy social capital and the capacity for collective problem solving. Civic results play a key role in building well performing and governable societies.[11]

Societies with well performing institutions and people able to collaborate and overcome their differences are better positioned to take risks, innovate and overcome the challenges brought about by an uncertain environment. A civic capacity for collective problem solving explains why similar reforms lead to very different results in different countries and why some countries are able to overcome difficulties and prosper in the face of adversity, while others flounder. It has a significant impact on the ability of government to initiate an ambitious agenda and achieve results that require the active contribution of citizens because it reduces the cost of frictions and improves the likelihood of success of collective efforts.

At the most fundamental level, civic results make societies governable. The relationship that binds the State, citizens and society is at the very heart of public administration.[12] This relationship reflects values and principles that have been forged over time but are also constantly changing. People are not born citizens but become citizens as they accept the constraints and take on the responsibilities that stem from being members of a broader human community.[13] As citizens, people can rise above their differences because some of their most fundamental interests can only be fulfilled as members of a larger community. This is the case for people's quest for a peaceful life and personal safety, their aspiration for a good life or for ensuring the well-being of their children.

One of the most fundamental roles of the State is to transform people into citizens.[14] The State produces citizens in several ways, through education, a common judicial system, economic and social policies as well as common rules and norms.[15] Public institutions contribute to building societies where people live under a common rule to resolve their differences peacefully and voluntarily accept not to take justice into their own hands. The State gives meaning to a concept of citizenship that becomes real in practice. It plays an important role in creating a broader community and mediating differences of views among citizens in increasingly pluralistic societies.

Globalisation, mass migration, new public threats, rising inequalities and many other factors are transforming the relationship between government and citizens. In many countries, there are increasing signs of malaise such as growing cynicism about politics, declining electoral turnout, deterioration of public discourse and the rise of entrenched positions. This signals the need to re-think and re-frame the relationship between citizens and government in contemporary terms.

In the public administration of the 20th century, people were credited with limited ability to solve public problems. They were voters, taxpayers with obligations under the law, users of public services, beneficiaries or obligates as the case may be. Governments were the providers of services to citizens who had no or limited involvement in the development of public policies or the design of public services. This view was a dominant tenet of the public administration of the industrial age. This has a number of perverse consequences. For one, it crowds out the contribution of citizens in solving collective problems.[16] Second, public policies and programmes that make poor use of people's assets reduce the range of options available to government and impose a higher cost than necessary on society.

In reality, citizens are the main public value creators in an increasing number of domains, ranging from public health or literacy to environmental protection. Communities are the drivers of viable solutions to encourage public safety, reduce energy consumption or initiate corrective actions to mitigate the impact of climatic changes. No country, even with deep pockets, can achieve these results through legislative and coercive measures alone. These results require an active role by government, the collective will and civic capacity of citizens to act as problem solvers, and communities as agents of change.[17] It is worth noting that the best results in such areas are not achieved by countries with the highest spending level as a percent of GDP but by countries that successfully enrol the active contribution of citizens as public value creators. People build societies worth living in by the decisions they make and the actions they take with others. Their contribution is the real "Wealth of Nations".[18] People's investment in building well performing societies far outweighs all other forms of investment, be they public or private.

The NS Framework brings a *citizen-centric perspective* to public policy making and service delivery. This helps explore how a different relationship between government, citizens and community, based on mutuality and shared responsibilities, may yield better public and civic results.

Governing in a period of high uncertainty and finding solutions to complex problems require a broader mental map to optimise societal results and a different relationship between government and citizens to bring about viable and sustainable solutions.

Focussing on public and civic results ensures that public sector leaders are grounded in the fundamental principles of public administration. Public results bring a societal perspective and civic results bring a citizen-centric perspective to the role of public institutions and the choices open to government. For public sector leaders, public purpose and citizens come first.[19]

AN EXPANDED VIEW OF THE ROLE OF GOVERNMENT

An increasing number of challenges are beyond the reach of government working alone. Governing in the 21st century extends beyond governments' own reach and requires incorporating what can be achieved by enrolling the contribution of others. The solutions to a number of contemporary problems require pooling resources, knowledge and capabilities wherever they may reside, across government or beyond.

There will always be cases where it is necessary for government to take action on its own. Governments must know when to act alone and when results can only be achieved by enrolling the contribution of others. Working across multiple boundaries and interfaces is a defining characteristic of modern governance.[20] This in turn has implications for public administration: the more dispersed the exercise of power in society, the more important the stewardship role of the State.[21] This includes the capacity to monitor and detect emerging issues and opportunities, and introduce corrective or mitigating actions in a timely way to improve the likelihood of generating a more favourable outcome for society.

The Authority of the State

In most countries, a small group of people have the legal right to use the authority of the State to produce results. This includes the authority to make laws and enforce them, use coercive measures, tax and spend public funds. They owe this privilege to the position they hold. People become public office holders in various ways depending on the governance system in place in their country. In democratic societies, public office holders include elected officials and professional public servants appointed through some form of a meritorious system.

The authority of the State rests with public institutions. The separation between institutions and public office holders is an important principle of public administration. Loyalty is owed to the institutions – that is the positions of Prime Minister or President, Cabinet Ministers, or other positions of public office rather than to the incumbents.[22] This separation makes it possible to ensure the continuity of the State while encouraging renewal and orderly political transitions.

The ultimate responsibility of public office holders is to exercise the authority of the State to promote the collective interest.[23] What constitutes the collective interest does not begin or end with the government in office. The laws that govern society today reflect democratic choices that were mediated through political debates over long periods of time. They form part of today's governance system and are the democratic expression of prior democratic choices. Not everything is changing and not every choice needs to be renegotiated after each election.

Public office holders simultaneously administer programmes and services inherited from the past, transform existing systems and practices to adapt to changing circumstances, and introduce new initiatives aimed at addressing contemporary problems in a way that reflects the priorities of the government in office.

Public office holders must ensure the continuity of the State while at the same time generating solutions to new and emerging public challenges. The stability provided by public institutions is a necessary condition for public, private and civic innovation.

Governing is a delicate process of constructive deconstruction where the authority of the State is used to ensure stability and initiate actions to transform society.

The Collective Power of Society

While the authority of the State is exercised by a relatively small number of public office holders, the power to change the course of events in society is vastly distributed. Multiple agents in the private sphere, civic organisations, other governments, international and multi-lateral organisations, and media and interest groups bring about changes that transform the economic, technological, environmental and socio-political environment.[24] These changes transform society, the role of government and the approaches needed for problem solving. From this perspective, governing is a search for a delicate balance that is never entirely achieved and where all elements are interacting with each other and perpetually changing.

In today's world, governments are facing issues that span multiple dimensions. The economic, social, political, technological and environmental dimensions of complex issues are intertwined. Complex issues do not and will not fit within the boundaries of any single organisation, a single government or even a single country. Governments cannot re-organise themselves out of this dilemma; instead re-organisation simply creates new boundaries that need to be overcome.

Viable solutions require a mix of interventions, some by the public sector and many by other agents in society. They require public organisations with the capacity to work collaboratively across a web of interrelation-ships, across government and across sectors in order to generate practical solutions by making the best possible use of existing resources, means and capabilities.

One key finding of the NS fieldwork to date is that there are always enough resources around to make progress if we are smart enough to leverage the power of others. Building on the strength of others requires a dynamic view of the role of government, where government interventions form part of long chains of intermediate results and where the actions of multiple agents must converge. Addressing systemic challenges such as poverty reduction, public security or public health requires the active contribution of multiple agents in society. In all these cases, *the authority of the State is used as a lever to elicit the contribution of others and to transform behaviours.*

* * *

Public results shift the focus of attention from an agency-centric perspective to a societal perspective. *Civic results* encourage a citizen-centric perspective to public administration that opens up avenues for a different sharing of responsibilities between government and citizens.

The *authority of the State* is the lever used to harness the *collective power* of society. This shifts the focus of attention from a government-centric perspective (what government can do) to a governance perspective (what can we do collectively) to ensure the well-being of society.

A DYNAMIC GOVERNING SYSTEM

At the crossroads of these vectors there are tensions to manage, conflicts to resolve and an infinite number of possible permutations.[25] A dynamic exploration of such an expanding space of possibilities helps to uncover pathways with a greater potential to generate better futures.

The NS Framework is far from the mechanistic view of public administration inherited from the industrial age. There is not one right way nor even one option, but a broad range of possible choices to invent solutions to the problems that stem from living in a post-industrial era.

Government is an actor like no other but it is not the only one able to influence the course of events. Government actions, decisions and interventions are deliberately designed to modify behaviours and transform the interactions between the public, private and civic spheres. Governments are meta-system designers. Their actions influence interacting systems that in turn shape life in society. Public organisations and institutions are mandated to shape the environment to achieve desirable public outcomes.

Some desirable results can be produced by government actions through public agencies. Other requires the pooling of capacity across government. Other still require the coming together of multiple agents from other levels of government, the private or civic sectors working as one to generate the desired public outcomes. Some of the most important public results can only be produced with the active support and contribution of citizens, families and communities. Governing and building a well performing society result from multiple interactions that transform the environment and the behaviour of people operating within it.

A compliance function: Well performing societies depend on public institutions able to govern, make laws and enforce them to prevent lawlessness. These functions contribute to stability and reduce uncertainties. This ensures that a society is governed by the rule of law. It provides a normative frame of reference based on the constitution, rules, norms and conventions that govern how we live in society and define how a society governs itself. Well performing societies require a compliance function. This requires institutional capacity.

A performance function: Well performing public organisations must be able to produce results of high public value by using public means and public resources. They must display a concern for efficiency, productivity as well as a concern for the wellbeing of citizens, users or obligates of public services. They must display respect for democracy, integrity and accountability. In contemporary terms, they must also have the capacity to work across multiple boundaries both inside government and in collaboration with the private and civic sectors or other levels of government. A performance function transform government priorities and public policy ideas into reality. This requires a high level of organisational capacity.

An emergence function: Well performing governments need the capacity to detect and anticipate emerging issues and phenomena and to proactively intervene to mitigate risks and improve the likelihood of more favourable outcomes. Well performing societies need strong inventive and innovative capacity. Government can create an environment that encourages collaboration, collective problem solving and public innovation. This helps ensure that the private, civic and public spheres work in a synergistic way. These interrelationships and the resulting ecosystem contribute to building the innovative capacity of society. The emergence function improves the capacity of government and society and lays the basis to invent solutions to the problems of life in society.

A resilience function: Resilience is the ultimate reality check of a well performing society that benefits from skilful government stewardship. This includes the capacity to adapt to changing needs and circumstances and to generate sustainable futures. It is manifest in the capacity to adapt, absorb disturbances and prosper even in the face of unforeseen or unpredictable circumstances. Resilience requires well developed civic capabilities and the civic will to deploy these capabilities to advance the collective interest. Government is and remains the steward of the collective interest in all circumstances whether or not it is actively involved.

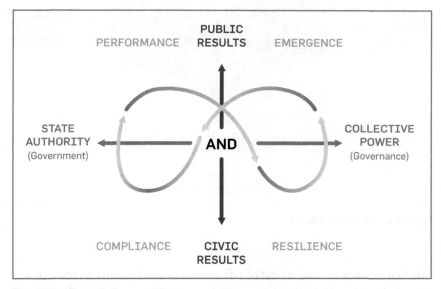

Figure 3.2: A Dynamic System of Governance

Taken together these functions map out an open, dynamic interactive system of governance where an infinite number of choices and permutations are possible. The challenge is to ensure that the overall balance serves the collective interest, generates solutions, encourages collective problem solving and propels society towards a better future.

The participants in NS workshops have over the years generated many visual representations of the NS interacting elements and functions. For reason of simplicity, a diagram in two dimensions is used while in fact there are dynamic interactions evolving over time. This diagram does not capture the dynamic nature of the NS Framework.

The following picture goes some distance in capturing aspects of the dynamic at play. It has the merit of illustrating several key aspects.

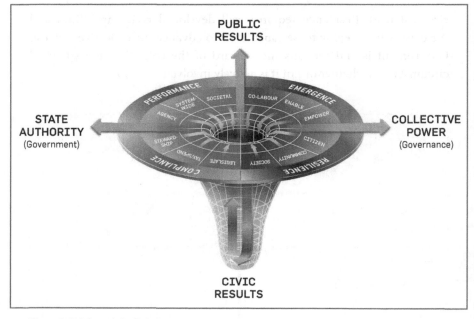

Figure 3.3: A Search for Balance

The first is that what comes out of a dynamic system depends on what comes into it. In this illustration, the compliance, performance, resilience and emergence functions are at play simultaneously. Government is playing an active role and so are other agents of society and citizens themselves. This mix is used to generate public results of value for society.

The second useful aspect of the diagram is that actions and interactions create ripple effects. It could be small and reach only the people directly affected or have vast affects throughout society. The concept of ripple effects appears in one of the cases presented in Appendix A at the end of this book.

Finally, this diagram points out that civic results play a unique role in the functioning of the overall governance system. Civic results are outputs, inputs and contribute to societal outcomes.

Civic results are an *output* as the active engagement of citizens has intrinsic value in itself. This contributes to building the capacity of people to act as citizens. Citizens are active beings that behave in ways that serve their interest and the collective interest.

Civic results are an *input*. Civic results build the capacity to act collectively and to mobilise behind a shared purpose. The greater the civic capacity and the stronger the civic will to deploy this capacity, the greater the likelihood of success of an ambitious change agenda. Civic results reduce the costs of friction in society.

Civic results provide the fuel to generate societal outcomes. In this case, people are doing the heavy lifting. The efforts of government and people are aligned and moving in the same direction. There is less need to rely on enforcement because voluntary compliance and self-organisation are prevalent. In the diagram, the civic results arrows point downward (accumulating civic results in abundance) and upward (joining efforts with government and others to move society forward).

The NS Framework recognises the need for law and order, and well performing public institutions and organisations. The State must be able to ensure stability and governments must be able to govern. But it also recognises the limits of what can be accomplished by relying primarily on the authority of the State. *Governing is a search for balance.* The mastery most needed by public sector leaders is the capacity to harness the unique and irreplaceable contributions of the public, private and civic spheres in society to advance the collective interest.

The following chapters will describe what was learned from practitioners as they searched for a pathway towards a better future in their respective contexts.

PART II
THE NS EXPLORATORY PROCESS

The NS Exploratory Process presented in Chapter 4 to 7 is the result of several years of work with practitioners and public sector leaders facing very different challenges and different sets of circumstances in various countries. This phase of the NS Initiative was aimed at discovering what practitioners could do with the concepts of the NS Framework outlined in Chapter 3. Would it be relevant to them? Would it allow them to create better solutions and better results?

This was an enriching and yet demanding period for the NS Team. The team was focussing on learning how public sector leaders explore, uncover and invent solutions to the problems they are facing in practice. Beyond the differences in context and missions, similar phases became progressively discernible.

The NS Exploratory Process captures *the essential elements of a systematic, dynamic and iterative discovery process* aimed at finding a pathway towards a better future. The process is *systematic* because it brings together in a comprehensive way a number of phases leading to innovative solutions. It is *dynamic* because all the elements are interacting and influencing one another. The actions taken by governments influence the course of events, transform behaviours and the interactions between the public, private and civic spheres of life in society. Changes in the environment affect the perceptions of the issues and, as a result, the expectations and actions of other actors. The environment and the actions of government, citizens and multiple actors in society are intertwined.

The discovery process is *iterative* because public sector leaders leading public transformation are likely to go through the various phases several times as the exploration progresses and more people come on board. For the sake of clarity, the various exploratory phases are introduced one after the other. In reality, the positioning, leveraging, engaging and synthesising phases presented in the following chapters are influencing and interacting with each other.

Public sector leaders are pragmatic people. In their hands, relevant principles become tools and a conceptual framework becomes a map to explore new avenues to fulfil their mission. This is what happened during the most recent phase of the NS Initiative. This is the story of this part of the book.

A NS exploration becomes real when the key concepts are applied to a practical situation. The search for a solution can only be conducted by public sector leaders facing a challenge in practice. This exploration requires a commitment to bringing about change by using the resources and levers available to them.

The challenges faced by practitioners are called *live cases* in the context of NS labs and workshops to distinguish them from case studies with neither a direct relationship nor an emotional engagement between a public sector leader and an issue. The people involved in a NS exploratory journey are not separate from the results they are trying to achieve. They form part of the context they aspire to transform. The changes they want to bring about are unlikely to happen without an active engagement on their part.

There are no restrictions about what may constitute a live case. For example, the challenge faced by a head of a forestry department may be to reduce and prevent illegal logging, a head of a civil service may aspire to build the capacity for government-wide coordination, a manager of a prison system may be looking for ways to reduce recidivism, and a supervisor of a child protection agency may be facing increasing workloads and declining resources. A more detailed discussion of how case studies and live cases are used in developing the NS Exploratory Process is included in the Appendix.

Public sector leaders are frequently confronted with untenable situations where conventional approaches are insufficient to yield the desired public outcomes. This is the case when governments find themselves repeatedly in a reactive position, unable to anticipate or prevent crises before a high cost or significant impact is borne by the most vulnerable members of society. This is also the case when public sector leaders are confronted with ever increasing demands, where doing more with less leads to a dead end and doing more of the same, even with more resources, is not a viable option. In some situations, a job well done is not the answer.

Some successful public programmes are leaving behind unresolved issues and pockets of underserved citizens because the problems they are facing do not fit the general mould. Other public programmes and services generate unintended consequences that must be detected and corrected. Public programmes, even the most successful ones, will eventually become a source of problems if they are left unchanged over long periods of time and become maladapted to changing circumstances. In all these cases, a different way of thinking and an ability to frame issues from a broader perspective are needed to uncover solutions to seemingly intractable problems and challenges.

No problem is too big or too small for a NS exploratory journey. However, there are *rules of engagement*. One of them has already been mentioned; the challenge must be real for the people engaged in the discovery process. There must be a real commitment to use the resources and levers available to them to bring about the change they aspire to generate. NS explorations accept no "ifs" or "buts" and no conditionality. Concretely, this means that the proposed solutions do not depend on others acting first, getting more resources or waiting for ideal circumstances such as a more powerful minister or a better public service than the one that currently exists. A NS exploration takes shape in the here and now. It deals with the situation as it is rather than how one may like it to be. It uses the resources and capabilities available at the time to generate better public results and build the capacity to achieve better outcomes over time.

High aspirations are not sufficient to change the world and bring about a better future; they must be supported by public organisations and public sector leaders who are able to make them a reality.

CHAPTER 4

THE POWER OF A BROADER MENTAL MAP – POSITIONING

Public sector leaders must articulate the broad public purpose of the change they aspire to bring about in order to mobilise action and enlist the contribution of others. Framing an issue in societal terms is an essential step for leading public transformation or managing a change process of some significance. It helps answer questions such as: Why does this matter? What difference would this make for society? How would this bring about a better future? In a word – why should we care?

MOVING UP A VALUE CHAIN OF PUBLIC RESULTS

Articulating the higher public purpose brings greater clarity to government actions and decisions. It provides guidance to practitioners serving in a context characterised by complexity and a high level of uncertainty. In essence, the public purpose is the North Star of public administration; it provides a general direction. It helps ensure coherence and convergence between aspirations, actions and decisions at multiple levels, across multiple boundaries and vast networks.

Positioning is about exploring the interrelationship between agency, system-wide and societal results to gain an appreciation of the overall effects of government interventions, and their impacts on the interactions between the public, private and civic spheres. Positioning government interventions in the context of societal outcomes reveals the mix of instruments most likely to enable progress and to bring about the desired public outcomes. The challenge is to explore what can be done, using the resources and capabilities currently available, *to move up the value chain of public results*. This means generating better government-wide, system–wide and societal results (see Figure 4.1).[1]

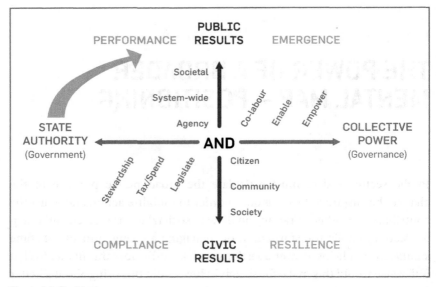

Figure 4.1: Positioning

Agency results: Practitioners are well familiar with agency results; the outcomes of individual organisations effectively delivering services or administering programs. These results provide a basis for reconciling inputs and outputs. They define clear responsibilities and accountabilities for the use of taxpayer money and the exercise of delegated authority. Agency results encourage efficiency and productivity. Public sector leaders have a responsibility for ensuring the efficiency of public organisations, the careful use of public resources and compliance with the laws and regulations generated over the years. They have a responsibility to improve agency performance and build the capacity of the organisation they lead. Taxes must be collected without leakage, public services must be exempt from corruption and government services must treat all in accordance with the law. Focussing on agency results reveals a *spirit of performance*.

Important as agency results may be, they capture only part of the story. Public agencies must position their contribution to generate better system-wide results and societal outcomes.

System-wide results: System-wide results exceed the capacity of any single agency or even government as a whole. They require the active contribution of a number of agencies across government, other levels of government and multiple agents in the public, private and civic spheres. This collaboration requires the capacity to work across boundaries. The responsibility of public sector leaders does not stop at the frontiers of the organisation they lead. They have a *shared responsibility* to work with others to produce better system-wide results. This includes supporting government-wide priorities, contributing to public service-wide initiatives and generating results through vast networks of collaboration in government and beyond.

System-wide results require a constant exploration of new and better ways to combine issues, means and capabilities to generate better public results. It entails bringing together the strength of hierarchical public organisations and the power of vast and distributed networks.

For instance, all hospitals provide health care services; some also provide community services, while others conduct medical research. Whatever their mandate, they all form part of a broader health care system. They share a responsibility to contribute to better healthcare and better health outcomes. Efficient and well-managed schools do not guarantee that people will benefit from an accessible and affordable education system nor guarantee a population with a high level of literacy. Collective actions allow for the achievement of results beyond the reach of any single agent on its own. System-wide results are shared results. Focussing on system-wide results reveals a *spirit of invention*.

Societal results: Public results, at the highest level, benefit society as a whole. They are a measure of the overall performance of society. They reveal the impact of government interventions over time to ensure that the public, private and civic spheres operate synergistically to advance the overall interests of society. They are the results that matter most to citizens. At the highest level of aggregation, societal results include results such as economic prosperity, improved human conditions, cross-generational fairness and a sustainable biosphere.

Public office holders have a collective responsibility to optimise societal results and to advance the collective interest. They bear a special responsibility for using the authority of the State to steer society through an ongoing process of change, create a better future and prepare public institutions that are fit for the future. Focussing on societal results reveals a *spirit of stewardship*.

As in the examples mentioned above, the results that matter most for people in the health and education sectors are *societal results*; these include better health outcomes, low and declining child mortality, long and productive lives, a high level of literacy, and the acquisition of the skills and knowledge to benefit from participation in the global economy.

Public servants, public organisations and public institutions serve a *public purpose*. If this were not the case, there would be good reason to ask whether these activities belong in the public sector in the first instance. This higher purpose transcends the programme public servants manage, the services they provide and the organisations they run. Agency, system-wide and societal results are interrelated. The continuum running from agency to system-wide and to societal results is scalable. The words agency and system-wide have different meanings depending on the issue and context. An agency may be a unit within a department, a department within a large ministry, a ministry within the public sector, or even a government among others in the case of a multilateral effort.

The interrelationships between agency, system-wide and societal results are not linear; they interact with each other. Articulating the higher public purpose in societal terms and defining what success means for society will influence the way one conceives of a system-wide effort and the contribution needed from various public agencies. Conversely, an initiative at the agency level may have a ripple effect across government or across systems and may even transform society. A public transformation process may start at any level. It can be top-down, as is the case with government priorities, or bottom-up, when the initiative starts on a smaller scale and expands.

THINK PUBLIC PURPOSE, FOCUS ON SOCIETAL RESULTS

In NS workshops positioning exercises are used to help practitioners articulate the broad public purpose and frame the desired public outcomes of their actions in societal terms. Positioning is the starting point of a NS exploration.

At one level, government interventions operate in the context of a vast administrative ecosystem comprised of other government agencies and other levels of government. Public sector leaders must focus on the big picture to invent solutions that will work in practice.

At another level, the impact of government interventions will be felt at various levels in society and influence the actions and behaviours of other social agents. Clarity of purpose guides the actions and decisions of governments. Understanding the context and articulating the broad public purpose improves the likelihood of success of government interventions.

An agency-centric perspective is likely to miss the multidimensional nature of an issue and the potential for progress. It limits the ability of government to discover solutions that lie in the *space between* the contributions of individual agencies and other agents in society. An agency-centric focus is all too common. It is the first difficulty to overcome to generate innovative solutions.

When a situation becomes unsustainable, when a challenge cannot be solved by doing more of the same no matter how hard people try, this is the time to *re-frame* the issue, *re-think* the approach and *re-position* the contribution of the organisation.

In these circumstances, a broader mental map is most helpful. The following story is based on the experiences of three different child protection units operating in Australia, Singapore and the UK. Taken together, they provide a useful illustration of *the power of a broader mental map* to generate innovative solutions.

Learning from Practice: Serving a Broader Public Purpose
Children at Risk

Child protection agencies have the legal authority to take measures to protect children from significant harm.[2] Many countries have a special unit with the authority to investigate allegations of child abuse and to remove children from their family environment if there is plausible or probable evidence of harm or risk of harm.

*Like many government agencies, the child protection service unit in this case faced an increasing workload and declining resources.[3] This led to high staff turnover that put the ability of the organisation to fulfil its mandate at risk. The manager initially framed the issue from an agency perspective; the challenge was to find ways to **improve staff retention** and make better use of resources.*

Framing the issue narrowly forecloses the possibility of discovering a better way of addressing the issue. Framing the challenge as a retention issue means that the problem rests entirely with team members and their manager; no one outside this group can help or be part of the solution. One can easily predict the team will continue to struggle and that the situation will deteriorate – caseloads will increase and the children at risk will face longer wait times. The approach envisaged does not address the root cause of the problem. There are other ways to look at the situation. Focussing on societal results could lead to a very different approach and yield very different results.

Further discussion led the unit to realise that increasing its efficiency and reducing turnover would not solve the issue. The unit was only able to act after-the-fact, once harm had been done, and even at that, it was losing ground. Interventions were delayed due to a shortage of staff. The unit was in crisis and becoming an emergency responder, intervening only in the most severe situations. A different way of thinking and a different approach were needed if the unit was to serve its higher public purpose to protect children from harm. This could only be fulfilled if the unit shifted some resources from casework to prevention. Information was needed to identify risks factors, detect pockets of risk and take proactive measures that were in the hands of social services, schools, the police, community organisations and other actors. Interagency collaboration takes time and there is no guarantee that it will improve prevention and reduce risks.

The unit chose to free up some resources, knowing that this affected its efficiency in the short-term and could affect children in the process.

There are important implications to a shift from an agency-centric perspective to a focus on system-wide and societal results. The first is that such a shift takes courage because significant trade-offs are involved. In this case, the benefits of focussing on societal results of higher public value are unproven and will only materialise over time while the short-term consequences of reallocating resources will be immediate and very visible.

Another important observation is that one cannot optimise both agency and societal results; a choice must be made. The question for public sector leaders faced with such difficult decisions is: what principle should guide them? A commitment to serving a broad public purpose means that the choice should be to *optimise* results of higher value for society.

A third observation is that public agencies that consume the totality of their resources to deal with daily operations are by definition inefficient organisations because they lack the capacity to anticipate or respond to emerging needs that would generate better results for society. They are stuck in a trap that undermines the very purpose they were created to serve. This problem is compounded by the fact that administrative systems frequently reflect a different era, when agencies were expected to operate more or less in isolation from each other. As a result, administrative systems inhibit collaborative efforts aimed at generating better government-wide, system-wide and societal results.

*The early work of the unit in collaboration with others led to the identification of six determinants of risk: a history of family violence, poverty, poor attachment to the labour force, illiteracy, juvenile parents and teenage pregnancy. This work was the first step towards the early detection of pockets of risks, which encouraged other organisations to join forces with the child protection unit. A focus on child protection was giving rise to a system-wide approach where each agency remained responsible for delivering on their respective mandate, but also shared a responsibility with others to contribute to a common purpose. The group was moving up a **value chain of public results**. The unit later discovered that many of the factors linked to children at risk were also predictors of families at risk. These findings were valuable to social service agencies dealing with the reintegration of ex-offenders and family violence. This encouraged inter-agency co-operation on a larger scale. The unit is now exploring what can be done to improve the capacity of families at risk to fulfil their caretaker role. A broader perspective and a shared purpose opened the door to collaborative and innovative approaches. It created hope and helped resolve the retention problem.*[4]

Not every case will lead to such positive outcomes but the conclusions that can be drawn may be similar. An agency-centric focus leads to sub-optimal results and reduces the range of available options. A broader view reveals the multidimensional nature of the issues at play and opens new avenues for collaboration. Clarity of purpose is needed to address the tensions between agency, system-wide and societal results, as it gives meaning to government actions and decisions. A commitment to serving a higher public purpose encourages public decision makers to optimise results of increasing value for society. *For public sector leaders, public purpose comes first.*

THINK TOTAL SYSTEM

In the previous example, the transformation process was initiated by the public service. It gained political support as the work progressed. Many phases were well within the authority of officials and could be undertaken without seeking political support or additional authority. In other cases, a public transformation process requires the early involvement of elected officials at the highest level.

The following example illustrates political leadership as well as professional leadership. It is sometimes argued that law enforcement agencies have less potential to introduce innovative practices. The fieldwork conducted to date reveals that law enforcement agencies have innovative capacities on par with any other public agency and that they may even display a stronger will to explore innovative practices.

Most public agencies are created by statutes. These statutes define their mandate in broad terms, delineate the authorities they can exercise and in some cases set parameters for the use of these authorities. The broad public purpose that a government initiative is seeking to achieve must be framed and actualised taking into account the circumstances, the political context and prevailing government priorities at the time.

Having the legal authority to act and using it are two very different things. Clarity of purpose and an articulation of desired societal outcomes help public sector leaders discern how authority may be used to greatest effect. Clarity of purpose is needed to guide practitioners' actions and decisions.

Learning from Practice: The Effectiveness of the Whole
Illegal Logging

The State of Sarawak in Malaysia is endowed with rich and diverse forest resources; 80 percent of its 12.4 million hectares are still under forest cover.[5] This forest resource offers a huge economic, social and environmental potential that could benefit present and future generations. Illegal logging is emerging as a serious threat.

The Forest Department was given the objective of reducing the number of offenses by 20 percent in 2015. By the end of December 2014, the Department had handled 210 cases; there were 109 cases of illegal logging, 87 cases of tax evasion and 14 cases of various offenses committed by sawmills. The Department was quick to realise that achieving the departmental objectives would not resolve the problem of illegal logging or adequately protect forest lands. Consequently, it decided to focus on **government-wide results** *and put in place a "sustainable forest management system". This system required the involvement of a broad range of agencies with responsibilities in a variety of related fields, including enumeration and tagging, log tracking, royalties, remote sensing and geospatial analytics.*[6]

Public initiatives take place in the context of a vast ecosystem of existing laws, regulations, programmes and services. Understanding this ecosystem is necessary in order to discover viable solutions and encourage collaboration. Mapping the existing administrative system across agencies may be time consuming, but it is invaluable to gain a holistic view of an issue. It reveals the intricate legal and administrative requirements in place, the diversity of agencies involved and the conflicting demands and priorities of various government agencies. This helps identify the administrative deficiencies that may curtail the capacity of government to bring about desirable societal results. The important point is that administrative deficiencies will not resolve themselves. They need to be identified and addressed to achieve the desired societal outcomes. This forms part of an effort for leading public transformation.

A sustainable forest management system could operate in very different ways depending on the desired societal outcomes. Some societal choices could only be made at the political level because they involved conflicting priorities and required that the government arbitrate between the logging industry, the tourism industry, the palm oil industry, local communities and aboriginal groups. Under the guidance of the Chief Minister, the State of Sarawak chose to focus on **"the protection and conservation of the forests for the benefit of present and future generations"**. *As a result, the approach to forest management by the government of Sarawak now includes conservation, protection, public* *education, enforcement and the enrolment of people as "custodians of the forest". The public purpose is driving the design and implementation of a government-wide effort.*[7]

Some important observations may be drawn from this example for the benefit of practitioners leading public transformations. One is that a public agency can meet its key performance indicators and fail to serve its broader public purpose. Another lesson is that better public results cannot be achieved by improving only the productivity and efficiency of individual agencies. The focus instead must be on measures that improve the overall effectiveness of a collective effort that brings together a number of agencies, contributors and partners to achieve the desired societal outcome. In the end, *what matters most from a societal perspective is not the efficiency of the parts but the effectiveness of the whole.*

In summary, thinking through the positioning of government policies, programmes, services or new initiatives provides an opportunity to articulate the higher public purpose and explore the interrelationships between agency, system-wide and societal results. It opens up a broader space of possibilities. Discovering and articulating the higher public purpose is the starting point of a journey of discovery aimed at inventing solutions to the problems we face as a society.

LOOKING BACK AND MOVING FORWARD

A number of practical exercises, tools and templates have been designed over the years for participants in NS workshops and Labs. Some were generated for a specific purpose but most were created to capture what was learned by observing practitioners engaged in framing and articulating the higher public purpose of the change they sought to bring about. This material is available to participants in NS workshops.[8] For the purpose of this book, the examples presented so far should be sufficient to provide the reader with an appreciation of the concepts involved.

In closing, it is useful to mention some of the most frequent difficulties encountered by practitioners attempting to shift from an agency-centric focus to a societal perspective in developing solutions to the problems they are facing in practice. The most common mistake is *to underestimate their authority* to bring about change. In a nutshell, this means that public sector leaders have a propensity to ask for permission even when they have all the necessary authority to initiate actions. They also have a propensity to wait for others to take action.

There are many reasons for this behaviour, but, contrary to a prevailing opinion, this has not much to do with risk taking or risk management. These behaviours reveal a low tolerance for blame or criticism. This is an issue that deserves the attention of senior public sector leaders since leading public transformation requires a willingness to make full use of existing authority to generate better public results.

Another frequent mistake is that public sector leaders have a tendency to *overestimate the constraints* they face, legal, fiscal or otherwise, and to *underestimate the assets available* to bring about change. We have found that the simple exercise of making a list of barriers and validating whether these barriers actually reflect a legal obligation or merely the perception of one, had a significant corrective effect. Constraints, which so frequently frustrate public administrators, often emanate from within their own organisations. In a sense, they are self-inflicted and self-perpetuating unless they are challenged. Other constraints and requirements, such as those imposed by central agencies, departmental reporting requirements or management control systems, do not have the same importance as legal requirements. Some control mechanisms may have been introduced to address issues that have long since disappeared. *They can and should be challenged* if they are an impediment to producing better public results.

Constraints are not barriers to public innovation per se. Public organisations operate under heavy constraints. This is a fact. These constraints may be legal, financial or administrative in nature. Public organisations operate with limited resources: there will never be enough resources to meet all needs. Public agencies must therefore balance demands and needs as well as the urgent and the important. This will not change.

Public organisations must therefore invent solutions within their constraints. These constraints set the parameters within which public innovation must take place. The challenge is to invent solutions that offer the greatest potential for public impact using existing resources, capabilities and authorities to the fullest. NS fieldwork has revealed time and time again that there is always a way to make progress, notwithstanding these constraints.

This requires public sector leaders knowledgeable about the full extent of their authority and willing to use it to the fullest. One often finds that public administrators do not make full use of their existing authority and that they have a tendency to wait for others to take the first step. Significant opportunities are missed this way. Public administrators have access to considerable assets to bring about change and lead public transformation. To generate results of increasing public value, the starting point is a clarity of purpose. The next phase is to harness the authority of the State to leverage the collective capacity of society to build a better future.

CHAPTER 5

THE POWER OF OTHERS – LEVERAGING

The previous chapter discussed the need to explore the interrelationships between agency, system-wide and societal results to generate outcomes of increasing value to society. This chapter explores how existing assets and the authority of the State may be used to enlist the contribution of other state and non-state actors to make progress on matters of public interest. Government does not need to accomplish everything itself for the collective interest to be well served. Producing better public results and building a better future are a shared responsibility. It requires a collective effort, the participation of the public, private and civic sectors as well as the active contribution of citizens themselves.

The capacity of government to build on the strength of others and to enrol the contribution of others to promote the collective interest characterises *smart governments;* those able to achieve desirable societal results with a parsimony of effort, economy of time and resources and with a minimal amount of unintended consequences. Smart governments are those that have learned to build on the strength of others and have the capacity to sustain collaborative efforts across vast networks.

In most countries, a small group of people have the legal right to use the authority of the State to generate results. This includes the authority to make laws and enforce them, use coercive measures, and to tax and use public funds, all to advance the overall interest of society. Governments have considerable assets for enlisting the contributions of others.

Working across organisational boundaries and ensuring collaborative efforts across vast networks of actors are characteristic of public organisations fit for the challenges of serving in a post-industrial era. A lack of capacity in this regard erodes public confidence in the ability of government to bring about viable solutions to complex issues that require a holistic approach to problem solving and decision making.

WHAT IS THE CONCEPT OF LEVERAGING?

Leveraging is a search for practical solutions to multifaceted problems using existing resources, means and capabilities. It is an exploratory process aimed at pooling capabilities and resources across a network of social actors, as well as multiple organisational boundaries, to achieve results of higher value at a lower overall cost to society. From this perspective, government interventions form part of long chains of intermediate results where the contribution of multiple agents is garnered to achieve the desired societal outcomes. Relying on conventional approaches is insufficient to generate sustainable solutions to an increasing number of public policy challenges.

One of the key findings of the NS fieldwork is that public organisations are not limited to acting within the constraints of their limited resources; there are always enough resources around to make progress if we are smart enough to leverage the power of others.

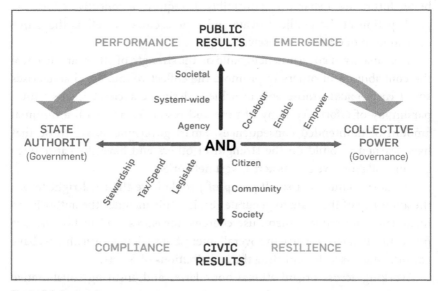

Figure 5.1: Leveraging

The NS Framework provides a map for exploring how different permutations of actions by government and others may yield better results. A map does not dictate the journey but enables public sector leaders and decision makers to look ahead.

The decisions that matter can only be made by the people with the authority to act, in the context and circumstances prevailing at the time. The way they frame an issue will have a direct impact on the solutions that will be envisaged and the results that will be achieved. A broader view and a collaborative perspective expand the range of options open to government.

The following Brazilian case provides an example of a government exploring a broadened space of possibilities and leveraging collective capacities to shape an emergent solution.

Learning from Practice: The Potent Combination of State Authority and Collective Power
Brazil's Response to HIV/AIDS[1]
In the 1980s, Brazil was experiencing an HIV/AIDS epidemic. The number of cases of citizens with HIV/AIDS was increasing at an alarming rate.[2] The Government of Brazil was facing a number of challenges in its fight against this epidemic, including limited fiscal capacity, the high cost of treatment, limited health infrastructure and a shortage of medical personnel. The challenge was compounded by difficulties reaching at-risk populations due to factors such as high levels of illiteracy, poverty and a dispersed population spread across a vast territory with a large number of Brazilians living in remote communities. In light of such challenging circumstances, experts advised the government to protect future generations by concentrating its efforts on prevention.[3] Essentially, the opinion of experts at the time was that Brazil did not have the capacity to do much for people already infected with HIV. Eventually, the pandemic would run its course. The priority should be to protect the next generation.

Governing is never easy but some circumstances are more challenging than others. Fortunately, public sector leaders are not always confronted with issues of life and death as was the case in this example. The advice of experts, to let the pandemic run its course, may seem cold-hearted but it was nonetheless a fact that the government of Brazil did not have the capacity and the resources to resolve the situation on its own. There were problems of affordability; their fiscal capacity was insufficient to pay for expensive drugs.

There were problems of capacity; not enough hospital beds and qualified personnel, including nurses and doctors. Making the situation even more complex, there were problems of access. A vast country with a large number of communities makes it especially challenging to reach the affected people and prevent the spread of the disease. These difficulties were compounded by a high level of illiteracy and poverty prevailing in many remote communities at the time. If there was ever a time for out-of-the-box thinking and exploring avenues beyond conventional approaches, this was it.

> *The Government of Brazil opted for an approach that combined awareness, prevention and care. Such an approach was unprecedented at the time. Experts in the field were of the view that this strategy was unaffordable and unlikely to succeed. The Government sought to ensure that "**no one would be left behind**" no matter how poor or illiterate and in spite of limited resources and challenging circumstances. Unlike other countries, the Government of Brazil acknowledged the issue early and went public about it. Public awareness generated the conditions for broad based mobilization. A **national effort** was launched that enrolled the contribution of government organisations, healthcare workers, community based organisations, non-governmental organisations (NGOs) and religious organisations. Treatment would be provided to all who needed it. Prevention strategies enlisted the support of those already affected to encourage behavioural changes even in the most remote communities.*

Many of the elements involved in this example are relevant to a discussion about the capacity of government to leverage the contribution of organisations in the private and civic spheres. First, the role of government is not limited or even defined by what government can do on its own but by what it can make happen.

In this case, the government played a key role in setting a clear course of action and a clear purpose. This was essential for mobilising everyone's effort. It provided leadership when needed and relied on the contribution of others wherever possible. To drive down the cost of expensive antiretroviral medications, the Brazilian government enlisted the support of the World Trade Organization to produce and donate generic versions of expensive drugs. To address the problem of low medical capacity, the government enlisted 600 NGOs, churches and food distribution centres to support hospitals and clinics. This network was able to reach those affected, even in the most remote areas, thus providing health care to people who did not have access to the traditional hospital-based system.

The strategy was multifaceted. Complex issues are multidimensional and as a result they require a mix of actions to generate a viable solution. No single action and no single agent, government or otherwise, could have generated the desired societal outcome. Brazil's response to the HIV/AIDS epidemic is the story of a collective effort. It is a powerful illustration that there is always enough capacity around to make progress if we are smart enough to harness the collective capabilities and resourcefulness of people in challenging situations. A country may have deficient infrastructure or have limited fiscal capacity but have strong ties of solidarity that can be drawn upon to unleash a concerted and collective action that can change the course of events.

The results were impressive. In 2001, it was estimated that a $232 million investment by government had resulted in total savings of $1.1 billion for society as a whole.[4] By 2002, the rate of HIV infection in Brazil was stable at 0.6 percent, the mortality rate had fallen by 50 percent, and in-patient hospital days had fallen by 70-80 percent.[5] In 2014, UNAIDS reported that the HIV prevalence rate in Brazil remained stable at 0.6 percent.[6] In 2013, Brazil added a new dimension to its strategy to ensure that all people with HIV have access to anti-retroviral therapy regardless of the virus' progress. That same year, Brazil passed a law criminalising discrimination based on HIV status; the first of this kind in the world. Brazil remains at the forefront in the fight against HIV.

Transformations on this scale require deliberate and proactive government interventions. The Brazilian government's journey to bring about a viable solution began by generating broad public awareness of the HIV epidemic. Public awareness was the starting point of a multifaceted collective effort that unfolded over many years. The government needed simultaneously to enlist the contribution of multiple agents from public, private and civic spheres at home and abroad. Much has been written about this case and abundant literature is available.[7]

An important lesson is that governments that display the capability to leverage the contribution of others, work collaboratively across boundaries and build on the strengths of partners have a heightened capacity to invent solutions to the problems of society no matter how bleak the situation may seem at the time.

WORKING ACROSS MULTIPLE BOUNDARIES

Fortunately, most public sector leaders are not facing issues of this scale. Most often, the collaboration needed is across agencies operating in the same government, across levels of government or across private, public and civic sectors within the same region. These situations may appear to be less challenging but sustaining a collaborative effort across multiple agencies requires many of the same capabilities.

A leveraging strategy often begins by identifying the partners needed to achieve desirable results and framing issues in ways that provides partners with a compelling reason to collaborate. Understanding potential partners' situations, motivations and capabilities as well as the constraints they face is crucial to initiating a collaborative effort that spans across multiple organisations.

Collaboration does not happen by accident. Competition among agencies, even in the same government, is often the norm. Collaboration may be sometimes met with resistance because the agencies involved in a collaborative effort must relinquish some degree of control. Furthermore, working across agencies is difficult because the administrative systems needed to encourage collaboration are frequently lacking. Systems such as performance management, performance pay or annual reporting generally encourage agency-centric behaviours.

Deliberate effort is required to counter agency-centric tendencies. Collaborative effort requires skilful leadership and managerial abilities to put in place the mechanisms needed to sustain the efforts of the group. Ground rules and a degree of procedural definition are needed to enable co-decisions, resolve differences of view and encourage the co-creation of solutions. Leveraging the contributions of others and working across boundaries are necessary conditions for addressing an increasing number of issues of public concern.

The following example from a Children's hospital in Canada shows how the cooperation of several different health organisations lead to results that none of the organization could have achieved on their own.

Learning from Practice: Designed for Collaboration
Children's Hospital of Eastern Ontario [8]

Technological and clinical breakthroughs in life-extending treatments for children have improved the prognosis of many previously fatal conditions.[9] Children who suffer from complex medical conditions typically require extensive treatment involving life-sustaining equipment, therapeutic services, regular paediatric care and consultations with a large number of medical specialists. These children make frequent visits to emergency centres and require regular hospitalisation.[10]

*About 3,700 children with complex medical conditions, representing 0.14 percent of all children in Ontario, account for 50 percent of the province's paediatric in-patient expenditures. On average, these children require services provided by up to 11 medical specialists. Most of them (93.8 percent) require access to special medical equipment. Their medical conditions create inter-agency and inter-service coordination problems. It puts a heavy burden on their family. Parents, particularly mothers, often end up leaving the workforce to become full-time caregivers. This situation places a high level of stress on all family members, including siblings. **Health care costs** may be disproportionate but the **social costs** are even greater. The health care system was not designed for children with complex medical conditions. These patients need a co-ordinated approach across multiple disciplines and organisations.*

In 2009, the chief executive officer (CEO) of the Children's Hospital of Eastern Ontario (CHEO) committed to finding a way to help these children and their families.[11] He prepared the way for an inter-agency collaborative effort by convening and enlisting the support of his colleagues. The partners co-designed a three-year pilot programme based on a 'family-centred' approach. This approach included several innovative practices such as the designation of a multi-agency case manager and a "most responsible physician" to co-ordinate medical care. The partners initially funded the programme without support from the Ontario Ministry of Health.

The programme's results show that enhanced coordination across disciplines and among service providers improved access to care and provided better support for families. The programme led to shorter wait times and reduced service redundancies. The streamlining of health and social care systems allowed more patients to live at home, attend school and participate in community activities, thereby elevating their overall quality of life. The pilot phase of this initiative demonstrated how similar projects could achieve significant benefits for the children involved, their families and society as a whole at a relatively low cost.

Cases such as this one, in which enhanced collaboration improved services, are not rare. We can readily identify similar situations from personal experience. The people involved in these situations are well aware of the problems. They know what works and what constraints prevent cross–agency collaboration. This case provides an illustration of the key factors for the success of such collaborative endeavours. Leveraging strategies have a number of common characteristics.

A point of leverage: A rallying point is needed to unleash a collaborative effort across multiple agencies. The purpose must be worthy of engagement and be relevant to the organisations invited to join the collaborative effort. This rallying cause defines and embodies the reason why partners are committed to working together. It is shared, significant and used to bring partners on board. The rallying point for CHEO and its partners was the overarching needs of children with complex medical conditions.

An important observation is that collaboration does not constrain the freedom of action of partner organisations in other areas. Partners remain independent. They go their separate ways and may even compete against one another, but in a specific area and for a specific purpose, they agree to work collaboratively.

Framing for collaboration: Leveraging strategies require identifying the key partners needed to ensure the success of collaborative efforts. Who are they? What would motivate them or hinder their participation? The capacity to enrol the contribution of others is enhanced by an understanding of their positions and a willingness to take their concerns on board. These considerations frequently lead the initiators of a collaborative effort to re-frame the issue to embody the collective interests of the contributing partners beyond the view of the initiating agency.

A leadership of proximity: Collaborative efforts require a special form of leadership. A leadership of proximity involves being close enough to detect the issue, committed enough to act and credible enough to secure the contribution of others. Many issues requiring inter-agency collaboration cannot be resolved by decisions taken at the highest level of government. Instead, leaders gain support by taking action and demonstrating the benefits of their initiative.

A coalition: Collaborative efforts must start somewhere. Regardless of whether the initiators are an individual, a group or an agency, they must build a coalition to guide the collective effort during the early phases. The coalition will most likely include the main organisations as well as a number of interested external groups. In this case, the CEO of the CHEO was the initiator and the initial coalition included several organisations in the region as well as family representatives.

Reputation and relationships are leveraging assets: Reputation and relationships provide public sector leaders with the legitimacy to initiate actions that span beyond the scope of their organisations. The power to invite colleagues and partners beyond one's formal authority to explore the potential for collaborative initiatives. The *power to convene* is a powerful asset.

Institutionalising collaboration: Working across boundaries and leveraging the contribution of multiple agencies take more than good will and heroic efforts. It requires good management and problem-solving mechanisms. The case mentioned above required fairly heavy procedural machinery to support the group's efforts. These mechanisms were co-created by the partners and designed to sustain a collaborative effort over time.

A different approach to cost-benefit analyses: The greatest difficulty in sustaining collaborative efforts is how to reconcile agency costs and societal benefits. Everybody benefited from the collaborative effort launched by CHEO. Children enjoyed a better quality of life, their parents were better supported and employers were less affected by the frequent absenteeism of the parents of children with complex medical conditions. The benefits are vastly distributed and accrue to society as a whole. But what about the costs? By and large, the participating agencies are saddled with the additional costs. Herein lies one of the most important barriers to inter-agency collaboration. The accounting costs of public initiatives are programme-based, agency-based and government-centric and the benefits that accrue to society are not taken into account. There has been little effort dedicated to revamping the accounting and budgeting systems of government to bring them in line with the need to focus on system-wide and societal results. There is an urgent need for a systematic re-thinking in this area.

LEARNING AS ONE FOR SERVING AS ONE

Leveraging strategies explore how to pool assets to generate better results and invent solutions to problems that had previously remained intractable when using conventional approaches. Leveraging different assets yields different benefits and requires different considerations.

The fieldwork with law enforcement agencies has stressed the importance of leveraging knowledge assets. They help agencies deploy their limited resources to areas with the greatest potential of impact. For instance, law enforcement agencies looked for risk patterns in order to develop strategies aimed at unravelling clusters of illegal behaviours.[12] In these cases, the starting point of a leveraging strategy is the pooling of knowledge assets available in relevant government agencies and other levels of government.

Leveraging knowledge assets across government agencies ensures that government gains a comprehensive knowledge of what it already knows in a disaggregated way. There may be some limitations to sharing information across agencies, but, by and large, these problems are not insurmountable. Aggregating and leveraging information from across government are important steps to improve the likelihood of success of targeted government interventions. Analytical tools and techniques are available to help practitioners extract meaning and detect patterns from large data sets.

The next two cases provide examples where administrative data collected by multiple public organisations was brought together to detect patterns of harm and to develop a holistic strategy in response.

Learning from Practice: Detecting Patterns of Risk
Metal Thefts
A law enforcement agency in Sarawak, Malaysia trying to prevent metal thefts discovered a direct correlation between incidents and the value of metal on the stock market. A majority of the theft was of copper cabling and threatened the stability of the power supply and telecom systems. A more detailed analysis allowed the agency to detect patterns of infractions

at the community level and on specific construction sites. Using this information in combination with existing data on licensed resellers and the origin of materials, the agency was able to deploy successful enforcement interventions targeting high-risk areas.[13]

Learning from Practice: Evidence-Based Re-thinking Road Policies

The Government of Australia's 10-year road strategy aims to reduce the number of fatalities to zero. While road causalities have declined by 25 percent between 2003 and 2013, data showed that vulnerable populations such as pedestrians, motorcyclists and cyclists remain at risk. The discrepancy between declining car fatalities and incidents involving other road users suggested enforcement efforts focussing on 'irresponsible' drivers were unlikely to remedy the situation. Conventional safety strategies place accident responsibility primarily on driver behaviour and human error, however, a more detailed analysis revealed that poor road system design and other factors had a more significant impact on vulnerable users. Recommendations were made to design a "Safe System" that accepts the possibility of human error when trying to reduce crash risks as much as possible.[14]

Big data analysis may still be in its infancy in government but it has significant potential for improving decision making. Data is collected by government at all levels, statistical agencies and multiple international organisations. Academic research and private organisations collect data for their own purposes. Web browsers are meta-data collectors. Polls and surveys of all kinds are conducted regularly. Making good use of data is challenging because of the availability of large volumes of data from multiple sources generated with high velocity and in a variety of forms. The greatest potential of big data is to confirm or invalidate the hypothesis underlying government actions and decisions.

Despite the increasing need for co-operation, leveraging exercises reveal very few systems designed to serve across boundaries. The administrative systems in place today were designed at a time when departments and ministries were expected to carry out most of their business on their own. The good news is that what was put in place by those in authority at a prior time can be changed by those in authority at this time. Administrative systems are not immutable and must change to adapt to changing circumstances.

There is a need to complement the administrative systems that have worked well in the past with ramps and connectors to support government-wide activities, ensure strategic coherence and create solutions with others. Modern public administrations going forward should be recognised for their capacity to *serve as one, act as one and learn as one.*

LOOKING BACK AND MOVING FORWARD

Positioning shifts the focus of attention from agency results to societal outcomes. This encourages public sector leaders to focus on the big picture and on the higher public purpose they serve. Focussing on societal results reveals the multidimensional nature of complex issues and the need for co-operation across boundaries. This is the power of a broader mental map.

A *leveraging* strategy encourages collaboration across government and across sectors. This shifts the focus of attention from a government-centric search for solutions to a governance-centric perspective; from what governments can do on their own, to how better results can be achieved by building on the *strength of others* and pooling existing resources and capabilities.

While positioning and leveraging concepts have been introduced sequentially, in reality they interact with one another as the search for solutions progresses. It is not uncommon in practice to reframe an issue several times as the exploration progresses and new insights are garnered through discussions among interested organisations and partners.

As with positioning, there are common mistakes practitioners make in developing a leveraging strategy. Too often public sector leaders seek permission to make decision within the space of their authority. They do not use their authority to the fullest. An effective leveraging strategy requires a real commitment to leverage change using whatever resources are available. Public sector leaders unnecessarily limit themselves if their actions are conditional, whether dependent on others acting first or on others granting permission.

Leveraging resources is a collaborative effort. Unfortunately, practitioners often attempt to exert control over the relationship, merely 'inform' partners of their plans and approach the collaboration with minimal flexibility in desired means or ends. Entering a collaborative effort with a view to improve agency results misses the larger purpose, and jeopardises the relations needed for serving across boundaries.

Clarity of purpose is the starting point of an NS exploration aimed at addressing issues of concern for society. What would success look like in societal terms? Why does it matter and what difference would this make for the future? Who cares enough about the issue to put time, energy and resources behind this?

Every government intervention is aimed at transforming the world we live in. They are designed to transform behaviours and the interrelationships between the public, private and civic sectors. Public interventions are experiments in progress aimed at generating results judged desirable for society. Government uses the authority of the State as a lever to bring about the desired societal outcomes. Small changes may have a vast ripple effect at multiple levels and across systems. In some ways, governments are meta-system designers where every action and decision is intended to change the behaviour of other systems.

The NS Exploratory Process is designed to help public sector leaders figure out what mix of actions and decisions will bring about, in the most effective way, the desired public outcomes with a minimum of unintended consequences or disruption of society. This is where the leveraging capabilities of government and public organisations make a world of difference between grand ideas that will never materialise and those that will, in some ways, change the course of events for the better.

CHAPTER 6

THE POWER OF CITIZENS AS PUBLIC VALUE CREATORS – ENGAGING

Serving a public purpose and using the authority of the State to promote the collective interest are two principles public sector leaders can rely on to guide their actions. A third and equally important principle is that governing entails a *relationship that binds the State and citizens together*.[1] This relationship plays a critical role in building a governable society. It is a determinant of whether government has the capacity to govern without excessive reliance on the use of coercive measures.

The conventional view saw citizens in a subservient relationship with the State. According to this view, people have a limited capacity to address the public challenges that bedevil society.[2] At the most basic level, citizens are expected to pay taxes, obey the law and participate in elections from time to time.[3] They are not expected, nor encouraged, to play a significant role in shaping public policies or programmes, problem solving or decision making with government even in the areas of greatest interest to them.[4] This view has had a number of adverse consequences over the years, not the least of which has been a crowding out of the contribution of citizens and an erosion of the natural resilience of society.[5]

Civic results reflect a civic capacity for collective problem solving and a civic will to put these capabilities to productive use. Civic results are the dark matter of well performing and governable societies. These results are forged by citizens in their interactions with each other and with government. A society displays a high level of civic capacity when its members are able and willing to accomplish shared goals and build a better future together.[6] It is manifest in the collective capacity to forge a level of consensus that encourages collective actions. Conventional public administration has given insufficient attention to the importance of civic results. Pursuing the analogy of dark matter in astronomy, it is said that dark matter amounts to 75 to 85 percent of all matter in the universe; it is not directly observable but its influence is felt across the universe. Similarly, civic results are intangible; they are not easily measurable but their influence is felt across society. Their importance is most obvious in period of rapid change or when society is under stress. Civic capacity makes it possible to align live forces within society in a convergent direction to address collective issues. It reduces the cost of frictions between groups and the tensions among people and government.

Civic results are much more than civility in interpersonal relations or a sense of belonging – even though these factors help avoid behaviours that erode the civic capacity for problem solving. Civic results include self-confident individuals able to deal with the circumstances of life in society. They possess the self-confidence necessary to make choices and participate in society including the political affairs of public life.

Civic results include resilient communities with a deep reservoir of solidarity and a capability for collective problem solving,[7] and a civic spirit that infuses every aspect of people's lives as members of a broader human community.[8] Civic results contribute to societal cohesion and build the capacity for collective action.

The importance of civic capacity is most noticeable when it is most needed. The civic capacity of the people of South Africa was on display in the post-apartheid period where political leadership, institutional support and community engagement all played a prominent role in the reconciliation process.

It was also evident in the fight against the HIV/AIDS pandemic in Brazil that was discussed in Chapter 5. A combination of public leadership, institutional capacity, community based support as well as public mobilisation was needed to change the course of events. Other situations reveal that one or several of these elements are lacking. For instance, the leadership and community support systems to enable collective action were lacking in the aftermath of hurricane Katrina in New Orleans in 2005.[9] *Civic results and collective problem solving require a blend of public leadership, institutional capabilities, civic will and civic capacity.*

Public mobilisation without institutional capacity to harness the collective efforts or the civic capacity to converge towards a common solution is unlikely to generate viable solutions. This was on display in recent years in a number of Arab states and in particular in Egypt where popular uprisings in favour of greater liberalisation were co-opted by groups with greater organisational capability on the ground, even though their priorities ran in the opposite direction from many of the people who had initiated the protest movement. In a different way, violent events in France, Ferguson, Dallas and Baton Rouge also reveal a lack of capacity for collective problem solving. Mobilisation and spontaneous expressions of solidarity did not lead to a growing consensus to address the challenge of ensuring public safety without curtailing the rights and freedom of citizens. In fact, these events have led to deeper divides and a more polarised society.

Civic results are generated day by day through the actions individuals take in partnership with others and with government to find solutions to problems of concern to them and society.[10] Governments bear a special responsibility for building the civic capacity to problem solve and invent solutions to collective problems. Governing in the 21st century requires re-thinking the relationship between government and citizens from the subservient relationship that characterised governance during most of the 19th and 20th centuries to a relationship that encourages mutuality, shared responsibility for results and shared accountability for collective actions.

This requires a *citizen-centric perspective* to policy making and service delivery as well as a recognition of the role of citizens and communities as public value creators. The NS Exploratory Process uses a systematic approach to discover how a different relationship between government and citizens may yield better public and civic results.

CITIZEN-CENTRICITY

A citizen-centric perspective is quite different from a focus on user satisfaction. A high level of user satisfaction is not a guarantee that the results generated are of increasing value for society. As individuals, people pursue their own interests and the interests of those closest to them. As citizens, people are called upon to reconcile their individual preferences with the pursuit of the collective interest, because they can only fulfil certain fundamental aspirations by belonging to a larger community.[11] This is the case for people's aspiration for a peaceful life or for ensuring the well-being of their children. One of the most fundamental roles of the State is to transform people into citizens.[12] The relationship that binds the State and its citizens is at the very heart of public administration.[13]

Serving in the 21st century requires re-conceptualising the relationship between the State and its citizens. The NS Initiative does not express a view about who should or should not become a legal citizen, nor does it speculate about the bundles of rights, entitlements and responsibilities that ought to be associated with modern concepts of citizenship. The NS Initiative focusses instead on the relationship between the public sector and citizens. A NS exploration to engage citizens as public value creators begins with the proposition that citizens, their families and communities are the most important public value creators in society.

The term 'citizen' in the NS context refers to all persons living in a country whether or not they meet the legal definition of citizenship. In part this is justified by the fact that government interacts with those inside its geographic jurisdiction whether or not they are legal citizens. From the NS perspective, citizens are those whose interests are involved in the collective projects of their communities. The pursuit of the collective interest cannot strictly delineate between legal citizens and other members of society.

There are many reasons and situations where it is advisable for government to explore the benefits of a different sharing of responsibilities with citizens.[14] For instance, some government programmes have become *unaffordable* as they are no longer adapted to current circumstances and make limited use of their beneficiaries' own capacities to contribute towards desired public outcomes. A typical example would be the impact of an aging population on the cost of health care services or the affordability of pension programmes. In the case of pension reforms, a government-centric perspective typically leads towards two unsatisfactory answers – reducing costs (by increasing the age of pensions and cutting benefits) or spending more (by raising taxes or increasing contributions). Similarly, confronted with the rising costs of elder care services, a conventional approach is to contain costs in order to avoid raising taxes or to reduce the investments needed in other priority areas.

In other cases, government initiatives are *unsustainable* without the participation of citizens. Reducing energy and water consumption or preventing the obesity pandemic require the active contribution of a diversity of actors, including individuals, families, community organisations, and the private and public sectors. Government can regulate, educate and set favourable conditions, but ultimately, these results involve behavioural changes. In such cases, the desirable outcomes will either be co-produced or not produced at all.

Finally, some government policies and programmes have created *dependencies*. These programmes erode people's capacity to control the circumstances of their lives and the natural resilience of society to adapt to changing circumstances. For example, an efficient in-home healthcare programme may discourage recipients' autonomy if not structured to develop individual capacities. These situations are not limited to social programmes, and extend to any organisation, association or entity dependent on government support to exist or sustain its activities. Eliminating these programmes is not always the most effective way forward. A different sharing of responsibility may yield better results.

Public policy challenges look very different from a citizen perspective and from the perspective of the users and beneficiaries of public services. What if engaging the people most knowledgeable about their own circumstances in the design of public policies and services intended to support them could lead to better outcomes, lower costs and improved user satisfaction? The fieldwork revealed that this is exactly what some public sector leaders have been able to achieve by bringing a citizen-centric perspective to their search for solutions.

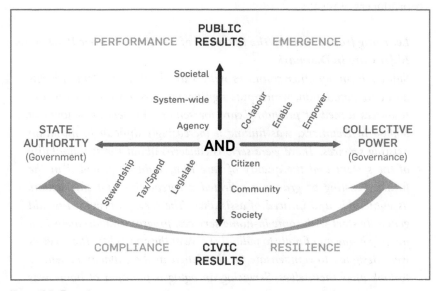

Figure 6.1: Engaging

Citizen engagement has intrinsic and instrumental value. Providing opportunities for people to act as citizens, and by doing so building an active citizenry, is a public good in itself whether or not it also translates into other public results. Citizen engagement opens new avenues for creating public results that avoid overreliance on government or overconfidence in market forces.[15]

A strategy for citizen engagement can take many forms depending on the purpose, context and circumstances. The possibilities span a broad spectrum, ranging from familiar practices that contribute to a shared awareness of issues, like shared information, communication or consultation, to more ambitious arrangements that entail a deeper relationship such as co-creation, co-production and self-organisation.

Ultimately, the responsibility for selecting an approach that engages citizens as problem solvers and as value creators rests with government. Public sector leaders must know when and how to engage citizens in order to make better use of society's most valuable assets: people's time and ingenuity.

This case from Denmark shows how better public outcomes are possible when the individuals directly affected are included in policy making and are co-producers of results.

Learning from Practice: The Potential of a Citizen-Centric Perspective Elder Care in Denmark[16]

Similar to many other countries with a low birth rate, Denmark has an aging population, which puts significant pressures on services and resources aimed at providing care for seniors. Fredericia, a town of 50,000 in Denmark, was finding it increasingly difficult to maintain existing services. There were serious concerns about the sustainability of the system and the quality of care that could be provided in the future. Existing programmes reflected a perspective that saw seniors as vulnerable and in need of assistance. The services provided would generally start with some in-home services, progress to placement in a nursing home and finally to palliative care at the end of life. The services were designed to compensate for the deficit in the capacity of seniors to look after themselves. Servicing an aging population at home was putting significant pressure on services and resources earmarked for elder care.

These services were becoming unaffordable for the municipality as the population was aging, but there were other reasons to worry beyond the cost factors. Some research revealed disturbing results. The programmes, though well intended, were a "care trap" where the beneficiaries progressively lost their ability to cope with everyday life. This research also showed that seniors who managed their daily life as long as possible had a happier life.[17] This was the starting point for unleashing an innovation process that led to a new approach to elder care based on personal strengths, self-reliance and resilience. It begins with a citizen-centric perspective to programme design and delivery. Given the chance to speak for themselves, seniors provided a very different perspective than the one embedded in existing programmes. The conversations with seniors turned several basic assumptions on their head. Many elders did not really care for some government-paid home care; they would rather care for themselves for as long as possible.[18]

The existing situation was unaffordable and had serious detrimental consequences. This was an opportunity to re-frame the issue from a different perspective. The Municipality made the decision to re-evaluate the situation from a user and a citizens' perspectives. Exploratory conversations with the users of the programme and their families revealed a serious disconnect between the assumptions underlying existing programmes and the aspirations of users. Not all services were appreciated by elders or needed. Elderly people may be frail but a clear message was that they aspire to maintain control over their life for as long as possible. Instead of demanding more 'care' services they wanted help to maintain their autonomy as long as possible.

This departure from conventional thinking was the starting point of radical welfare innovation based on the idea of empowering the elderly to take care of themselves by investing in developing competencies that would diminish the use of compensatory initiatives.[19] The purpose of the initiative was to encourage "Life Long Living" by building the capacity of seniors to maintain independent living as long as possible and as long as they wanted. The conversation with seniors centred on what they would like to be able to do again; the needs ranged from getting dressed, taking a bath by themselves, walking to the bank, going to the theatre or visiting their grandchildren. The programme developed a concept of daily rehabilitation, using every day activities as a way of regaining strengths and developing cognitive capacities. Another element of the programme were systematic re-evaluations of elderly users' needs to ascertain if they still needed the same level of assistance they were initially provided or if their condition had improved. This recognised that the situation will not inevitably deteriorate and may very well improve as the participants regained competencies and new capabilities.

There are important insights to draw from the experience of the Municipality of Fredericia:

Exploratory conversations: Citizen-centric exploratory conversations are focussed, targeted and methodical. They do not start with answers and a defined position as is so often the case with consultation initiatives. Rather, they begin with open-ended questions such as "what would you like to be able to do again?" The conversation focused on the human experience and the interactions between the elderly person and others. The life of people enrolled in the programme is the starting point of designing services to help them meet their life goals.

People's assets: Citizen-centric approaches recognise that people, even in difficult situations, have important assets to contribute. It is their aspirations and active engagement that will bring about the desired outcomes; in this case, this means to regain the strengths and abilities to live a functional life.

Flexibility: Citizen-centric services present particular challenges for public administrators. They require a high degree of flexibility on the part of the administration and the programmes may be open to challenges since not everyone will get the same services. It is worth noting that the Municipality of Fredericia changed its governance model as a result of this experience. They also decided to use a similar approach in other areas.

Co-creation and co-production: Co-creation and co-production transform the relationship between users and providers of public services.[20] Both groups play an active and essential role by building on each other's strengths and making use of each other's assets in order to generate better public outcomes.[21] There is no guarantee of success but a real possibility of discovering a better solution than the one that currently exists. There is nothing to lose when the status quo is untenable or unaffordable.

The results of the Danish elder care programme were impressive:

> *The programme empowered seniors to define the services they needed to pursue an active live on their own terms. They co-created a programme that freed substantial resources that could be redeployed in areas of greater need. Seniors involved in the programme share the responsibility to work with the various professionals involved in their care. It is their resolve and their efforts that make it possible for them to maintain an independent and fulfilling life for as long as life permits. Building on the strengths of seniors and making better use of their resourcefulness yielded significant results. An evaluation conducted in 2008 based on 778 participants in the programme revealed that 45.9 percent were able to live an independent life, 38.9 percent needed less help than initially requested and 84.8 percent expressed better quality of life and a resumption of desired life activities. Staff morale improved.[22] The programme has continued to evolve and has been replicated in other cities in Denmark and in other countries.*

Citizen engagement strategies open up the policy making cycle and service delivery processes to the people most directly affected. This provides invaluable insights into how people interact with government. It is at this point that public policy choices become real for most people. Citizen engagement strategies offer an opportunity for government to improve the impact of public initiatives by tapping into the knowledge and insights of users and sharing the responsibility for creating practical solutions with them.

A CONTINUUM OF CHOICES: KNOWING WHEN

There is no expectation that government should engage citizens in all circumstances. Governments have been elected to make decisions on people's behalf and they have access to powerful tools to bring about desired public results.

A key question for public sector leaders to know is when is it desirable to seek the active engagement of citizens and when is it preferable for governments to take action on their own? The answers to these questions depend on the purpose, context and circumstances as well as the culture of government. The following sections may help practitioners think their way through some of the choices open to them.

Participants in NS labs have found it useful to clarify when governments are best positioned to act alone and when there would be political reluctance to open up the decision-making process even if there is a high likelihood of generating better results. Governments are not all equally receptive to the idea of sharing decision making with citizens. The NS fieldwork has shown that it is preferable to move slowly and gain experience in co-creating solutions and co-producing results before generating expectations that cannot be fulfilled. Co–production is not applicable to every domain of activity and may even be counter-productive in contentious areas such as the protection of minority rights or in the case of ethnic or religious conflicts. It may inadvertently lead to more entrenched positions and deeper divisions.

Figure 6.2 was generated with participants in the context of NS labs. At one end, it summarises when governments are well positioned to act on their own and, at the other, when it is unlikely that the desired public outcomes can be achieved by governments acting alone. In between, there is a whole host of possibilities including information sharing, communication, consultations and cooperation.

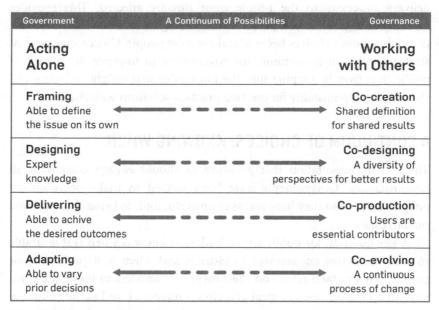

Government	A Continuum of Possibilities	Governance
Acting Alone		**Working with Others**
Framing Able to define the issue on its own		**Co-creation** Shared definition for shared results
Designing Expert knowledge		**Co-designing** A diversity of perspectives for better results
Delivering Able to achive the desired outcomes		**Co-production** Users are essential contributors
Adapting Able to vary prior decisions		**Co-evolving** A continuous process of change

Figure 6.2: A Continuum of Possibilities

Acting Alone

The NS fieldwork has identified three sets of conditions that reveal when government is well positioned to act on its own and achieve its desired outcomes. First, the case when the knowledge required to frame an issue is readily available to government and when the relevant tools are also in the hands of government. Tax issues come to mind as an example. Although taxation measures may be hotly debated and contested, government generally possesses all the relevant data and tools to model the impact of tax measures and assess the results in advance of making decisions.

Second, governments are in a strong position to act on their own if they have the exclusive use of the tools for achieving the desired policy outcomes or if they have preponderant influence on their use. For instance, governments have the exclusive use of some of the levers pertaining to border management, national defence, monetary policy, public safety and criminal justice. Some have significant influence on matters like trade agreements and treaty negotiations.

The third set of conditions is to be able to detect the early signs of problems and to initiate course corrections if necessary. These three conditions interact with one another. Some decisions, once acted upon, unleash a chain of events beyond the control of the initiating government. The history of the world is replete with examples of conflicts that arose as a result of government actions initiated with no fall-back position and no capacity to turn back the clock.

Government decisions and actions following conventional means will continue to be the preferred approach in a number of circumstances. Indeed, it is the most efficient approach to address many pressing needs, and it is the most efficient way to mass-produce services that benefit society as a whole.

A conventional approach sets a clear direction and gives an impetus for change, but it is not the only way nor the best way to govern in all circumstances. Governments fit for the challenge of governing in a post-industrial era must be able to simultaneously use a diversity of approaches: acting on their own when needed and working with others whenever it is both possible and desirable to do so. Public sector leaders must *know when* a different sharing of responsibility has the potential of advancing the overall interests of society and they must *know how* to do it well.

Co-labouring with Others

The participants in NS labs have also identified three sets of circumstances when there are compelling reasons for government to work with citizens, and by extension their families and communities, to generate desirable public outcomes.

Governments need to consider engagement strategies when a shared understanding of the issue is key to making progress. In some cases, the relevant framing of an issue is the one that will generate buy-in and encourage collective actions. The search for solutions starts by framing an issue in a way that helps overcome resistance and rise above entrenched positions. Such a problem definition must be co-created to achieve a shared understanding of the issue that is sufficiently broad to bring together people with starkly different perspectives. Debates about climate change, gun control and the use of the death penalty are of this kind. New knowledge or new data are unlikely to unfreeze the situation and law enforcement does not work in the face of deep public opposition.

Co-creation is also a promising avenue when no one has an adequate understanding of an issue and when government lacks the information to make informed decisions. The knowledge needed is distributed among various groups and the relevant information on the situation is in the hands of those closest to the action. A process that encourages shared knowledge is a necessary step to gain a shared understanding of the challenge. This in turn opens up previously undetected avenues for bringing about viable solutions.

The second set of circumstances prevails when a result requires a shared responsibility of government and citizens, families and communities working together. An increasing number of issues exceed the capacity of governments to bring about change on their own. Some changes require behavioural changes and broad cultural shifts; addressing the impact of an aging population and work force, reducing fossil fuel consumption and encouraging the use of public transportation come to mind.

Other challenges require a complex alchemy that brings together a mix of actions from the public, private and civic sectors. Reconstruction initiatives whether in Fort McMurray, Canada as a result of a devastating fire that affected 80,000 people or post-conflict reconstruction situations are examples of results that must be co-generated. They require collective action from multiple contributors, affected families, communities and government working together.

The third set of circumstances is a reminder of the need for government to co-evolve with society. Citizen engagement builds the civic capacity for collective problem solving, the adaptive capacity of government and the resilience of society.

A CONTINUUM OF CHOICES: KNOWING HOW

The approaches most frequently used by government officials that participated in NS workshops to engage citizens can be grouped into four broad categories: collaborative policy making, co-creation, co-production and self-organisation.

In the context of the NS Initiative, the terms co-creation and co-production are used selectively. One may find examples in the literature where these terms are used to describe any form of citizen engagement, including information sharing, communication or consultation. However, for the NS Initiative, the prefix "co-" is used only when there is evidence of a sharing of responsibility between the users and the public service agency in question.

Co-creation brings together a diversity of perspectives by drawing from the assets of public agencies, service providers and users. Users and service providers are directly involved in shaping a policy response adapted to the context where solutions will be implemented. Design thinking, ethnographic surveys and prototyping are frequently used to help users and service providers co-invent solutions adapted to the users' needs. Government generally sets the parameters for the collective effort, taking account of the legal, fiscal or administrative constraints that may otherwise limit action.

Co-production directly engages public service users, and by extension their families and communities, in the actual production of results by working with public agencies. It makes active use of people's assets and requires a shared responsibility for the outcomes. In contrast with co-creation, which requires no direct relationship with the ultimate users, co-production entails a direct relationship between the service provider and the service users. They co-produce the service together. Co-production builds a relationship between government and citizens characterised by mutuality and shared responsibility.

Self-organisation aims at generating the conditions to encourage citizens and communities to generate solutions to their concerns in a manner that also serves the collective interest. In these cases, government plays an active but supporting role that may include building the necessary infrastructure, fostering an enabling environment, sharing information or monitoring results. Technology-enabled self-organisation opens the door to new forms of mass collaboration.

Collaborative policy making brings citizens into the policy making cycle. These approaches contribute to building public awareness, generating a shared understanding of the consequences that various policy choices entail and building a broad-based consensus on a desired approach. Strictly speaking, these approaches do not necessarily entail a sharing of responsibility since governments retain the authority for making decisions, but they create an expectation and even a political imperative to take the results of the engagement process into account in future decisions. The credibility of the initiative and of future undertakings hinges on the decisions that are made following a collaborative policy making effort. Modern information and communication technologies open up new avenues for through mass collaboration, and other ways of collective problem solving.

In the end, it is the responsibility of governments and public sector leaders to select an approach adapted to the circumstances. It is also the responsibility of the public sector to ensure public servants have the skills and competencies needed to engage citizens effectively. Many countries have gained experience in recent years. However, citizen engagement strategies rarely figure in the curriculum or programmes designed for preparing future public sector leaders.

The NS fieldwork has generated a number of important insights for improving the likelihood of success of government initiatives aimed at engaging citizens as problem solvers and public value creators.

Meaningful engagement starts with a clarity of purpose. Successful citizen engagement strategies are open to a diversity of solutions but designed to serve a specific public purpose. What is the problem government is trying to address and that the engagement process is intended to resolve; why does it matter for society and citizens? This topic was previously discussed in Chapter 4.

Clear rules of engagement. It is the responsibility of government to explain how an engagement process will unfold, how input will be used and how decisions will be made. Clear rules of engagement reduce the risks of misunderstanding and avoid generating expectations that cannot be fulfilled.

A commensurate approach to the expected benefits. The engagement of citizens implies a reallocation of people's time from their private life to work with government. Citizens' time is an asset of considerable value. People use their time to earn a living, take care of their children or ageing parents, work in the community, rest or pursue activities of their choosing. Public sector leaders must therefore consider with care if the purpose they have in mind warrants displacing people's time from their current activities.

Synergy through a diversity. A diverse set of approaches working simultaneously is necessary to address complex issues. Viable solutions to complex issues require a mix of activities – some by government, some by others and others by citizens. This is a significant departure from conventional approaches to public policy making that focus primarily on government decisions. The public sector must ensure that these activities work synergistically to bring about the desired results.

In summary, public agencies that do not consider the potential for co-producing results with citizens reduce the range of options available to government for generating better public results at a lower cost for society. The following sections provide practical examples of the concepts discussed so far.

OPENING UP THE PUBLIC POLICY CYCLE

From time to time, governments choose to open up the policy making process by seeking the input of stakeholders and various interest groups. This is done to bring in valuable external insights at various points along the policy making cycle. External insights may help frame the issue from a broader perspective or adjust the design of programmes in a manner that takes into account the concerns of particular groups. External input may also be necessary to monitor results over time or to evaluate the impact of a policy initiative. These approaches are well known to government. They are represented by the dotted arrows in Figure 6.3. They do not entail a different sharing of responsibility per se since governments retain the authority for decision making.

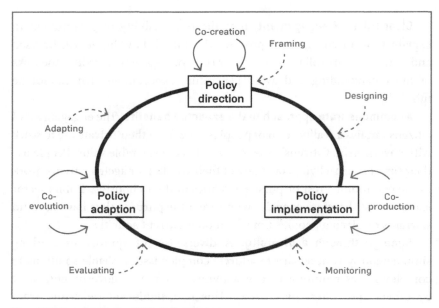

Figure 6.3: Opening Up the Public Policy Cycle

Other avenues are open to government. They are represented by the solid arrows in Figure 6.3. Co-creation and co-production initiatives are used to explore how government and citizens may make better use of each other's assets to address issues of concern to society. In these cases, government forgoes some degree of control over the solution that will be found because the solution will be created through a collective effort. Nonetheless, government retains a high degree of control over the overall process since it must decide if a co-created solution will be implemented at all and by what means.

A co-created solution may be implemented in conventional ways by a public agency, by an external service provider, by a public-private partnership or by any other means. Co-production is one more way of implementing a public policy response; it is a public-citizen production model between government and citizens where both play an active role and share the responsibility for the outcome.

It is important to note that the willingness of government to co-create a solution does not create an obligation to co-produce the services that will ensue. These are two distinct and independent decisions.[23]

A Public-Citizen Production Model

Co-production "open[s] up an alternative approach" to government-centric services and market solutions.[24] Deregulation, privatisation and public-private partnerships have been used extensively in recent years. In some cases, these measures were taken in response to fiscal pressures. In other cases, they reflect a search for a different balance between the roles of the State and the market.

Something of profound significance is at play when government is considering whether a service should be provided by the public sector or left to market forces. This decision is not simply about the choice of a delivery channel; it is about *the nature of the good*. Is it a public good available to all under certain circumstances or a private good produced if it is profitable to do so and accessible to those who can afford it?

Co-production expands the range of options open to government for the production of public goods. It is, in essence, a public–citizen production model.

The case of the *Swedish Clinic of Internal Medicine* illustrates how co-production was used to generate better health outcomes, better services and a better use of public resources.

Learning from Practice: Co-production
Swedish Clinic of Internal Medicine[25]
At the Highland Hospital in Eksjö, Sweden, long wait lists were preventing the clinic from offering timely treatment. This was a source of concern for both patients and staff of the gastroenterology unit. Regularly scheduled appointments were using most of the medical staff's time but were marginally useful in detecting the risks of imminent flare-ups and crises. These acute conditions typically arose between regular visits and necessitated visits to the emergency room. Long wait times were adversely affecting patients' health and increasing the likelihood of extended hospital stays.

The medical staff devised a new approach. They re-designed the system from the patient's perspective. The new system placed patients at the centre of two streams: a community stream, composed of family and friends, and a medical stream comprised of hospital staff. Patients were prepared to play an active role by monitoring their medical condition when their health condition was relatively stable and administering medication and treatment on their own or with the assistance of family and friends trained for this purpose. This reduced the need for routine visits and freed up the medical team's time so staff could dedicate more time to patients when their conditions deteriorated. Patients enrolled in the programme were guaranteed timely access to medical staff in the event of a sudden flare-up. Patients, with the support of their family, became co-producers of their health care services. This approach led to significantly improved results. "Waiting lists were eliminated, the number of unscheduled visits by patients with flare-ups declined from two per day in 2001 to two per week in 2005. This led to better patient access to treatment, improved health, lower morbidity rates and reduced stress on the unit's budget and staff".[26]

The participants of NS labs and workshops have drawn several lessons from their own experiences with co-production and from international examples. One of the most important lessons is that in many cases the riskiest option is the status quo while the least risky option is to try something different. In the above example, the status quo was affecting patients' health; there was nothing to lose and much to gain in exploring a different approach.

Conventional approaches place the expert – a physician in the example above and a public servant in other examples – at the centre of the service delivery function, with the user in a peripheral position and other staff in supporting roles. In cases of co-production, the services are re-thought from the users' perspective. The Swedish clinic's patients were in the middle of two service delivery streams: a community stream made up of family and friends and a medical stream composed of hospital staff. Activities were re-thought "to involve patients more intensively in their own care" and "give them greater personal responsibility for their health".[27] In this context, patients become co-producers. They partner with the medical team and share the responsibility for their treatment.

Co-production does not diminish professional responsibility. Conventional practices and new approaches co-exist. In the above case, patients enjoyed a high degree of control when their health was relatively stable, but medical staff exercised professional oversight of their health conditions and control over medical treatment.

Extensive data collection and ongoing evaluation are needed to monitor co-production initiatives. This is needed to assess the impact of new approaches and ensure their sustainability. In the above case, the information collected over the last ten years provides a reliable baseline to monitor the progress achieved by the Highland Clinic compared to other clinics in Sweden.

A Public-Community Production Model

At the outset, the NS Initiative focussed on co-production involving government and the users of public services. Fieldwork has revealed, however, that a community-based co-production model also deserves special attention.

Communities played a key role in most of the strategies crafted by participants of NS workshops. Communities, rather than individual users, were the co-producers of results in several areas ranging from border and water management to crime prevention. Community-based co-production initiatives share a number of common characteristics. They bring decisions closer to users and improve the collective capacity for timely adjustments or course corrections.

Community co-production cases are not devolution initiatives where power and resources are transferred from a legal government entity at a higher level to one at the local level. They involve a real sharing of responsibility which enables formal, informal and community groups to play an active role that will change over time as circumstances change.

The importance of community-based co-production approaches appeared most clearly during a project undertaken in the spring of 2015 with the State of Sarawak, Malaysia.

Learning from Practice: Public-Community Production Model
Sarawak High Performance Teams, 2015
The participants were asked to discover solutions to some of the most intractable law enforcement challenges confronting the State. The initiative brought together heads of agencies and senior public officials from 109 government agencies, including 21 federal agencies, 51 State agencies, 28 statutory bodies and 9 government-owned or government-linked companies.[28] The initiative evolved over several months and led to a number of government-wide strategies that are currently being implemented.

The theme of the Sarawak HPT retreat 2015 was "Enforcement and Safety". Eleven teams were set up to find solutions to compliance issues of concern to the State. The topics selected were vast and diverse. They included illegal logging, illegal sand extraction, illegal activities in retail outlets, waste management, the management of water catchment areas, road safety, illegal dumping, open burning, the illegal entry of foreign nationals, illegal palm oil fruit harvesting and metal thefts.

These topics were selected because of the negative impact they were having on the well-being of the State of Sarawak as well as on government revenues, the environment, society and Sarawak's reputation. Participants recognised, from the outset, that these complex issues required a government-wide approach and that citizen and communities support would be needed to make progress.

The teams used the NS Framework to craft their enforcement strategies. The proposed strategies used a diversity of approaches and most included some form of co-production arrangement at the community level. The strategies to eradicate illegal dumping, improve road safety, reduce the use of open burning, prevent illegal logging and improve border management made explicit provisions for the engagement of communities and put in place working arrangements involving local agents and local authorities. The arrangements frequently included shared responsibility for detecting issues and monitoring results. Several included co-decision mechanisms. Others required the training of local groups and co-ordinated enforcement efforts. A broad sketch of the proposed strategies was published in the fall of 2015.[29] The strategies have since received Cabinet approval and are currently being implemented.

This work was an important reminder for the NS Team that co-production arrangements are not limited to a sharing of responsibility between government and individual users of public services. It is necessary to make better use of community assets to generate public and civic results of increasing value for society.

Other countries have also experienced the importance of a production model that brings together the innovative capacity of communities and the support role of government.

As this example from Finland shows, government need not be the primary driver behind a collaboration if it is willing to support emergent and self-organised solutions.

Learning from Practice: Public-Civic Production Model
Helsinki Cleaning Day
In early 2012, a resident of Helsinki, Finland posted a Facebook status with an idea to simplify urban recycling.[30] Helsinki had no equivalent to the citywide flea markets held in neighbouring countries that allowed citizens to sell second-hand items in public spaces without a permit.[31] The Facebook status proposed a community-organised, one-day flea market for citizens to sell, give away or exchange gently used items in public spaces across Helsinki.[32] The idea generated enthusiasm online as local citizens volunteered to co-ordinate activities and build an online platform to plan the event. The first Cleaning Day (Siivouspäivä) was held in Helsinki on May 12, 2012.[33]

The success of the first Cleaning Day encouraged collaboration from government, private corporations such as recycling plants, and the general public.[34] Following the success of the first Cleaning Day in Helsinki, residents from dozens of other Finnish towns and cities have organised similar flea market events and have drawn crowds of buyers and sellers from all over Europe.[35]

SELF-ORGANISATION AND MASS COLLABORATION

Self-organisation and mass collaboration are not phenomena unique to the 21st century. What is different in the 21st century are the tools and technology, like social media, that significantly lower the barriers to both forms of engagement.

Self-organisation

Self-organisation occurs all the time. People take initiative on their own or join voluntary organisations, committing time and energy to causes of interest to them. These are manifestations of a vibrant society populated by an active citizenry. Voluntarism and voluntary organisations operate with or without the support of government. These activities cover the whole spectrum of human interests whether they contribute to advancing a collective interest or promoting a single interest group.

In the context of the NS Initiative the focus of attention points in another direction. The key question is: *What can government do to encourage people to pursue their individual interests in a manner that also promotes the collective interest?* Of particular interest is how government can use modern information and communication technologies to enable and encourage self-organisation.

Some governments are actively exploring new avenues to enable citizens to self-organise and invent solutions to issues of concern to them. The following two examples, one from New Zealand and the other from the USA, illustrate the potential of technology-enabled self-organisation.

Learning from Practice: Self-organisation for Voluntary Compliance Fishery Compliance in New Zealand

The Ministry of Fisheries in New Zealand was facing compliance problems. Fishermen argued that they could not easily obtain official information about catch sizes, catch limits or changing rules and regulations relevant to each of the six fishing zones off the coast of New Zealand. In response, the Ministry designed a smart phone application that made it easier for fishermen to comply with the government's environmental protection laws and fishing requirements. The application allowed fishermen to receive real-time updates about changes to the minimum size of a fish, the number of fish that could be caught each day and the rules as they applied to different zones. Since releasing the application, the Ministry has reported a decline in formal warnings issued by enforcement staff and a reduction in criminal prosecutions.[36]

Most people want to do the right thing and aspire to be part of a collective effort that makes a difference to society. The key is to discover how to make it easier for people to behave as good citizens. In this example, the fishermen understand very well that their livelihood depends on preserving fish stocks. A successful enforcement strategy in this case is to give fishermen the tools and the information they need to act as conservation officers.

Learning from Practice: Public-Private-Civic Partnerships
Envision Charlotte

Envision Charlotte is an "alliance of employers, building owners and managers along with municipal and technology leaders" in Charlotte, North Carolina aiming to make smarter and more sustainable building choices through collaboration, innovation and community engagement.[37]

Through its Smart Energy Now initiative, Envision Charlotte aims to reduce energy consumption by using technologies that enable individuals and companies to monitor their energy usage in near real-time, thereby empowering them to make better decisions. The community can see data about its collective energy usage on digital displays in the city centre. As a result, people adjust their behaviour to reduce their individual costs leading to aggregate energy savings.

Envision Charlotte aspires to create "the most sustainable urban core in the nation".[38] *Its goal is to reduce energy consumption in the city's urban core by 20 percent over five years. Work is under way on a similar programme to reduce wastewater and develop innovative waste and air quality programmes.*[39]

In this case, organisations in public, private and civic sectors, as well as individual citizens were willing and able to modify their behaviour when provided an effective means of doing so. Overall, the sum of many small behavioural changes is having a significant impact on the city's overall goals.

Mass Collaboration

People are breaking out of a subservient relationship with government. They expect to have a say on matters of interest to them and play an active role in generating solutions to the issues that affect their well-being. Furthermore, modern technologies provide them with the means to ensure their voice is heard on matters of interest to them. This presents new challenges for government as well as significant opportunities to transform the relationship between government and citizens. Several initiatives involving mass collaboration have taken place in recent years. For Instance, this case from Singapore highlights how the credibility of government action is intertwined with engagement practices and subsequent action.

Learning from Practice: Collaborative Policy Making
"Our Singapore Conversation"

In 2012, Prime Minister Lee Hsien Loong launched an initiative called "Our Singapore Conversation". It was a national consultation process designed to engage Singaporeans in discussions about their aspirations for the future of their country. The purpose of the initiative was to build on the success of the last 50 years and chart a course to ensure the future prosperity and well-being of the citizens of Singapore.

The "Conversation" was held in two phases. In the first phase, open-ended questions were used in small group discussions to identify Singaporeans' views, aspirations and hopes for the future. In the second phase, public dialogues were used to explore the major themes that emerged from the small group discussions. Issues like housing, health, education and employment were raised as were concerns about the well-being of the pioneer generation and the need for a better balance between growth and wellness. The relevant public agencies and ministries organised the second phase of the "Conversation" by topic.

Over the course of the year, more than 47,000 Singaporeans from all walks of life participated in 660 dialogues.[40] Citizens were also encouraged to participate via social media platforms. A national face-to-face survey was conducted in four official languages to supplement the information gathered through dialogues and online channels. The initiative resulted in a change agenda framed around five core aspirations:

> ***Opportunities:*** *Building a society where anybody can "make a good living and pursue their aspirations" irrespective of their family background.*
>
> ***Purpose:*** *The value of "a balanced and fulfilling life" beyond economic success.*
>
> ***Assurance:*** *The assurance that "basic needs such as housing, health-care, and public transport" are affordable and within the reach of citizens.*
>
> ***Spirit:*** *Nurturing a common bond that develops "a deeper understanding of the challenges" faced by fellow Singaporeans.*
>
> ***Trust:*** *Deepening trust among Singaporeans and between government and citizens through effective engagement.[41]*

This national consultation initiative strengthened the bond between people and government. A number of new programmes and policies in the areas of health, housing, pensions and immigration were launched as a result. This assured the credibility of such exercises, should others be launched in the future. Collaborative efforts on such a large scale create expectations that may be hard to fulfil and generate a moral obligation for government to take action and explain the decisions that ensue. They require a willingness to trade some degree of control in exchange for the likelihood of forging a broad based public consensus for action. In many cases the risks are well worth the efforts.

The case from Seoul, South Korea is a good example of mass collaboration to forge a consensus on societal goals.

Learning from Practice: Mass Collaboration for Consensus Building Seoul Citizens' Welfare Standards in South Korea

In 2012, the Seoul Metropolitan Government adopted the Seoul Citizens' Welfare Standards with the goal of improving welfare conditions. Developing the standards was an exercise in collaborative policy making that brought together the perspectives of citizens, community organisations, private organisations, government agencies, academics and experts. Today, the City of Seoul is equipped with a policy framework that enjoys strong public support. This has provided the government with the political legitimacy to make difficult decisions and has built strong societal consensus in support of Seoul's welfare programmes.

The City of Seoul committed 30 percent of its 2013 budget to achieving the standards. The government identified 190,000 citizens in need of assistance. Support programmes were provided to improve the standard of living of the targeted population. The City launched a job creation programme aimed at creating 152,000 employment opportunities for youth, women and seniors living below the welfare standards.[42]

The demand for public engagement in collaborative policy making will continue to increase. That said, large-scale engagement initiatives must be used selectively. The NS fieldwork has revealed that consultative processes are a challenging form of citizen engagement and that, by comparison, co-production is a low risk and low cost option. This requires a word of explanation.

Consultation approaches are frequently used by government. Some are done well but many are conducted rather poorly. As a result, there is growing cynicism about government's real motives and increased fatigue with consultative approaches that take up people's time and amount to little in the end. The reality is that it is very difficult to design an effective consultation process. There are issues of representation. There is a need to ensure a diversity of views while avoiding the dominance of single interest groups and preventing the loudest voices or deepest pockets from taking control of the process. In comparison, a co-production process can be run on a small scale and is circumscribed to the users of a given service or to the people directly affected by a programme. Learning is generated as people gain experience and adjustments are made as necessary. If the initiative works well, it can then be expanded to a broader group or used in a different area. Compared to consultation, co-production is a low risk option because much is known about the people involved, and there is an existing relationship between users and service providers.

LOOKING BACK AND MOVING FORWARD

Positioning helps public sector leaders to focus on the big picture and reconnect to the public purpose that gives meaning to government actions and decisions. *Leveraging* reveals the impact of government actions across sectors and the interrelationships between the public, private and civic spheres of our life in society. *Engaging* encourages government to explore how to make better use of people's assets to invent solutions and generate better public and civic results.

At the end of the day everything must fit together. There are an unlimited number of ways to combine issues, means, resources and capabilities to invent solutions to the problems we are facing as a society. The "magic" resides in how all the elements are brought together and interact with each other to bring about a viable solution and propel society forward. This is what *synthesising* is about. Every "New Synthesis" is unique. It can only be created by the people with the authority to act in each circumstance. A *New Synthesis* is a pathway towards a better future. This is the topic of the next chapter.

CHAPTER 7

THE POWER OF A NARRATIVE OF CHANGE – SYNTHESISING

The choice of the words *New Synthesis,* used to describe the initiative launched in 2009, proved to be more thoughtful than was understood at the time. The initial intention was to signal a desire to integrate past practices of enduring value, lessons learned over many years of public sector reforms as well as new practices better aligned to the realities of practice today. As the fieldwork progressed, the NS Team realised that the name was well chosen for many reasons.

A partial answer to the question raised at the start of the NS Initiative – What can we do to ensure that the capacity of government to invent solutions will keep pace with the increasing complexity of the world we live in – is to build the capacity of government and public organisations to bring together in new ways the contributions of government, citizens and multiple agents in society. *A synthesis is needed.*

Some problems cannot be solved through analysis. This is the process of breaking down a matter into smaller parts or elements. It allows for a deeper knowledge of the constitutive elements of a problem and for inferences about the causal relationships among them. Synthesising calls on a different set of practices and skills. It is concerned with *generating a new whole* rather than gaining a deeper understanding of the parts. It is the act of putting a diversity of elements together to form a new pathway, or a new approach for solving problems. Public organisations are known for their analytical capabilities. Going forward, they should also be known for their mastery in combining a diverse set of elements in new ways to generate viable solutions to complex issues and seemingly intractable problems.

Complex problems cannot be solved through analysis alone because there is no direct cause and effect relationship. Multiple factors are at play that interact dynamically with each other and transform the context and the behaviours of relevant actors. These issues do not fit within the boundaries of any single agency. They require public organisations with the ability to invent new pathways leading to better futures. These organisations must be able to pool knowledge and insights that are vastly distributed in society and to enrol the contribution of others. There is a need to build a public sector recognised for an ability to generate new ways to conceptualise issues and an ability to map out a trajectory to address them.

The NS Initiative helps public sector leaders to invent *their own "New Synthesis"*, one that is relevant to their needs and circumstances in order to steer society through a process of change. This involves uncovering practical solutions to the problems that stem from living in a global, hyperconnected and disorderly world.

The previous chapters have illustrated how a systematic exploratory approach to public problem solving can be used to make progress in a measured and pragmatic way. The key elements of the NS journey must be systematically explored, created and put in place in order to make progress. This begins with a clarity of purpose to set the general direction, followed by the use of the authority of the State as lever to enrol the commitment of others, and make use of people's assets, creativity and inventiveness to fulfil collective aspirations for a better future.

In this book, the NS Team has attempted to document lessons learned from public sector leaders who were successful at changing the course of events. They introduced seemingly small changes that unleashed a sequence of events with a disproportionate impact. They focus on emerging issues, detect the early signs of problems, search for solutions, tap the knowledge and expertise of others, try new approaches, monitor results and learn as they go.

The key to preparing public institutions fit for the challenges of governing in the 21st century *is to do systematically and consciously what many public sector leaders do instinctively from time to time*. This is what the NS Exploratory Process is about.

Change can begin in a diversity of places and at any level within the public sector. Success does not depend on the capacity to impose a top-down solution but rather on the ability to bring together into a coherent whole those actions and decisions with the catalytic potential to change the course of events. The exploratory phases presented in the previous chapters were introduced sequentially. In practice, however, they interact with each other. The various elements are modified and combined in different ways until a trajectory gains sufficient support from those people committed to leading the change process. Similarly, the examples presented in the previous chapters were used to illustrate a particular concept, but as we will see in this chapter the positioning, leveraging and engaging dimensions are present in all of them.

A "New Synthesis" brings together, in a coherent whole, the key elements necessary to make progress in addressing a public challenge in a particular context. In the end, everything must fit together and the ideas that describe the general trajectory must be shared to enlist the collaboration of others. Public sector leaders must therefore articulate a narrative of change that takes into account the current reality and the aspirations for a better future. Their "New Synthesis" describes a new reality that does not yet exist but is within the collective capacity to create.

WHAT IS A NEW SYNTHESIS?

A *New Synthesis* integrates the findings of the earlier phases of the NS Exploratory Process outlined in Chapters 3, 4, 5, and 6 around four interacting sets of principles. The NS Framework, depicted again in Figure 7.1, maps out a space of possibility. In determining a course of action within this space, government needs to pay special attention to four key lessons drawn from the earlier chapters:

A public purpose: Public institutions and organisations serve a public purpose. This purpose should encapsulate how the transformation process will lead to a better future, improve the quality of life of citizens and promote the collective interest. Articulating the higher public purpose sets a broad trajectory. This is necessary to generate momentum and enlist the contribution of others. Public purpose comes first in leading public transformation. This brings a *public perspective* to a collective effort.

Societal outcomes: Public organisations bear a responsibility for generating public and civic results of ever increasing value. These contribute to building a well performing and governable society. Framing issues in term of the results for society ensures that public sector leaders stay focused on the big picture and on the results that matter most. This brings a *societal perspective* to public sector actions and decisions.

The authority of the State: This is the lever used by public sector leaders to steer society through a process of change and to invent solutions to problems of public interest. The instruments of the State are used to harness the collective power of society, influence behaviours and transform the relationship between the public, private and civic spheres of life in society. This brings a *meta-system perspective* to the role of government.

Citizens as public value creators: The responsibility for producing results of value to society is shared between government, citizens and all agents in society. This responsibility also extends to present and future generations. Policies and programmes can be designed to make better use of people's assets and to encourage self-organisation. This brings a *citizen-centric perspective* to problem solving and decision making.

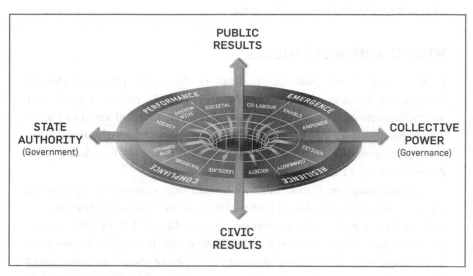

Figure 7.1: Synthesising

The NS Exploratory Process is designed as a systematic approach to uncover and put in place the key elements of a trajectory leading to better public and civic results. It helps practitioners weave together the many strands and elements needed to lead a group down such a path. It provides a way to do systematically what many leaders are doing instinctively, that is, discover *a pathway to a better future*.

A Pathway to a Better Future

Each "New Synthesis" is unique. It must be crafted by people with the authority to launch a public transformation designed to bring about a desired public outcome in a specific context and set of circumstances by using the levers of the State.

Government interventions are designed to transform people's behaviours and the interrelationships between the public, private and civic spheres in the hope that they will generate more desirable outcomes for society. During an NS Exploration Process, public sector leaders are searching for a way to open up a pathway towards a better future. This pathway will be made of multiple elements, some laid down by government, some by other agents in society and many by citizens themselves.

A key question at this point of the exploration process is to figure out how all the elements will fit together. A practical approach is to learn from those who have successfully opened a *pathway to a better future* like in the examples presented in the previous chapters. One such initiative is the Singapore Prison case. It illustrates all the phases of the NS Exploratory Process. A more detailed description is presented in Appendix A. This case was first documented in the early days of the NS Initiative. An update has recently been published by the Singapore Civil Service College.[1] This initiative has been unfolding for more than 15 years and therefore it provides evidence that is not available in the case of initiatives launched more recently.

Learning from Practice: The Singapore Prison Service
Re-think, Re-frame, and Re-invent
In 1998, the Singapore Prison Service (SPS) was a secure and safe institution with a zero-escape rate. From that perspective, SPS was fulfilling its basic mission. But at the same time, all was not well at SPS. Overcrowding was putting a strain on infrastructure and resources. SPS was suffering from a shortage of labour due to staff retention and recruitment problems. From a societal perspective, the situation was even worse. The recidivism rate was 44.4 percent, which meant that almost half of ex-offenders found themselves back in prison within two years.[2] In spite of all its hard work, SPS was not fulfilling its broader societal mission of building a safer society. Even more troubling was a disturbing trend that revealed the presence of "inter-generational prisoners"; the

children of inmates were becoming offenders.[3] Left unchecked, this trend suggested that SPS would consume an ever-increasing share of public resources while societal costs, resulting from the SPS' inability to re-integrate ex-offenders, would keep climbing. A vicious cycle was in full swing. The situation was unsustainable. How could a prison system contribute to reducing the risk of recidivism and repeat offences? How could a "high security ship" be used for rehabilitation with the help of officers, inmates, employers, inmates' families and the community?[4] How could SPS bring about such a fundamental societal change? Was this even SPS' role?

The initiative unfolded in several phases. A small group of committed officers and staff embraced the concept of rehabilitation. They took a number of measures that transformed the role of prison officers interested in experimenting with new approaches. At first, the group did not have the support of the Ministry of Home Affairs (MHA). The MHA believed that the "Prison Service had gone soft".[5] Nonetheless, the initiative followed its course and created a ripple effect; more officers were coming on board. One year later, in 1999, SPS unveiled its new mission: "to protect society through the safe custody and rehabilitation of offenders".[6] Prison officers had become agents of change.

The inmates created the second wave of change by enrolling in rehabilitation programmes despite their initial reluctance. More changes were introduced; rehabilitation profiles and programmes were created. In 2000, SPS started an educational institution, the operating philosophy of which was "School First, Prison Second".[7] Predictably, the change process generated tensions. There were dissenting voices. In addition, some experienced prison officers expressed concerns about the cost of the new initiatives and argued that the new way of doing things would make their work even more challenging. These were valid concerns. The prison guards' efforts would come to naught and the recidivism rate would not drop unless the community provided ex-offenders with a second chance. It was time for a third wave of change, one that required support beyond the confines of SPS. Ex-offenders needed the support of their families, potential employers, communities and the general public after their release from prison.

The Singapore Corporation of Rehabilitative Enterprises (SCORE) is a self-funding statutory board operating under the MHA. It plays a key role in finding employment for and providing training to ex-offenders. In 2002, SCORE joined forces with SPS and took on the role of "building bridges of hope for offenders and their families". It contributed to creating "a safe community by successfully reintegrating offenders".[8] SPS had found an important ally. The initiative was spilling out of the prison system and into the public domain. The message that was conveyed to the public focused on giving ex-offenders "a second chance" to become valuable members of society.[9] The public campaign called the Yellow Ribbon Project (YRP) was highly successful. It stressed that families, friends, neighbours, employers and communities hold the key to the "second prison".[10] A Yellow Ribbon Fund was created to provide support for reintegration and provide family assistance. Employers expressed interest in hiring ex-offenders. The number of volunteers involved in community support and after-care programmes grew from 76 in 2004 to 2,625 in 2013.[11] A fourth wave of change was afoot. This time, the challenge of re-integrating ex-offenders into society was seen as a collective responsibility and was broadly supported by the public.

The transformation process that started with a few committed individuals was changing the image Singaporeans had of themselves as a society. Fifteen years of data document the progress over time. The number of inmates who received training increased by 65 percent between 2009 and 2013. The recidivism rate dropped from 44.4 percent in 1998 to 27.4 percent in 2011. More than two thousand families received government assistance to support rehabilitation between 2010 to 2014. The Criminal Registration Act was amended to strike out criminal records for minor offences to facilitate the successful re-integration of ex-offenders. Employers contributed to the effort by offering employment opportunities. The number of employers in the "job bank" doubled between 2004 and 2013 and the number of inmates who secured jobs before they left prison more than doubled from 951 in 2009 to 2,114 in 2013.[12]

SPS invented a *pathway towards a better future* that benefited society as a whole as well as the inmates and the employees responsible for the prison system. It started with a few committed officers using the resources available to them at the time. Their actions reveal a clear sense of public purpose and the desire to make a difference. Focussing on societal results enabled SPS to see new possibilities, identify new partners and create space for others to contribute.[13]

While the broad direction was set at the start, most of the elements were invented along the way. Progressively, SPS' "New Synthesis" included custody, rehabilitation, prevention, after-care, a family support programme, a community-based programme, an employers' programme, training and so forth. This case provides a good illustration of how government interventions can and do transform society. It also shows the importance and the core elements of public innovation.

Focussing on societal results: The SPS transformed itself from an organisation focussed on keeping prisoners in jail to one centred on the successful re-integration of ex-offenders into society – societal results. For employees, this meant a shift in thinking: they went from ensuring that prison doors were "bolted and locked down" to becoming "captains of lives".[14]

Leveraging inside, across and beyond: Public transformation rarely enjoys overwhelming support from the start. Support is gained progressively as the initiative unfolds and generates evidence that it is worthy of support. In practice, there are always sufficient resources and capabilities available to get started. The rest will come as others come on board.

Shared and mutual responsibilities: Public innovation may start in many places; in government, at any level, or beyond in the private and civic spheres. In the end, a sustainable public innovation requires both the use of public instruments to transform an idea into a public good that benefits society as a whole and the public ownership of the idea so that these transformations end up reflecting the way people live and what they stand for as a society.

NARRATIVES OF CHANGE

Public sector leaders must give voice to the change they aspire to bring about and articulate a compelling narrative to create an impetus for change. This narrative exposes the gaps between the current reality and the desired outcome. It signals a commitment to do something about the situation.

Narratives are powerful statements.[15] In fact, numerous successful social movements in history have been driven by a narrative that inspired people to do amazing things.[16] Readers will remember Nelson Mandela's call for *"Healing Through Truth"* which helped put an end to apartheid while averting the risk of racial conflicts and insurrection, President Lula's declaration that *"No one will be left behind"* in the fight against HIV/AIDS,[17] or, in the above example, SPS employees' aspirations to be *"captains in the lives of offenders under our custody"*.[18]

Narratives reflect synthesising capabilities. They provide a distinctive way of organising ideas that communicates a new and purposeful direction.[19] They are integral to transformation because they engage people at an emotional level. Practitioners are often experts in a narrow area, a specific type of policy or body of knowledge. However, the skills emphasised in developing a degree of expertise, like a capacity for rigorous analysis, are not the same skills necessary for generating a compelling narrative. Moreover, expertise can lead to a misplaced focus of concern. Getting caught up in the background knowledge, or 'sweating the small stuff' does not justify why an action ought to be taken, or outline what problem it resolves. A narrative of change is intended to garner support from other actors who will not have the same degree of domain expertise.

A capacity for storytelling is hampered by a lack of clear purpose. Formulating a narrative of change is a discursive process that helps clarify choices and provides answers to fundamental questions such as: Why does this matter? Why should we take action? *Narratives reveal what an organisation stands for and the values that unite people as a community.*[20]

A narrative of change reconciles ambitions for a better future with concrete actions and helps generate a shared understanding of the differences between what is and what could be. It evolves as progress takes place and as people come on board.

NS Narratives

NS narratives are shared narratives. A common effort towards a desired public outcome does not mean that all actors share the same motivation. It does mean, however, that there is enough synergy among them to sustain the necessary collaboration and convergence of efforts. The *point of intersection* of the various perspectives becomes the shared story that supports the group's endeavour.

NS narratives are not stories in the traditional sense. Stories have a beginning, a plot and an end.[21] Instead, NS narratives are open-ended and adaptive. The outcome cannot be entirely predicted since it will take shape through collective actions. The NS fieldwork revealed that the narratives supporting public transformation initiatives go through multiple phases. The following diagram was generated in the context of NS Master Classes. It summarises some of the key phases.

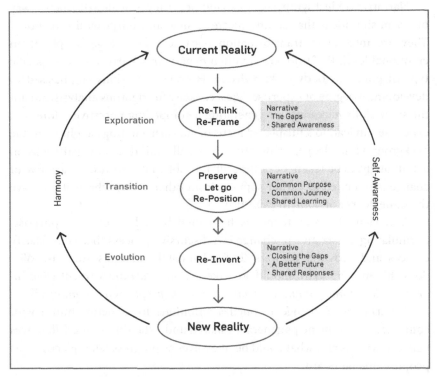

Figure 7.2: Leading Transformation – Narratives of Change

The exploration phase: During this initial phase, some people come to realise that things must change. The situation may be untenable or there may be untapped potential. The gaps between the current reality and future aspirations are becoming painfully obvious. Exploratory conversations generate a better understanding of the differences between the past, present and potential future situations. The *exploration phase* helps to generate a shared awareness of the challenges at hand as people re-think the issue from a different perspective, articulate the challenges in societal terms, and explore how to re-position their agency's contribution.

The transition phase: This phase is a challenging one. New activities are starting up but old ways of doing things are still in place and use up all available time and resources. Where will the resources come from to support new activities? How to make room for new approaches that are still unproven? Until the initiative shows some concrete results, it is unlikely that much assistance will be forthcoming beyond the coalition of people who initiated the effort. This was the situation faced by the initial coalition of supporters behind the CHEO and the SPS initiatives.

The transition phase tests the resolve of those who launched the change process. It may span over many years. CHEO's pilot project stretched over three years. In the case of the SPS, the transformation and all its interrelated dimensions took shape over the better part of ten years. During the transition phase, narratives are used to reinforce the common sense of purpose, capture the collective journey, celebrate the group's efforts and articulate why the initiative is worthy of support.

The transformation phase: This phase presents a different set of challenges. A new reality is taking hold and is replacing the one that existed before. If the initiative has been successful up to this point, there is a compelling story to tell about how it has contributed to a better future and generated better results for citizens. This is the time when key elements are consolidated, changes institutionalised and measures introduced to ensure the sustainability of the new reality. The narrative during this phase encourages broad ownership and support.

The results of a long cycle of change come to fruition. It started with a few committed individuals and ended up in the hands of a vast number of people. But this is also the beginning of a new cycle of change. A successful transformation builds the capacity to adapt, evolve and lay the basis for the changes to come ... and so, the journey continues.

Factor-YOU

During the NS labs and workshops conducted between 2012 and 2015, the participants and the NS Team started to talk about the *Factor-YOU* of public administration to describe the importance of the role played by public sector leaders as initiators or supporters of public innovation. The concept has since been integrated into the key findings generated by the NS Initiative.

Public sector leaders are not separate from the transformation processes they lead; they are part of it. *The way they think* about their role and the role of government has a direct impact on the solutions they will find and the results they will achieve with the help and support of others. *A narrow view* of the role of government in society hinders the optimal use of the levers of the State. Such a minimalist view of government's role may erode the capacity of public institutions and organisations to detect emerging issues or to intervene proactively in order to influence the course of events in a more favourable direction. There are countless examples of situations where governments have been taken by surprise and have only taken action when the costs to society were at their highest.

A narrow view of the role of the public sector is unlikely to lead to uncovering solutions that lie just beyond the border of hierarchical organisations. It reduces the range of options open to government. In fact, the broader the view, the easier it is to connect issues, knowledge, know-how, resources and capabilities in new and creative ways.

A narrow view of the role of public servants replicates a narrow view of the contribution of citizens. Both lead to making poor use of people's assets. No country is rich enough to waste resources by not making use of people's talents, inventiveness and resourcefulness.[22]

The way public sector leaders think about the role of the State and the way they frame public policy challenges opens up or closes off possibilities. The leaders form part of the context they aspire to change and part of the transformation process they lead. This is the *Factor-YOU* of public administration.

To open up a pathway to a better future, one must be grounded in the fundamental principles that make the contribution of the public sector unique, irreplaceable and most valuable for society. Government actions and decisions are deliberately intended to change the course of events in society. These actions are initiated with imperfect knowledge and with no safety net. Moreover, the pace and complexity of government interventions is likely to increase in response to the increasing complexity and hyperconnectivity of the world we live in.

The NS Exploratory Process attempts to ground practitioners with a *systematic approach* to explore and invent solutions to the problems of society. The concepts underlying the NS Framework and the NS Exploratory Process challenge existing administrative systems and practices. The systems and practices inherited from a prior time must evolve to make it easier for government to explore, experiment and invent solutions.

NS as a conceptual framework invites us to re-conceptualise public innovation, problem solving, public policy making and public leadership development. However, the need for reconceptualising extends well beyond public administration. In fact, it goes to the very core of re-thinking the kind of societies people want to build for the future. How do we want to be governed? What is the future of democracy and the role of politics in a post-industrial era? These, and other related issues, bring us beyond the scope of the NS Initiative.

PART III

RE-THINK, RE-FRAME AND RE-INVENT

The first part of this book made the case for the need of a New Synthesis of public administration to serve in the 21st century. Serving in a post-industrial era may not be more difficult in absolute terms than before; it is different. Prior generations of public sector leaders experienced their fair share of challenges. They lived through two world wars, a cold war and a great recession. They witnessed the devastating effects of colonisation, navigated through the reconstruction of Europe, saw the fall of the Berlin wall, the end of the Union of Soviet Socialist Republics (USSR) and the post-apartheid reconciliation process in South Africa. The rise of China pulled millions of people out of poverty. There has been unprecedented growth in South East Asia and in some parts of Latin America and Africa. These are some of the events that have marked the 20th century. Governing at the best of times is difficult. Governments are always confronted with challenging circumstances.

That said, there are unique characteristics to serving in a post-industrial era. As a result, new ways of thinking and governing are needed to face the challenges that stem from living in an increasingly global, interdependent, hyperconnected and disorderly world where the life support for a soon to be nine billion people depends on a fragile biosphere.

There comes a time when ideas and practices that have worked reasonably well in the past must give way to a profound realignment of ideas. *We live in such a time*. This is a time to re-think the role of government in society in light of the lessons learned over the past fifty years and to re-conceptualise public policy issues from a different perspective. The ideas and governance models inherited from the industrial age will be insufficient to face the challenges of society in a post-industrial era. Leading public transformations and finding solutions to the challenges of this time start by challenging conventional ideas and practices that played a useful role in the past but fail to explain the issues and challenges people are experiencing today.

The second part of this book introduced the reader to the NS Framework and the NS Exploratory Process. It is the result of a number of years invested in learning from practitioners searching for solutions to problems they are facing in practice. Leading public transformation is deeply circumstantial and contextual. And yet, the fieldwork has revealed that while each initiative is unique in its context and the outcomes it generated, there are important similarities in the process of discovery leading to innovative solutions. Part II captures the essence of this *systematic process of discovery*.

The NS Exploratory Process expands the range of possibilities open to government, improves the likelihood of success of government interventions and builds the capacity for collective problem solving. It is aimed at providing practitioners with a deliberate approach to think their way through complex issues and find their way towards results of increasing public and civic value. The approach is grounded in four sets of dynamically interacting principles to guide government decisions and actions.

This last part is different. There comes a time where more reform and incremental adjustments are unlikely to bring about the desired outcomes. In many countries, governments have reached the end of a long cycle of reforms. Several reforms were government-centric and focussed on the inner workings of government. Many led to the introduction of incremental adjustments to existing systems and practices, leaving unchallenged the underlying ideas and assumptions inherited from a prior time. They did not provide answers to the "big questions" that need to be addressed to find new ways to govern peacefully, reduce tensions and uncover solutions to the problems that bedevil societies in the fast-changing landscape of the 21st century.

There is a need to re-think the role of government and the interrelationship of the public, private and civic spheres of life in society in contemporary terms; to re-frame public challenges in a manner that is congruent with the emerging reality on the ground rather than a theoretical construct inherited from a prior time; and to re-discover the fundamental principles that make societies governable and *re-invent the conditions for building a better future together*.

The re-thinking needed extends well beyond the scope of this book. For instance, this is a time for re-thinking the functioning of a market economy and the underlying assumption that innovation, productivity, growth, employment and income growth work synergistically together. The evidence of the last 20 years points in the opposite direction. There is a need and an opportunity to re-conceptualise the mix of policy instruments to encourage distributed growth and shared prosperity. A clear-eyed diagnostic of the overall benefits of global trade and of the local dislocation that the process entails is long overdue. This is needed to conceptualise measures to improve the absorptive capacity of communities and mitigate the impact for the most vulnerable in society. It is also needed to alleviate public fears about the future and the capacity of government to guide society through an unprecedented process of change.

There is a pressing need to re-discover the irreplaceable contribution of the State to a well performing society and economy and to articulate a concept of that State adapted to serving in the 21st century. This is neither an overbearing nor a minimalist State but one with sufficient confidence in its role to use the levers of the State to serve the collective interest.

Ideas and principles matter. The way one thinks has a direct impact on the solutions that will be found and the results that will be achieved. Part III signals the need for a set of important conversations. First, it explores some of the ramifications of the NS Framework. It proposes new lines of inquiry to re-think public innovation. Second, it argues that there is a need to re-frame the conversation about leadership in a public sector setting. Going beyond NS, it raises probing questions that signal the need to re-think economic theories and democratic principles.

It is left to the reader to think their way through the most difficult questions. In the end, it comes down to articulating in contemporary terms a view about fundamental philosophical questions that have inspired prior generations. What concept of the State and society will guide collective actions? What gives meaning to our belonging to a broader community? What is the meaning of just society and a good life in this early part of the 21st century?

This last part is an invitation to the reader to *re-think, re-frame,* and *re-invent* the ideas that will guide them in building the future they aspire to build.

CHAPTER 8

RE-THINKING PUBLIC INNOVATION AS A COLLECTIVE ENTERPRISE

Innovation in government has received much attention over the years. For the most part, the focus has been introspective, giving special attention to the modernisation of public sector systems and practices as well as the service delivery functions of government. Primarily, this has been accomplished through the use of modern information and communication technologies and an increasingly diverse set of delivery channels.

There is a view that public organisations are slow adopters of new technologies and innovative practices and that they are lagging behind their counterparts in the private sector. The focus of attention in these conversations is on *innovation in government* and as a result may have missed the most important contributions of government to innovation.

INNOVATION IN GOVERNMENT

The narrative one generally finds in government literature and in academic work about innovation in government runs along the following lines: innovation in a public sector setting is inherently more difficult than in a private sector one because it is operating under a heavier burden of constraints and controls.[1] The political environment is described as generally hostile to public innovation due to short political cycles and the need to respond to political pressures.[2] As a result, the culture of the public service is inherently risk averse and risk-avoiding.[3] Introducing innovative practices in a public sector setting may even be a risky enterprise;[4] mistakes may lead to political embarrassment and bring about negative repercussions for the initiators. Ultimately, the legislative requirements, under which all public organisations must operate, act as barriers to new and innovative practices.[5]

As a result, the literature tends to focus on finding ways to remove barriers to the introduction of innovative practices. These measures include creating special units, such as laboratories and innovation hubs, to house innovative practices outside of the mainstream of the public sector. Other approaches include encouraging disintermediation through the use of modern communication technologies and promoting a greater role for the private sector or for public-private partnerships.[6]

In every narrative, there are elements of truth, and this is the case here. However, while this narrative about innovation in government may reflect some aspects of reality, it is missing the importance of public innovation. A focus on innovation in government is unlikely to help government keep pace with the increasing complexity of society or yield solutions to issues ranging from climate change, increasing income and employment inequalities or the impact of an aging population. These challenges will not go away without some form of government intervention.[7]

A conversation framed around *innovation in government* suffers from too narrow a focus to reveal the significance of *public innovation*. It underestimates the importance of the role of government for building an innovative society and to invent solutions to emerging issues with unknown consequences.

Strange as it may sound, we are lacking a narrative about public innovation that reflects an understanding of the fundamental role of the State and of public institutions in society. One that brings together the role of government to promote the collective interest, as well as the contribution of citizens and other agents in society to advance societal progress by pursuing their interests in a manner that also advances the collective good.[8]

PUBLIC INNOVATION

Governments innovate; this is the starting point for a broader conversation on public innovation. The capacity of governments to guide society through an ongoing process of change depends on their capacity to invent solutions to the problems we collectively face.

The public sector is responsible for many of the innovations that have given shape to our modern societies, including the nation state, the rule of law, checks and balances in the exercise of power and a regime of public accountability. Governments have created the policies and programmes that have contributed to building modern societies and have steered these societies as they underwent profound transformations resulting from the industrial revolution and post-industrial challenges. They have created social safety nets that have contributed to the prosperity of market based economies and the increasing standard of living of an increasing segment of the world's population. They have designed and operated public health and education systems, public pension plans and various support programmes to assist citizens most in need. They have designed the rules to harness the potential of a market economy while mitigating their negative impact on society, including laws governing labour relations, the protection of consumer rights, the safeguarding of intellectual property, and the regulation of financial institutions. Public organisations have funded and built the roads, harbours and airports required for a modern society to function properly and the information and communication technology infrastructure needed to meet the demands of the global economy.[9]

Government interventions and investments can be traced behind the radical technological innovations that have fuelled the "New Economy" from the internet, to nanotechnology, Global Positioning System (GPS), touch screens and voice activated systems. More recently, government interventions were used to rescue the financial sector. Monetary policies are currently used in unprecedented ways to stimulate the world economy in the hope of mitigating the impact of the "great recession" that began in 2008. These interventions have given new meaning to private risks and collective responsibility. Government interventions constantly mediate and redraw the boundaries between the private and public spheres of life in society. [10]

Public innovation is much more than the introduction of innovative practices in government. Reducing the conversation to this aspect is to miss its most important dimension. The most significant impact of public innovation is external to government. To reframe the conversation about innovation from a public sector perspective is to position it in the broader context of the role of the State and the contribution of government to society. *Public innovation is a core mission of government* – that is, to invent solutions to the challenges faced by society that cannot be solved without some form of government intervention.

In recent years, a number of organisations have contributed to a broadening of the conversation about the public dimensions of innovation, the importance of social innovation and the role of government in encouraging innovative ideas. Nesta, a UK based charity, is among them. It describes public innovation as "creating, developing and implementing practical ideas that achieve a public benefit".[11] Other organisations have focussed on encouraging social innovation that may be described as the "conscious effort of bringing novel ideas and processes in a way that creates valuable impact on society".[12] The European Commission has done much work to encourage innovation in government and in society. It defines social innovations as "innovations that are both social in their ends and their means".[13]

In the context of the NS Initiative, public innovation is defined as *"innovative solutions serving a public purpose that require the use of public means".[14]* In doing so, public innovation is conceptualized as intimately linked to government actions and to the use of the instruments of the State. This distinguishes public innovation from social innovation by focussing on innovations that require the use of public means to convert ideas into public goods that benefit society as a whole or that are available to all in similar circumstances.

This definition brings together public innovation and public interventions as two interconnected concepts. The State intervenes to create change to the existing order and transform society. In essence, it is a process of experimentation, invention and innovation that is authorised by the State.

From this perspective, far from being risk averse, *the State is the ultimate risk taker in society.* Government takes risks on a scale that no other sector or agent in society could take on and intervenes in areas where the forces of the market or the capacity of civil society would be unable to go. Furthermore, government is expected to act as the steward of society and the insurer of last resort of the ultimate risks and failures in society whether the result of natural disasters, global shocks or disturbances from the actions of others where the State had no part.

This broader perspective about public innovation and the role of government reveals some of the distinctive characteristics of public innovation.

Distinctive Characteristics of Public Innovation

Public innovation has distinctive characteristics that make it irreplaceable. These characteristics are linked to the authority of the State and the legitimacy of government to intervene in the public sphere to change the course of events in a manner that is judged to be preferable for society. They distinguish public innovation from innovations in any other sector.

A Macro-scale of Interventions: Unlike in the private, academic or civic spheres, public innovations often take place at the largest macro scale. They apply to the whole territory under the jurisdiction of the governing entity and to everyone under the authority of the State.[15] New laws apply to all. New programmes and services define the entitlements of eligible citizens and create new rights enjoyed by all citizens in similar circumstances. The law is a necessary enabler to act in this manner and on this scale. No other actor in society can intervene in such a way and on such a scale.

Macro-scale interventions create particular difficulties for government. Companies will generally test innovative ideas on a small scale before scaling them up. This reduces risks and improves the likelihood of a successful launch of a new product or service. Governments face the opposite challenge; they must find ways to scale down an initiative in order to learn more before launching it on a national scale. This is more difficult than it seems at first glance. For instance, scaling down an initiative to a geographical area or a smaller group of people may give rise to ethical dilemmas or to legal challenges if an initiative benefits some citizens and not others. The equal treatment of all citizens is an important consideration for government. In some countries, legal constraints may even limit the use of pilot projects. In other cases, testing ideas on a smaller scale could lead to speculative behaviours and unfair competition. As a result, governments have a tendency to deploy new initiatives on a national scale and thus with the highest level of risk. *Governments* are *inherently risk takers* when it comes to initiating new policies, programmes and services.

Every intervention entails the promise of generating better outcomes as well as the risk of producing unknown, unintended or unwanted consequences. The challenge is to discover how to improve the likelihood of successful government intervention while reducing the risks of generating unintended consequences.

Imperfect knowledge and unknown impact: Government intervenes with imperfect knowledge. Despite efforts to encourage evidence-based decision making, data analytics to extract meaning and detect patterns and other techniques to improve decisions – ultimately, governments will make decisions with the knowledge available to them at the time a decision is made.

Policy decisions, new programmes and services are not definitive answers, but the beginning of long chains of interrelated actions intended to influence behaviours in a given direction. From that perspective, success may not depend so much on what was known at the time the decision was made, but on the ability of public organisations to capture new insights of what is happening in practice in order to adjust the initial design to achieve the desired impact over time.

Governments intervene to create a better future from a place of incomplete and imperfect knowledge. In most cases, the full impact of a government intervention is unknown at its inception and will only become known over many years. Public organisations with a strong inventive capacity must be able to monitor results over long periods of time to recalibrate the initial intervention as circumstances change and new knowledge becomes available. Government interventions are experiments in progress.

Enabled by law and politics: Public innovation does not happen in spite of politics and the law but is enabled by them. Government interventions derive their legitimacy from a mix of democratic principles, political leadership and the rule of law. Government possesses the legitimacy to intervene on behalf of society.

Public innovation takes place at the crossroads of a reliance on the law that encourages predictability, and experimentation to discover new and better ways of achieving results of value to society.[16] A particular difficulty for government is balancing the need for continuity and stability with the need for change to meet the challenges ahead. There is a need to ensure the continuity of the State while initiating potentially disruptive interventions; public innovation is a process of constructive deconstruction that must be calibrated with care to engender the necessary public support.

In summary, reframing the conversation about public innovation opens up a broader perspective about the importance of government interventions to address problems that cannot be solved and to produce results that would not exist without making use of the levers of the State.

Public Innovation through Public Intervention

Every action and decision taken by government is deliberately designed to transform some aspects of society. Government interventions are intended to modify behaviours and influence the way people live their lives or to transform the interactions between the public, private and civic spheres. At times, these actions are a response to pressing challenges, in other cases, they are proactive measures aimed at securing a better future. In either case, government interventions are intended to influence the course of events and transform the world we live in. The impact of government interventions can be felt across vast systems and at times well beyond the country of origin.

At their core, public innovation and government intervention are related concepts.[17] Government intervenes in the current state of affairs to invent a new reality distinct in some ways from the one that existed previously. This is a process of change and innovation. Jesper Christiansen, in *The Irrealities of Public Administration,* reminds us that it is through government intervention that innovations "come in" the public sphere and "come between" various actors in society.[18]

Public organisations are mandated to shape the environment and to steer society through a change process to achieve desirable public outcomes.[19] Such interventions may require regulatory support or make use of the spending power of the State. Public means can be used to guide collective actions, encourage collaboration or prevent behaviours detrimental to society through coercive measures. Public innovation is both the goal and the process of generating public solutions that frequently exceed what government can do on its own but could not be achieved without the use of the levers of the State.

Some initiatives will achieve their desired outcomes, some will work reasonably well for a time but require periodic adjustments, and others will fail. In some cases, the reasons for failure may rest with government. This is the case when the lack of progress is due to a poor understanding of the issue, an inadequate selection of instruments or a poorly designed intervention. In other cases, the lack of progress is due to a lack of synergy between public, private and civic actions.

Inventing solutions to complex problems of the kind discussed in the previous chapters requires a collective effort to ensure that the actions taken by governments, citizens and various agents in society work synergistically to bring about the desired public outcomes. Innovation benefits from an ecosystem where the State plays a key role in building dynamic linkages among multiple organisations at the local, national and global levels.

THE STATE AS ENGINE FOR INNOVATION

A conversation about public innovation could be framed along several dimensions. One, as was discussed in the previous section, is to consider public innovation as the use of public means to generate innovative solutions serving a public purpose.[20] Another dimension would be to consider government's role when the public purpose is to build *an innovative economy and society*.

There has been a noticeable retrenchment of the State in some countries over the last 30 years. In some cases, this came about as part of efforts to reduce government spending, deficit and debt. In other cases, the underlying assumption is that constraining the role of the State would unleash the entrepreneurship and innovative power of society and of the private sector in particular. It is argued that this in turn would help build a more vibrant and innovative economy and society. In recent years, this view has been most powerfully put forward in the USA, the UK, and some other developed countries.[21]

A cursory look at the recent past reveals that the same countries held a different view of the role of the State for most of the 19th and 20th centuries and that the State acted as a force for innovation in generating the technologies that are now associated with the "New Economy".

Exploratory conversations about the role of the State in building an innovative economy and society give rise to a number of questions of interest for public decision makers. Is it possible to build an innovative economy and society without an active leadership role by the State? Could developed economies maintain their dominant position in technologically advanced areas without the support of the State? What conditions would make it possible for the State to re-capture its investments to sustain its capacity to make public investments in new areas in the future?

An active role by the State to encourage innovation, which has been described by Mariana Mazzucato as the "*Entrepreneurial State*",[22] has been on display in recent years in China, many South East Asian countries and some Latin American countries, where governments are making intensive use of state instruments and collaborative mechanisms between the public and private sectors. It is noteworthy that in fifty years, through planning and active public policies, many East Asian economies were able to catch up with the most developed countries in many technologically advanced industrial areas.[23]

As discussed in Chapter 7, the way one thinks about the role of government in society has a significant impact on the use of the levers of the State, the nature of the collaboration between the public, private and civic spheres, the solutions that will be put forward as well as the results that will be achieved. Divergent approaches among countries provide a fertile ground for experimentation and learning from practice.

The State as Radical Risk Taker: Going Where Markets will not Go

The State can make things happen that otherwise would not. Governments are periodically criticized for being unable to pick winners. It may be so, but this is hardly the most relevant question to reframe the conversation about the role of the State in encouraging innovation and building an innovative economy and society.

Public funds have been and continue to be used to create future winners by taking on the riskiest investments to create new technologies, generate new products and services and build markets that did not previously exist. The State has funded and undertaken the riskiest fundamental and applied research that led to aviation, space exploration, information technologies and the discovery of nuclear energy. By exploring uncharted areas, the State has initiated the innovation process that ultimately led to the development of new industries and the mass production of new goods and services.[24]

The State played a leadership role in railroad construction and the development of the rail industry sector in the 19th century. It conducted and funded the research that contributed to the development of the agricultural, aeronautical and aviation sectors in the 20th century. Governments played a leadership role in the development of the life sciences and key biotechnologies. Public laboratories and publicly funded research are at the origin of some of the most important pharmaceutical discoveries behind the success of the pharmaceutical industry in the 21st century.

There is ample evidence about the leadership and even visionary role played by successive governments in some countries in supporting leading edge research and generating new technologies that transformed the world economy. The visible role of the State has been operating well before the invisible hand of the market could take on a role. In "Political Structures and the Making of US Biotechnology", the authors concluded that "the new knowledge economy was not born but made".[25]

Encouraging radical risk taking means to *rely on the State to go where the market cannot go*. It is associated with risks that exceed the capacity or the willingness of the private sector to bear. It requires a long-term commitment with no guarantee of return on investments over a horizon that defies most corporate entities' tolerance for risk taking. Accepting such risks is an important public policy decision about the role of government in society.

An alternative view would see the private sector as the primary engine to generate the innovations needed to fuel future prosperity. In this scenario, the State plays a more limited role including the conventional responsibility of correcting market failures. This approach entails considerable risks.[26] In theory, it implies limiting the use of the powerful instruments of the State to encourage innovation or promote future growth and prosperity.

In practice, even in countries like the USA, where some argue most forcefully in favour of freeing the private sector from the shackles of the State, the reality is quite different. The political discourse about limiting the role of the State did not lead to a reduction of public investments in the USA. The most significant impact seems to have been limiting the capacity of government to capture a reasonable return from the investment of public funds in risky initiatives. [27]

There are risks to a relationship between government and the private sector where the State takes on the riskiest responsibilities while firms extract the benefits from state-funded technologies and state-funded research. It is not uncommon for successful global firms, which have benefited most from publicly-funded research, to use their newly-earned dominant position to argue in favour of paying less tax, thus constraining the capacity of government to fund innovative technologies in new areas in the future.[28]

In the private sector, it is generally accepted that there should be a relationship between risk taking and returns.[29] This logic seems to break down when it comes to the risks taken by government on behalf of society and to the return citizens should expect for the investment of their tax dollars.

One of the challenges that governments will need to address to encourage innovation in the changing landscape of the 21st century will be to figure out how to capture a rent for the investments of public funds in developing the technologies that fuel the new economy. In the context of the "Old Economy", arrangements progressively evolved that contributed to a sharing of risks and benefits. The world has not yet figured out how to share more equitably the risks and benefits of the "New Economy" and to distribute the benefits of technological innovation and the digital revolution across society.

A system that socialises risks and privatises rewards is not sustainable in the long run.[30] It leads to rising inequalities, increasing social tensions and a less governable society. Rising inequalities are not inevitable and some countries are doing much better than others at encouraging shared prosperity.[31] Smart, inclusive and sustainable growth will not happen on its own or without government action. It takes a State willing to take the risks of making this happen.

INNOVATION AS A COLLECTIVE UNDERTAKING

The *Entrepreneurial State* that Mazzucato talks about is "one able to take risks and create highly networked systems of actors to harness the best of the private sector for the national good over the medium to long term time horizon".[32] It recognises innovation as a *collective enterprise* and that the State plays a key role in building systems of innovation that have sectorial, regional, national or global dimensions. The dynamic links among multiple actors contribute to building a symbiotic innovation system.[33] A familiar example is the pharmaceutical industry where the large pharmaceutical companies, small biotechnology firms, universities and governments all form part of the ecology of the industry. Similar ecosystems exist in the aeronautic or aerospace industries.

A system view of innovation is very much in line with the New Synthesis of public administration that sees the role of government in the context of a dynamic system of governance where the State plays a crucial role in influencing the coming together of multiple agents to achieve results of increasing value for society.[34] Focussing on system-wide and societal results helps clarify the options open to government and the consequences that various choices entail. A system perspective draws attention to the interrelated steps that contribute to knowledge creation and its diffusion in society. The actions that generate innovation are part of a collective set of activities occurring through a network of actors where every step and every contribution together make the outcome possible.

A confident State is more likely to create a symbiotic system in which both society and the private sector benefit and avoid the risks of a detrimental system where some reap most of the benefits at the expense of those who have made all the riskiest investments.[35] This in turn can weaken the innovative capacity of society by rewarding those involved in the very last step of an innovation process – bringing ideas to market – at the expense of all those who contributed to a collective effort and have shouldered the brunt of the effort over many years.

Reframing the conversation on innovation means focussing on societal results and exploring how the authority of the State can be put to optimal use to lever a collective effort that encourages the sharing of responsibilities and rewards for contributing to a common desirable outcome. It brings a societal and citizen perspective to assessing government choices.

There is no doubt that government has the legitimacy to intervene in the public sphere. The role of the State includes intervening in areas where private and civic organisations will not or cannot bring about change.

The NS Initiative invites a re-framing of the conversation on public innovation and a repositioning of public innovation in the broader context of the role of the State. This chapter raised questions about the potential for government to bear risks beyond the market's tolerance in order to promote the public good. It identified a series of inquiries to explore how government could leverage social agents to build an innovative economy and society.

The task of re-thinking the role of government in public innovation is in no way limited to the questions mentioned above. A dominant economic view holds that the primary role of the State is to resolve market failures. However, growing income and wealth inequality calls into question conventional thinking on economic growth. There are other ways to produce public good that can be explored.[36] How can government ensure the conditions necessary for shared prosperity and inclusive growth? How can government re-link economic growth and employment or productivity and wages?

In essence, the NS Initiative provides an opportunity to explore, and to re-think, past assumptions that may limit future practice. Thinking through the role of government in public innovation is an opportunity to re-articulate its public purpose in a changing context and to examine the system of relationships between public, private and civic spheres that produce societal results. It widens initial perceptions of the role of government and opens up a broader space of possibilities.

As the challenges faced by society grow increasingly complex, the contribution of the public sector remains of critical importance both to develop innovative solutions and to create an innovative system of governance better able to adapt to the changing landscape of the 21st century.

CHAPTER 9

RE-FRAMING THE CONVERSATION ABOUT LEADERSHIP

The expression *public sector leaders* has been used in this book to describe *public office holders*. These are people with the right to use the authority of the State to promote the collective interest. They owe this privilege to the position they hold in the public sector, whether they are elected officials or appointed to the professional public service. The expression public sector leaders in this context describes people in position of authority rather than their leadership abilities.

A position-based perspective is useful in some regards, but this is not the best way to frame a conversation about the implications of the New Synthesis for public sector leaders, public sector leadership and public leadership. One question is whether there are distinctive characteristics to leadership in a public sector setting compared to other spheres of activity. Another is to explore the relationships between *public sector leadership* – the capacity to lead people, organisations and changes in a public sector setting – and *public leadership* – a broadly distributed capacity to advance a common purpose and generate public results.

Public leadership capabilities are not limited to government. The power to create a common purpose or take actions that generate something of public value is distributed across society and across the public, private and civic spheres. A relevant question is: what can government do to build the collective capacity for public leadership?

There is an abundant literature on leadership. Rather than reviewing the literature, this chapter will share some of the insights about public sector leadership that were generated in the context of the NS labs and workshops conducted between 2011 and 2015. Where relevant, it will blend observations from practice with insights from the literature on leadership.

THE DIMENSIONS OF PUBLIC SECTOR LEADERSHIP

In the 1950s, 1960s and early 1970s, leadership was seen to be more or less the same in any setting, public or private. As a result, public sector managers were encouraged to run the public sector like a business.[1] Leadership in the public sector was primarily discussed in terms of organisational development and focussed on enhancing organisational productivity and efficiency.[2]

Public sector leadership was later recognised as a distinct and specialised area of study.[3] Recent studies have brought forward many concepts particularly relevant to the public sector that take account of the increasing complexity of the environment faced by government. Concepts such as collaborative leadership, adaptive leadership and catalytic leadership are all complementary to NS findings to date.

The abundance of concepts can be overwhelming for practitioners. Thankfully, the work of Montgomery Van Wart, Ronald Heifetz, J.S. Luke and others help to draw linkages between different concepts. Often the academic study of leadership focuses on the formal leadership of organisations.[4] However, recent studies of leadership have kept pace with the challenges of leading in the hyperconnected and disorderly world of the 21st century.

Notwithstanding current progress, practitioners participating in NS workshops struggled to describe a concept of leadership that would embrace the breadth of their roles and responsibilities. The feeling was that some dimensions were missing in conversations about public sector leadership that too often focussed on leading public organisations at the expense of other dimensions. The participants were searching for a frame of reference broad enough to provide a holistic perspective about the interrelated dimensions of their role as public sector leaders and precise enough to provide practical guidance in the exercise of their responsibilities and the development of future leaders.

The concerns raised by participants were also echoed in the literature. While recent studies have gotten closer to a frame of reference integrating various dimensions of leadership relevant to the public sector, "none, [however,] have developed a model that addresses the nature of leadership for enabling network dynamics, one whose epistemology is consistent with *connective, distributed, dynamic* and *contextual* views of leadership".[5]

A NS workshop "for people at the top" was first conducted in the spring of 2014 and later replicated in two other countries in 2015. These workshops were designed to push the conversation further and explore various dimensions of public sector leadership. The following sections describe the key concepts generated as a result of this work as well as some of the advance work done by the NS Team in preparation for these events.

One Leader, Four Roles

Public sector leaders play multiple roles and exercise vast authority. The starting point of a broader conversation about leadership from a public sector perspective is to distinguish among these multiple roles and draw some initial observations about their interrelationships.

Public servants first: People in positions of authority in the public sector are public servants, public administrators and public sector managers acting on occasions as leaders and in many other circumstances as followers and enablers of the leadership of others in government and beyond.

At the most fundamental level, public sector leaders are first and foremost public servants. This role provides the foundation for other roles. At a philosophical level, this provides public sector leaders with core principles to guide their actions and the exercise of their authority. They must understand and embrace concepts of public service, public good and collective interest. They must show respect for democratic principles and citizens' rights, and live up to public values including dedication to public service, integrity and trustworthiness.[6]

People serving in government come from all walks of life and have a diversity of backgrounds. This diversity is an asset. Some have no prior experience or formal training in public administration before joining the public sector or being elected. A very real challenge is therefore to ensure that individuals who accept the responsibility to serve their fellow citizens become public servants able to put the collective interest above all else.

This dimension applies to elected and appointed officials. The roles mentioned in the following sections are exercised by public servants depending on the positions they hold.

Public administrators: Public office holders must be knowledgeable public administrators. They set or influence the setting of the rules and norms that govern society. They are responsible for ensuring that the law is administered fairly and applies to all without exception. They must achieve proper public aims in a suitable way and select the public means most appropriate for the task. This dimension of the role of public sector leaders speaks to the sovereign functions of the State and the importance of the law, and social rules and norms.[7] Every government depends on a state apparatus able to get things done and convert government priorities into reality in a legitimate way.

Public sector managers: Like their counterparts in the private or not-for-profit sectors, people in positions of authority in the public sector must be skilful managers. They manage vast organisations and networks of organisations. They must produce results, make the best use of resources, talents and skills, and prepare their organisations for the challenges ahead. The expectations for people in managerial positions in government are similar to what one finds in other sectors of activity – this includes the ability to set a vision, provide direction, influence others, gain employees' support and build organisational capacity.

Public office holders may display leadership abilities in the exercise of their responsibilities as public servants, public administrators or public sector managers. In every area and at all levels, there are opportunities for leadership. There is an important external dimension to the role of people in positions of authority in the public sector; a measure of success of public sector leaders is their contribution to building the *public leadership* capacity in society.

Public leaders: *Public leadership* transcends government and deemphasises the role of individuals while emphasising the importance of networks, communities and collective action.[8] It focusses on the capacity to forge a common purpose and act collectively to generate desirable public results.[9] Public leaders value collaboration and the collaborative problem solving that is necessary to address the complex issues and "wicked" problems that bedevil society.[10] This collaborative form of leadership does not replace the need for hierarchical organisations, competent public administration or efficient management, but it is a necessary complement to other approaches and forms of leadership.

This view enriches the NS Framework because it focusses on the interrelationships between government, citizens and multiple agents in society in order to generate results of increasing public value. This concept of public leadership helped the participants in NS workshops to imagine a concept of leadership that more successfully integrates several dimensions of their role and connects the finality of their actions to building the collective capacity to act.

AN INTEGRATED CONCEPT OF PUBLIC LEADERSHIP

People in positions of authority in the public sector simultaneously have *individual* responsibilities for the department, agency or unit that they oversee, *shared responsibilities* with other public sector leaders for achieving results that cut across several agencies, and *collective responsibilities* to prepare public institutions fit for the times and a society fit for the challenges that lay ahead.[11]

One implication is that public organisations cannot fulfil their missions if their actions are limited to what they can achieve on their own. They form part of a broader system of governance and therefore must position their contribution in the broader context of system-wide results and societal impact. Public sector leaders serve a public purpose whose ultimate expression is to build a better future and improve human conditions.

People in positions of authority have responsibilities that transcend their organisations. They must strike a balance and gain appreciation for how these roles interact with one another and contribute to building the collective capacity for generating better public results over time.

The following figure was generated in the context of NS labs conducted in 2014. It illustrates the key concepts and the interrelationships between various forms of public sector leadership.[12] In performing their responsibilities, public sector leaders exercise transactional, transformational and public stewardship forms of leadership. Furthermore, their actions contribute to building public leadership capabilities – that is, the collective capacity to solve problems and generate the public results that the collective desires.

The concepts of transactional and transformational leadership already exist in the literature.[13] The participants in NS workshops and labs modified these concepts to better reflect their realities. The concepts have also been adjusted by the NS Team to reflect conversations held with people at the most senior levels of government. Furthermore, the concept of "catalytic leadership" put forward by J.S. Luke was found to be relevant to the three dimensions identified by the participants that are presented in Figure 9.1 and briefly discussed in the following sections.

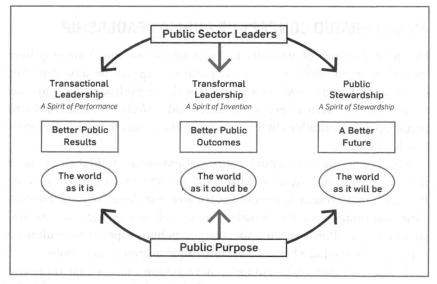

Figure 9.1: Public Sector Leadership

Transactional Leadership

Public sector leaders exercise responsibility for the organisation they lead. They must optimise the use of the resources and capabilities of their organisation to fulfil their mandate and produce results. They have a concern for productivity, efficiency, the careful use of taxpayers' money and the legitimate use of authority.

Public sector leaders operate under stringent conditions that impose limitations on their actions. Producing results in a public sector setting requires compliance with the law, regulations, norms and the control mechanisms designed to ensure transparency and accountability. Transactional leadership is agency-centric, user-focussed and politically sensitive to government priorities as well as the prevailing political circumstances. This reveals *a spirit of performance.*

It is a demanding task to lead public organisations at the best of times and to continually strive to improve performance and respond to changing needs and priorities.[14] In fact, it is increasingly difficult. Many organisations are struggling to reconcile increasing demands and declining resources. The increasing speed of transactions leaves little time for reflection, which in turn increases the risk of error. At the same time, the tolerance for error is declining and public criticism is mounting.

It takes very skilful managers and insightful public administrators to navigate through the conflicting demands placed on public organisations, set a course of action, motivate staff in the most challenging circumstances and get the best out of everything and everyone in serving the mission of a public organisation. It requires people able to adjust their leadership style to the culture of the organisation they lead and the circumstances prevailing at the time, using a mix of hierarchical authority, top down leadership when necessary, collaboration whenever desirable and empowering greater autonomy when possible. Exerting transactional leadership involves a commitment to improving agency performance through building organisational capacity.[15]

Public sector leaders are familiar with focussing on agency results. This provides the basis for reconciling inputs, outputs and responsibilities. It sets a basis for accountability and for improving efficiency. Yet, transactional leadership only captures part of the role played by public sector leaders.

Transformational Leadership

The responsibility of public sector leaders does not stop at the frontiers of their organisation. They have a responsibility to generate better public outcomes. This highlights the need to work across multiple boundaries and manage multiple interfaces to pool knowledge, insights, resources, tools and capabilities to support government-wide priorities and achieve better public outcomes.[16]

Transactional leadership deals with the world as it is and reveals a commitment to generate better agency results. Transformational leadership bridges the gap between our current reality and the *world as it could be* by making use of available assets across government and society, and by building on the strength of others to propel society forward.

This shifts the focus of attention from agency results to achieving outcomes of higher societal value. It moves the organisation along a public value chain to serve a higher public purpose by giving greater attention to system-wide results and societal outcomes. To reiterate the examples from Chapter 4, it is not sufficient to run effective hospitals, public sector leaders must also ensure that their actions contribute to an effective health system and improve public health outcomes. In the education sector, the challenge extends beyond having well-run schools to ensuring that the education system generates the high level of literacies needed for individuals and society to prosper in a post-industrial era.

Leading public transformation implies building the systems and capabilities needed for collaboration across government and across sectors. Transformational leadership values collaboration, co-creation, co-production and the sharing of responsibility to generate results of higher public value. It recognises that no organisation – public, private or civic – possesses all the tools necessary to generate the public outcomes the collective aspires to create.[17] This reflects a *spirit of invention*. It is necessary to support a process of ongoing transformation and re-invention. Transformational leadership never ends, but lays the basis for the changes to come and contributes to ensuring the ongoing relevance of the public sector.

Transformational leadership requires a system perspective. This means the capacity to frame issues in terms of desired societal outcomes, see the interconnections and linkages across issues, identify the key agents needed to pursue a shared interest and identify the strategic point of leverage. It also requires system-wide capabilities to encourage the early detection of potential risks or opportunities, shared knowledge, the pooling of resources and capabilities and collective decision making.

Public sector leaders exercise influence over a vast ecosystem of interdependent relationships that bring together the contribution of government, citizens and a multitude of actors across sectors. These assets are needed to make progress on issues of public interest. Public sector leaders must display the capacity to engage and work with multiple agents, users, beneficiaries and communities in public problem solving and solution making. Transformational leadership capabilities are necessary to serve in an interconnected and interdependent world.

Transformational leadership complements transactional leadership but does not replace it. The capacity of public sector leaders to lead public transformation is less likely to manifest itself in an environment where transactional leadership is seriously deficient. Both dimensions are needed in different proportions depending on the situation.[18]

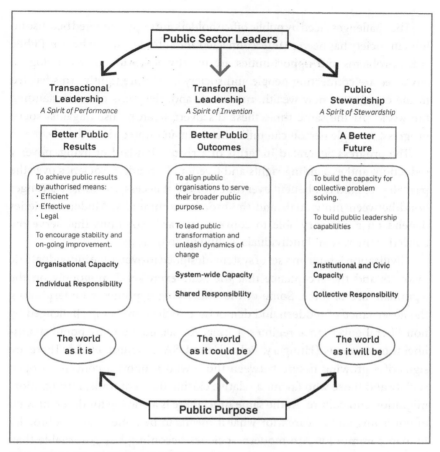

Figure 9.2: Leading Public Transformation

Public Stewardship

Literature on public stewardship is scarce, but the topic played a key role in the discussion of participants in NS labs. This reveals a growing concern about the factors that make societies more or less governable and what government can do in this regard. Public stewardship is a meta form of leadership. It is concerned with *building governable societies capable of collective problem solving and the public institutions to govern them.*[19]

This includes building a resilient society able to adapt to changing circumstances, public institutions fit for the times and a citizenry able and willing to build a future together.

The challenges faced by public office holders are unprecedented because no human society has been so interconnected and interdependent before. Public risks, problems and opportunities are intertwined. Modern technological advances are connecting people and society ever more tightly. This has led to the creation of new wealth, new cures and new ways of understanding the world. At the same time, these discoveries can be used against social progress. A single person can inflict harm on an unprecedented scale.

The progress generated in terms of a rising standard of living, poverty reduction, and expanding rights and freedom in modern societies over the past 50 years did not benefit everyone nor did it necessarily forge a stronger bond between individuals and the broader community. Modern societies depend on a citizenry able to converge towards solutions that serve the collective interest and individuals willing to do their part.

Civilisation is built on a set of systems designed to overcome individualistic instincts and the acceptance that the State exercises a monopoly on the legitimate use of force. Some of the underlying hypotheses underpinning the governance of modern and democratic society are being challenged by non-liberal governance regimes (China, Russia, etc.) and by populist anti-liberal movements (Hungary, Poland, the USA, Belgium, etc.).[20] There are signs of a growing fissure between those who support a concept of open society and those who favour a relative closing down of trade, immigration, migration and culture. At the same time, there is a craving for different ways of governing and a search for what it means to be a member of a broader human community. Are modern societies becoming less governable than before? And what can government do to build the collective capacity for problem solving and a cohesive citizenry capable of collective action in an increasingly pluralistic society?

The stewardship role of government may be one of the most demanding tasks for people in government today. The greatest risks for building governable societies start when people lose hope in government's capacity to build a better future and lose confidence in the capacity of public institutions to serve their interests.[21] *Public leadership* has received limited attention to date, but it is one of the factors that will play a significant role in the future governance of modern liberal societies.

Public sector leadership has traditionally been focused on ensuring productivity and efficiency. Management theory and sociological data combine to advise public sector leaders on how to lead their agencies for the efficient production of outputs. A narrow focus on these aspects of leadership misses something important.

Public sector leaders have responsibilities beyond the boundaries of their agencies. This recognition requires a shift in our understanding of the purpose of public sector leadership. Transactional leadership is important as well-managed departments are a necessary condition for fulfilling a public purpose. Transformational leadership is important because it allows the generation of public outcomes that would not otherwise be possible. Public stewardship contributes to the making of a governable society. The NS Initiative proposes that these types of leadership are interconnected and woven by the common thread of public purpose, a conception of public service and promoting the collective interest.

These are fundamental principles of public administration, yet they are not static concepts. They must be re-discovered, and re-articulated by public leaders to fit a time and context. Building a governable society is perpetually a work in progress. Public leadership contributes to this ongoing process as a capacity for people to take charge of issues of concern and find solutions by working collaboratively with others and with government.[22] In many ways, a measure of success of public sector leaders is their contribution in building a public leadership capacity in society.

CHAPTER 10
GOING BEYOND NS

The first part of this book posits that there are unique characteristics to serving in an increasingly global, interdependent, hyperconnected and disorderly world. As a result, conventional ideas and practices are reaching their useful limits; people in positions of authority know it, although they do not always acknowledge it publicly. People in all walks of life feel it and are searching for leaders to give voice to their concerns.

We are witnessing the breakdown of a number of beliefs about what has worked in the past and the end of assumptions supporting key public policies. This is a time for a profound re-thinking about what it may mean to govern a modern, liberal and democratic society in the future.

The NS Framework and the NS Exploratory Process provide a dynamic and multi-centric perspective to governing and problem solving in society. They recognise the importance of the authority of the State to get things done, ensure stability and encourage predictability, as well as the importance of co-generating innovative solutions. They recognise the need for institutional capacity as well as civic capacity to build governable societies.

The NS Exploratory Process helps practitioners challenge conventional ideas, re-frame public policy challenges from a broader perspective and re-position the contribution of public organisations to generate public results. In essence, it affirms that the New Public Management has run its course. It provides a useful perspective for issues that require managerial solutions, but does not provide much help to think through the "big questions" facing those who shoulder the responsibilities of governing in the 21st century. It is time to re-think public administration from a broader perspective, one that sees the dynamic interrelationships between the State, citizens and society as the fundamental element to governing modern societies. The NS Initiative focusses on the need to re-conceptualise public administration to guide the actions and decisions of public office holders. However, the re-thinking needed extends well beyond the scope of this book, the field of public administration and the NS Initiative.

There is a need to re-think the architecture and the functioning of the social, economic and political state.[1] This involves re-conceptualising the functioning of the market economy to avoid the dangers of an ideological attachment to polices that do not produce the desired results when put into practice. It also requires a deep re-thinking about what makes societies governable. Challenging trends are emerging that will affect future models of governance. The role of politics in building democratic societies is changing. A democratic society requires more than the running of elections or the periodic selection of a governing party. Elections can be used to promote a democratic agenda as surely as they can be used to promote an autocratic agenda.

There is a need to articulate in contemporary terms what conditions contribute to building modern societies and the governance of open, pluralistic and democratic societies. This requires reconciling in new ways the promotion of individual interests with the pursuit of ambitious collective aspirations.

Some ideas are too narrow to embrace the current reality, too inward-looking to extract meaning from emerging trends and too tentative to steer society through an unprecedented process of change. This is a good time to re-think, re-frame and re-invent. The need for a different way of thinking is great, but it remains an open question whether modern democratic societies will have the wherewithal to re-invent in a timely way their approach to governing.

In many parts of the world, there is experimentation underway. Some are aimed at re-inventing the social state, others at re-conceptualising the market economy. Some scholars and thought leaders are coming forward with new research that challenges conventional thinking. Others are putting forward novel ideas to bridge the gaps between prevailing ideas and the reality that people experience in their daily lives. This is the case, to name but a few, of the recent work by Marianna Mazzucato and Michael Jacobs on re-thinking capitalism, William Lazonick on the new economy, Joseph E. Stiglitz on unequal societies, Joseph Heath on the making of civilised society, Xavier de Souza Briggs on democracy as problem solving or Bernard Cricks on politics.[2]

In the public realm, there are increasing signs of concerns about the current state of affairs. People are manifesting their discontent and declining respect for the elites and institutions that are supposed to lead them. The public dissatisfaction on display in many countries is changing the political landscape and the political discourse. It is generating circumstances that can be used to roll back rights and liberties earned over long periods of time.

Public dissatisfaction can sometimes lead to progress. This energy may be channelled to bring about needed changes under some conditions, including existing institutional capacity, a reservoir of civic will necessary for collective action and skilful political stewardship. However, fear and anxiety are rarely a source of progress. The same circumstances may unleash a sequence of events with disastrous consequences when one or several of these enabling conditions are lacking. Rising tensions were most notable during the referendum on Brexit in the UK and in the USA during the 2016 presidential campaign. Similar phenomena are present in several other countries.

The greatest risk, in periods of profound transformation, is when people lose confidence in the capacity of public institutions to serve their interests and lose hope in their ability to benefit from the emerging world order. This is the time we live in.

This closing chapter is used to expand the conversation beyond the scope of the NS Initiative. It does not propose answers nor even a research agenda. It simply adds a voice to others who argue there is need to *re-think* the modern state, *re-frame* our expectations for a well performing society and economy, and *re-invent* in contemporary terms what it means to be part of a modern, liberal, pluralistic and democratic society. The re-thinking needed is profound. Building a democratic society is a collective enterprise.

RE-THINK ECONOMIC THEORIES

Economics and politics are never far apart. One of the expectations of governments is that their actions will contribute to improving the well-being of society and the quality of life of their citizens. The evidence about the need to re-invent economics has been abundant for a long time but overwhelming since the 2008 financial crisis. With all the advances in economics, why do governments do so poorly at managing the economy? Why did no one see the financial crisis coming? Why was so little done to prevent it and mitigate the impact for the most vulnerable in society?[3]

The financial crisis exposed fundamental weaknesses in the functioning of the global financial system. Many countries undertook financial liberalisation in the 1970s and 1980s and there has since been a marked increase in the frequency of banking crises.[4] The financial crisis revealed the weaknesses of prevailing concepts and resistance to the change necessary to prevent similar problems from re-occurring. When the defence of ideas resists mounting evidence about their deficiencies, they become ideological and stop being useful in shaping public policy.

Repeated policy failures signal that all is not well with the underlying assumptions that have guided economic policy decisions. *Policy failures are failures of concepts.* Repeated failures using a similar approach in a diversity of countries are not indicative of implementation difficulties; they reveal that the conceptual framework needs to be re-thought. In such circumstances, repeating the same approach is irresponsible, and not challenging basic assumptions in spite of mounting evidence is ideological. As mentioned by Stiglitz "the world has paid a high price for this devotion to the religion of market fundamentalism".[5] A number of economic assumptions have been discredited in practice.

Inequality and democracy: One of the striking features of the past four decades is that, even when growth has been strong, the majority of households have not seen commensurate increases in their real incomes.[6] During the period from 1985 to 2013, the Gini coefficient measuring income inequality increased in 17 OECD countries and wealth inequality has grown even more.[7] In the last decade, income inequality grew even in traditionally more egalitarian countries like Germany, Sweden and Denmark.[8]

The conventional view was that technological advances work alongside wage increases; this has not been the case in practice.[9] Recently, median wages have stopped matching productivity gains. The reality is that a small fraction of people capture an increasing portion of the benefits of growth. People worry that the economy does not work for them. In the past three decades, wages have grown much less than productivity. This fact is difficult to reconcile with the claims of marginal productivity theory.

Today we know that economic growth is not a "rising tide that lifts all boats". It does not inevitably bring increasing wealth and higher standards of living for all, and the benefits of growth unevenly distributed do not necessarily "trickle down" to the rest of the population. The trend toward greater equality of incomes, which characterised the post-war period, has been reversed and inequality has been rising. Past theories need re-thinking.

For many years, people were told to work hard, get the right skills and play by the rules to move ahead and achieve middle class status. Quoting Thomas Friedman, "this is just not true anymore".[10] Inequality has a number of economic, social and political implications. It weakens demand and therefore kills jobs. It weakens the fabric of society in ways that must be taken into account in the re-design of taxation and redistribution policies. Rising inequalities have serious implications for the well-being of future generations and for democracy.

The theory of democratic equality among citizens is under pressure. Some voting systems give more weight to the vote of some citizens than others. This is frequently the case in first past the post systems that give greater weight to rural constituencies than urban ones. These difficulties can be overcome. There are more serious challenges.

The principle of democratic equality is also being challenged by court decisions that give corporate citizens the same "inalienable" rights as individual citizens. De facto, this means that money plays a more significant role in the financing of electoral campaigns and the capacity of individuals to run for office. This gives more capacity to the wealthiest to influence the political agenda and enhances the capacity of corporate citizens to influence the electoral process.

Increasing income and wealth inequality compounds these problems. The question is: what can or should be done to preserve democratic equality? At what point does a democratic society become a democracy in name rather than in reality? At what point does rising inequality of influence undermine the capacity of a governing system to remain democratic?[11] Rising inequalities are not unavoidable but they require re-thinking the principles governing the economic sphere and the interface between the social, political and civic spheres.

Colin Crouch has described post-democracy as a society where the forms of democracy continue, including the rule of law, but where civil society is too weak to challenge corporate interests in influencing government.[12] Others are asking what does it mean to be a democracy, if citizens have no say over the issues they care the most about? This is the case when people have no say over the way their economic union is run,[13] or over trade agreements that affect their livelihood. Having a say is not the same as having a vote.

This is not an argument in favour of direct democracy or the use of blunt instruments like referendums, but a recognition of the need for meaningful involvement of citizens to build the capacity for collective action.

Globalisation and democracy: Globalisation and the supporting economic and trade agreements give rise to serious questions about how to preserve the capacity of governments to generate the public goods that their citizens value. The key concern is whether international economic and trade agreements will ultimately serve corporate interests, the collective interest or both.

At the macro-level, it is possible to demonstrate the beneficial results generated by opening markets and the positive impact of some international agreements. The problem is that people do not live their life at this macro level but in their community. What matters to them is the impact at the local level, the firms that provide them with employment opportunities, and their capacity to make a living and ensure the well-being of their children.

In a number of cases, the benefits of economic and trade agreements have been exaggerated and the impact on specific sectors and communities underestimated. People feel that they have been misled about the transition costs and the need for adjustments. The difficulties of the coal or agriculture sectors in the USA, automotive or meat industries in Europe and dairy or energy sectors in Canada are only too real for people losing their source of livelihood. Macroeconomic indicators do not pay the bills or put food on the table.

Economic and trade agreements are extremely complex and difficult to explain to the public. That said, a democratic society cannot be built by arguing that a matter is too complex to be discussed publicly, or by encouraging ignorance or distorting facts.

There is no denying that the dislocation brought about by the combined effect of globalisation and the digital revolution has been significant for some sectors. Disruptive changes have outpaced the absorptive capacity of society in some regions and in some sectors. *Acknowledging the need for adjustments is not a sign of weakness* but a necessary step for gaining public support to provide the assistance needed by fellow citizens in periods of rapid transformation. It is also needed to sustain public confidence in the capacity of government to steer society through a period of rapid change.

The rhetoric that economic globalisation is always beneficial and ultimately serves all people's interests need to be re-framed to display a greater sensitivity to the need for adjustment and the capacity of society to adapt.

This raises important questions about how to reap the benefit of an open and global economy while preserving the institutional and civic capacity to build a society of people's choosing. Economic globalisation is unlikely to succeed if it outpaces the absorptive capacity of society and without collective solidarity for those living through a rapid period of transformation.

Ideas and beliefs matter for political and societal projects. It is not enough to have faith in markets. A successful economy requires an understanding of the limitations of markets and what is required to make them work. It is not enough to have faith in the State for building a well performing society. An understanding of the unique contribution of State, market and citizens themselves is needed to re-invent the interrelationships that will best serve society in the future.

RE-THINK DEMOCRATIC PRINCIPLES

Re-thinking implies that the way one thinks and frames an issue transforms the approach that will be taken, the actions that will be needed and the results that will be achieved. *The way we think of democracy* transforms what it means to make it work and defines the potential for acting collectively and for collective problem solving.

For some, democracy is a contest among interest groups mediated by formal rules among elites or through a pluralist system.[14] For others, democracy is a deliberation process.[15] But there is another way to think of democracy that embraces both understandings and goes even further. Democracy is not limited to authorising a government to act, but it is "acting with it and beyond it".[16] From this perspective, democracy is the task of changing the state of the world. It is a collective effort that engages the shared responsibility of government, citizens and all agents in society.[17] The collective capacity for problem solving makes democracy work. Democracy is more than the capacity to deliberate or to set directions for government. Democracy is about *changing the state of the world through collective action*.

Xavier de Souza Briggs, in *Democracy as Problem Solving*, reminds us that collective action does not mean a consensual or conflict free approach to problem solving but rather the capacity to agree enough to make progress in some areas, while disagreeing in others. Mediating conflicting views is an important civic capacity.

A democratic society provides citizens with a sense of belonging but more importantly, it is recognised by the capacity of citizens to act collectively. This requires both the collective will to act and the civic capacity to take action. These capabilities are resources that can be deployed to solve collective problems. Civic capabilities are built day by day – they are developed or destroyed by the way societies are governed or the way we live our civil life. This brings to the fore important questions – *are we governed in ways that build the collective capacity for problem solving? As citizens, are we acting in ways that build or erode democracy?*

Freedom House found that "Freedom in the World" has consistently declined in each of the past 10 years.[18] This is the longest continuous decline in four decades. In 2015, 72 nations recorded a decline in freedoms, while 43 made progress. The number of electoral democracies in 2015 stood at 125, up slightly from a ten-year low of 116 in 2010.[19]

The retreat of democracy is not limited to developing countries. A number of countries of the European Union have taken measures limiting civic rights. Until recently, Hungary, Poland, the Czech Republic and Slovakia were considered success stories. The expectation was that they would join older democracies of Western Europe as well developed democratic societies. There has been some serious erosion since. In other parts of the world, there has been a significant rise of military regimes. This is the case in Thailand, Niger, Honduras and Pakistan, where the military restored its power as the central actor by dominating civilian governments.[20]

What should we learn from this? And what are the implications for the evolution of democracy and old "democracies"? The argument used to be that countries need to attain a certain level of development to create the conditions for a successful democracy to emerge.[21] The middle class was seen as the primary force behind democratic changes. This is not so obvious anymore.

In the late 1990s and early 2000s, the lack of economic growth in developing countries began to erode public confidence that democratisation would improve their living conditions. At the same time, China and other countries have shown that it is possible to combine State authority and market liberalisation in different ways. New ways of governing and alternative models are emerging.

The relative weaknesses of some of the most developed western democracies have raised concerns about the ability of democratic political regimes to govern in times of high uncertainty. Their inability to prevent the financial crisis, the long and protracted recovery that ensued, the rise of demagoguery and the rise of less than stellar leaders into positions of power are generating misgivings about the superiority of a governance model that is so unpredictable. Indeed, Freedom House reports that "division and doubts about global leadership among democratic powers around the world, result[ed] in wavering support for democracy beyond their borders".[22]

Democracy may be the best political system but it would be a mistake to believe that it is predestined to be the dominant system. So, how will the most prosperous democratic countries govern themselves in the future and how will they modernise their democratic society? How will they preserve the democratic values that contributed to their success while adjusting their governing practices to a changing world? Will "old democracies" be able to re-invent democracy for the knowledge age or will the trend lead instead to less democracy in practice? These are difficult questions that go to the heart of what it will mean to be a democracy in the future.

Civility and democracy: Joseph Heath in *Enlightenment 2.0* elegantly discussed the difficulty of governing in "The Age of Unreason".[23] His book gives voice to concerns raised by practitioners in many capitals around the world.

In a democracy, what people come to believe, whether it is true or not, has a potentially significant impact on the way policy choices are made and justified publicly. There are serious implications when evidence and facts are of declining relevance to public discourse, and what matters instead is the strength of emotion about a "believable" perception, whether real or unreal. This transforms public discourse from framing issues to encourage a greater public awareness of the benefits and consequences that various policy choices entail, to the creation of a plausible story to gain public support. "It used to be that everyone was entitled to their own opinion but not their own facts. But, this is not the case anymore. Perception is everything".[24] *Myths and untruths are becoming more powerful than facts.*

Politicians are discovering that with the use of social media, it is possible to repeat a statement over and over again until it becomes part of public perception whether it is true or not. Politicians are not the only ones to have discovered the potential of mass repetition. The same approach was used successfully by the tobacco industry over many years and by other lobby groups whether they were advocating for corporate tax cuts or arguing that there is no scientific evidence for global warming.

If democracy is the task of changing the state of the world through collective action and if civic capabilities for democracy are developed or destroyed by the way societies govern themselves and the way we act, then *what kind of societies are we building* when public discourse becomes disconnected from reality, and when public discourse makes no distinction between knowledge, expert opinion, scientific evidence and personal opinion? And what will happen if opinions and facts are given equal weight in the search for solutions to the problems we face as a society?[25]

The capacity to gather large crowds does not guarantee societal or democratic progress. The rise of the "angry hashtag activists" may be a force for change, but it is not necessarily civic nor civil. It operates as a network where outrage and anger are the currency used to galvanize people.[26] This may give more visibility to a cause but it also makes it more difficult to generate solutions that would serve the interest of the larger community. It leads to a hardening of positions as people with opposing views are portrayed as "enemies". This erodes democracy and alternatively encourages authoritative behaviours since at the end of the day, order must be maintained and someone must make a decision. *Can civilised democratic societies exist without civility* and respect for the views of others?

Politics and democracy: Politics may be an instrument for debating alternative futures and making choices in a peaceful way. Politics connects emotion and reason; this is why it is so powerful. Will the politics of "the knowledge age" disregard knowledge? Will politics in the future give greater weight to unleashing and fuelling emotions, and with what consequences?

Much progress was accomplished over a long period of time to improve the transparency and public accountability of government actions and decisions. It should be a concern for all when emerging trends encourage uncompromising and unbending positions. The rise of extremism and populism is a disturbing trend. The world has witnessed this trend before, but at a time when the tools for influencing public opinion were less powerful and the instruments for mass communication were in their infancy.

A democratic electoral process does not make a democratic society. It may be used to advance democracy or to give legitimacy to autocratic or oligarchic regimes. This was the case in the election in Germany in 1933, in Russia in 2004 and 2012, in Nicaragua in 2008 and in Turkey in 2015.

Politics arise from the simultaneous existence of different groups with different interests and different traditions within a territorial unit under a common rule. "It does not matter much how that unit came to be [...] what does matter is that its social structure, unlike some primitive societies, is sufficiently complex and divided to make politics a plausible response to the problem of governing".[27] Politics is one solution to the problem of order and by no means the only one. Tyranny (the rule of one person) and oligarchy (the rule of a group) are obvious alternatives. Whatever the difficulty of politics, it is radically different from tyranny, oligarchy, kingship, dictatorship, despotism and totalitarianism.

The promise of politics is that it is a more workable way of maintaining order. A political system uses politics to maintain order rather than relying primarily on the use of force.

A political process is not tied to a particular doctrine. Politics can work with democratic and undemocratic systems of government. In a sense, political parties are "oligarchical" organisations. Their role is to build popular support, sustain enthusiasm for the candidates they put forward, set machinery in place to gain support, and build ammunition against the candidates from other political parties. Political parties have shaped the political process for many years. What role will they play in the future? The strength of democratic society is its openness. This also makes it vulnerable to demagoguery. The democratic electoral processes can be usurped to serve an undemocratic purpose.

Democratic societies are made of many parts. They are governed by the rule of law. They value a separation of functions and powers. They need a well-functioning judicial system. They create and protect civic rights. These systems are designed to overcome individualist instincts and tribal interests. Democratic societies depend on a number of enabling conditions – public institutions able to govern and get things done, civic capability to share and build a better future together and, above all, people's will to live one's life as citizens of a democratic society with all the responsibilities, restraints and civic obligations that this entails. A democracy is a work in progress that never ends.

The New Synthesis focusses on re-thinking public administration ... in reality this is only a small part of the re-thinking needed to prepare government and society for the challenges of the 21st century.

CONCLUSION

CHALLENGING TIMES

The last 30 years have brought about profound changes to the world we live in. We have witnessed the end of the Cold War and the fall of the Berlin Wall.[1] The number of people living in extreme poverty worldwide fell by 70%.[2] The world is more global and interdependent than ever. In the last 10 years, the world has embraced the widespread use of the internet and information and communications technologies. The smart phone revolution has put internet connected computers in the hands of hundreds of millions of people.[3] Social media has exploded globally and connected everyone with an email address. Software innovations have enabled big data and cloud computing. In 2007 IBM launched Watson, the first cognitive computer. The world is undergoing a technological revolution that is transforming the economic, social and political spheres of life in society, the role of governments and citizens' expectations of their governments.

At the time of writing the final chapter of this book in November 2016, events on both sides of the Atlantic reveal the depth of public anxiety and the magnitude of social changes at play.

Within a few short months, voters in the United Kingdom (UK) and the United States of America (USA) repudiated their political establishments, shifted the fault line of Western politics to a more conservative position and voiced deep opposition to globalisation initiatives. In the wider world, authoritarian regimes are gaining prominence or are consolidating their positions. Far right parties and organisations are no longer fringe movements.[4] Voices that were silenced for a time are reasserting themselves carrying with them messages of intolerance. It seems that we are no longer moving towards a "point of inflexion" as discussed in chapter 1. Rather, *we are well into* it and events are likely to accelerate.

It would not take much to trigger a further escalation or a chain of events with unpredictable consequences. The risks of a terrorist attack, a fiscal crisis, or a possible bank failure are only too real in the coming years. Governments ready or not are called upon to guide and steer their society through an unprecedented process of change resulting from the combined effects of globalisation, a technological revolution, unprecedented population migration, and accelerating climate change. These factors are feeding on each other and accelerating the pace of change beyond the capacity of many people, communities or countries to cope. People in government today will need to find ways to reduce frictions, mitigate risks and invent solutions to society's problems in an increasingly polarised environment and with unfavourable circumstances.

Governing is never easy but this may prove to be an especially challenging time. Some problems that were left to fester for too long have seeded fear for the future and anxiety about people's capacity to adapt. The global economy has generated benefits for too few people. Rising income and wealth inequalities have fuelled resentment and are threatening stability. These circumstances present opportunities for renewal, but they may also lead to significant setbacks that curtail rights and make the world a more dangerous place.

Democratic societies are much more fragile than they seem on the surface. Some countries have conducted their affairs as if a democratic society could be subjected to abusive behaviours without risks or consequences. Liberal democracies are prone to the risk of demagoguery. This is well known. But new and even more potent risks have emerged for democratic societies. The USA provides the most recent and compelling example of the consequences of declining civility in society, a culture of violence, the effect of rage and outrage on public cohesion and the impact of lies, half-truth and untruths in public discourse. The presidential election in the USA and the Brexit vote in the UK to withdraw from the European Union constitute a single phenomenon with many common causes. The underlying forces have been bubbling up for years under the surface and are now coming into the open; the year 2016 may end up being an historical moment and a powerful reminder of the importance of building day by day the civic capacity for collective problem solving and a civic spirit conducive to collective action.

Every generation will chart an original path. Every generation faces the collective task of giving shape to a better future. This generation may be tested in unusual ways.

Different Times Require a Different Mental Map

Since the early 1980s public sector reforms have occupied a significant place in government agendas around the world. Many public sector reforms in the western world in particular were inward looking and government centric. They prioritised financial efficiency and the modernisation of the inner workings of government. Most paid little attention to the fast-changing landscape of the world we live in and how this was transforming the role of government or the expectations of citizens.[5] In some ways, some of these reforms have brought the State under attack. In some spheres the role of the State has been reduced, in others, eliminated entirely. The problem of a 'Hollow State' is that it devalues what makes the public sector unique and most valuable for society. It reduces the capacity of government to act even when it is most needed. These attempts at public sector reform have not prepared government for the challenges of serving in the 21st century, and have not built the capacity of society to face the challenges that lay ahead.

The New Synthesis (NS) Initiative was launched in 2009. At the time, it was already clear that there was some urgency in preparing government and society for the challenges of the 21st century. Several crises including the real estate crisis, financial crisis, sovereign debt crisis and the 'Big Recession' had revealed the weaknesses of public institutions and the inadequacy of several public policies. Governments were too frequently left in a reactive position, unable to anticipate shocks or to mitigate the impact for the most vulnerable in society. This in turn was eroding public confidence in the capacity of government to protect the collective interest and even to bring forward solutions to the increasingly complex problems that stem from living in an increasingly global and hyperconnected world.

The need to rethink public policies and the role of government in society was particularly obvious in countries that had benefited most from a governance model inherited from the industrial age. A different time requires a different mental map, ideas and practices, a capacity to challenge conventional ideas and practices and an openness to new and different ways of addressing collective problems. These conditions are not prevalent when there is a deep emotional or ideological attachment to existing ideas and practices even if there is mounting evidence that these ideas and practices are deficient or inadequate.

The New Synthesis Initiative: An Improbable Consensus

The NS Initiative brought together a diverse set of practitioners, academics and public sector leaders who shared both a commitment to modernising public administration in theory and in practice, and a common desire to prepare government to steer society through an unprecedented process of change.

The New Synthesis Initiative name was well chosen – a synthesis coherently integrates, in new ways, past theories, conventions, principles and practices of enduring value with new ones better aligned to the realities of today's practice and future challenges. In periods of deep transformation, it is of primary importance to rediscover the fundamental principles that contribute to good government and a well performing society, know what is worth preserving from the past and integrate new practices more appropriate to today's reality. At their limit, every discipline leads to fundamental philosophical principles; public administration is no different.

The NS work led to an "improbable consensus" considering the diversity of backgrounds, experience and perspectives of the participants drawn from four continents. It brought forward a conceptual framework that reconnects the role of government, citizens and multiple agents in society in a dynamic system of governance that can be used to propel society forward. It is a dynamic system where multiple interrelationships change the course of events and transform the environment; where success is not preordained and where multiple agents can neutralise each other's actions or find ways to act synergistically.

At its core, NS affirms the importance of the State and public institutions for a well preforming society. The State is an institution like no other. It plays an essential role in providing stability and ensuring peace and order. It is the guardian of rules, norms, values and conventions that make life in society possible. Irrespective of political orientation, public institutions must be able to adapt to changing circumstances to fulfil their mission.

The State is uniquely positioned to steer society and must ensure that the contribution of the public, civic and private spheres serve the collective interest. Not everything can be monetised, commercialised or managed as a product. Some public results of great importance for society cannot be generated by private and civic organisations on their own. Government plays a key role in building the capacity of society for collective problem solving.

Now more than ever, it is time to bring the role of the State back into the public discourse. Understood as a 'summative collection' of actors, entities, and institutions from government and throughout society, the State's *"raison d'être* is that of defining and pursuing the common interests of a given society".[6] As such, States reflect the entire system of laws, institutions, people and groups that together hold the responsibility for serving the collective interest and building a future worth living in.[7]

The way we think about the society we aspire to build shapes the reality we live in and the future that will be created. Ideas matter. They permeate our thinking. They influence government actions and decisions and define the relationship that binds government and citizens together.

This is a time when there is a need to re-think what it will mean to be a member of a modern democratic and pluralistic society in the future and what will be expected of government. Preparing a society that is fit to meet the complexity of the future will require re-thinking the role of the State in contemporary terms and re-integrating citizens into the practice of governing for the purpose of "building public institutions marked by integrity and responsiveness".[8]

Citizens are society's greatest assets. They can make and undo governance regimes. There are no law-abiding societies without law-abiding citizens. There are no peaceful societies without citizens able and willing to build a future together, no literate and knowledgeable societies without citizens willing to learn, and no public safety without citizens who care for one another. Citizens are public value creators and public value setters.

One of the most important roles of the State is to create a citizenry and to engage it in building a better future. People become citizens as they accept the constraints and responsibilities that stem from being a member of a broader community. In a democratic society, the capacity to act as citizens should transcend ideological boundaries.

Public sector leaders play a key role in creating the conditions that foster democratic citizenship. They set the tone for public conversations, and their actions may expand or reduce the space for civic action. Public leaders can be divisive; they can feed social insecurities and heighten the awareness of the differences between people. They can also use the authority of their position to unite people and help them rise above their differences. Some actions and behaviours erode the governability of a society. Civic capacity is the antidote to this risk.

Building Institutional and Civic Capacity

The *New Synthesis* provides a modest contribution to assist those tasked with leading society through this unprecedented period of transformation. Part I and Part II explain how a broader mental map can expand the options and opportunities open to government to address the complex problems we are facing as a society. Part III expands the conversation beyond the original scope of the NS Initiative to highlight the need to re-think, re-frame and re-invent the path towards a better future.

This book ends where the NS Initiative started. This means more questions requiring "new" answers. *What do we need to do to build the institutional and civic capacity of society so that people can build and share a better future together? What can we do to build the capacity of society for collaborative problem solving?*

These questions deserve attention. Institutional and civic capacity are likely to shape the next phase of the New Synthesis Initiative. *And so, the journey continues* ... for there is no end in our search for better government and better governance.

APPENDIX

LEARNING FROM THE "NEW SYNTHESIS" OF OTHERS

The use of case studies is a well-established practice in leadership development to prepare people to face challenging situations. There may be no simple solutions, but through a process of exchanging perspectives, and defending and building on others' ideas, participants develop their skills at analysing issues and making difficult decisions. The downside of case studies is that they are not *real* for the participants. There is no direct relationship between the participants and the issue, no emotional attachment and no obligation for results.

The NS Initiative uses *live cases* in the context of NS labs and workshops. A live case is a real challenge that public sector leaders are facing in practice in the context of the position they hold. This creates a direct relationship between the participants and the issue being explored. In this context, it is not sufficient to ask intelligent and probing questions; the purpose is to uncover a way forward that can be implemented and that would generate the desired results in practice. NS labs are used to generate practical solutions rather than building a bank of cases – although some will eventually be captured in that form to share what has been learned.

The NS Initiative also uses narratives that participants bring forward to illustrate real life challenges they are facing in practice. These narratives succinctly summarise a situation or an approach used in practice.

The NS Initiative has made a particular use of live cases in preparing this Fieldbook. The main focus of attention is not on the solution that was found or the results that were generated but *on the process of discovery* leading to a public change process. The key is to learn from public sector leaders about how they invented solutions to issues that had remained unresolved till then and how they managed to lead a transformation process to bring about this change. The scale and scope of the issue does not matter. In a sense, live cases are timeless because what matters most is how people at a given time and a given place invented solutions adapted to their context and circumstances.

The practitioners confronted with real life challenges are the teachers of the NS Team. It is their process of discovery that the NS Team has attempted to document and develop as a systematic way of doing what many public sector leaders do instinctively when they are searching for solutions to complex or seemingly intractable issues. How do they manage to see and frame issues from a different perspective and what can we learn from them? How do they gain traction and enrol the contribution of others? How do they work their way toward a viable solution through a maze of conflicting avenues and possibilities? How do they build support to ensure that a solution is owned by the largest number of people and end up reflecting who people are as a society and how they choose to live together? These are the questions of interest to the NS Team.

The essence of what was learned is presented in this Fieldbook. It is presented as the NS Exploratory Process. The key steps include positioning to rise above an agency-centric focus and reconnect actions and decisions to public purpose and societal results. It uses the authority of the State and available resources and capabilities for *leveraging* the contribution of others and propel society forward. *Engaging* and citizen-centricity unleash the civic capacity and the civic will for collective problem solving. This ensures that solutions are sustainable by sharing the responsibility with citizens and others. *Synthesising* is used to generate a powerful narrative of change. It is the narrative of a society, able and willing to invent solutions and to build a better future together.

The previous chapters have used some live cases and case studies to illustrate these concepts. Every example illustrates in its own way the concepts of positioning, leveraging, engaging and synthesising that are discussed in Chapters 4 to 7.

The Prison Management case, Singapore (Appendix A)

This case is a flagship for the NS Initiative. It was first documented and published during the early phase of the NS Initiative and has been recently updated by the Singapore Civil Service College. **Lena Leong** powerfully describes the evolution of a transformation that spans over many years. The questioning of the management team, about the value proposition of a prison system where no one escapes but where ex-offenders return to jail because they do not successfully re-integrate society, is inspiring. This is the starting point of a journey of discovery that will lead the team to transform public opinion, mobilise multiple actors, enrol inmates, families, communities and employers in a shared effort and reconceive the justice system. This case was used in Chapter 7 to illustrate the concept of synthesising. All the elements of the NS Exploratory Process figure prominently in the case.

The Champlain Complex Care Program, Canada (Appendix B)

This case was used in Chapter 5 to illustrate the concept of leveraging the power of others and enrolling the contribution of multiple organisations as well as community groups to bring about results that exceed the capacity of any single agency. **Michel Bilodeau** was the CEO mentioned in the case as well as the author of this chapter. He played a prominent role in launching and spearheading the initiative. He is therefore best positioned to look back and reflect on the lessons learned along the way. The positioning of the initiative focussed on the well-being of the children rather than the services provided by various agencies. This was the rallying point for collaboration. Michel Bilodeau shares lessons of critical importance for leveraging collaboration across multiple agencies, including the need to invent the machinery needed to sustain collaboration. He shares important insights about the inadequacies of financial systems in cases such as this one where the benefits of an initiative are dispersed across society while the costs accrue to a particular organisation.

Elder Care in Fredericia, Denmark (Appendix C)

This case was used to illustrate the importance of citizen-centricity in policy development and service design. It is also a compelling illustration of the power of co-creation and co-production to generate better public results, lower societal costs and improve user satisfaction. All four dimensions are illustrated in the case. The initial challenge was to re-frame the issue from a societal and user perspective. The positioning and engaging dimensions figure prominently in this case. The Municipality would not accept the inevitability of declining services due to increasing costs; a better solution was needed. The programmes were reframed from the perspective of users to support their desire to remain in charge of their lives for as long as possible. This opened a host of new possibilities. At the heart of the transformation process was the willingness of the City Council to change its governance model to accommodate a high level of variability to account for a diversity of needs, circumstances and capabilities. The results have been impressive and inspiring.

Cleaning Day in Helsinki, Finland (Appendix D)

Well performing societies have strong civic capacity and a strong civil will to put these capabilities to productive use in order to invent solutions that promote the collective interest. These civic capabilities figure prominently in this case. At the end of the day, the capacity for self-organisation and mobilisation must be met with public agencies able and willing to support community-based initiatives and self-organised solutions. This was also on display in this case. Collective capacity and public agency support the transformation of a good idea into a viable public innovation that will benefit society for years to come. This case is an illustration of collective problem solving and a reminder that issues are neither too big nor too small to benefit from a different way of thinking that leads to a different way of doing things. The NS Team learned about this initiative in the context of its ongoing work in Finland.

* * *

One thousand participants have been involved in some ways in the NS Initiative in the period between 2012-2015. One thousand journeys of discovery have been unfolding since. A small number of them were documented by the NS Team and an even smaller number ended up being mentioned in this Fieldbook. Most of the initiatives launched by participants in NS workshops during this period will remain unknown beyond the circle of people who invented them and maybe some of the people who benefited most directly from a new and better way of doing things. The NS Initiative and this Fieldbook are a way of reaching out to practitioners who did not participate in NS workshops but who might benefit from the findings to date.

The NS Exploratory Process transforms the way we think and understand public initiatives. Once the principles are understood and internalised, it opens up one's mind to the underlying complexity of public transformation initiatives and the accomplishment of the people leading them. Someone could read the following four cases and miss what matters most. After all, public servants in charge of prisons are expected to manage prisons and ensure that people will not escape. The CEO of the Children's Hospital of Eastern Ontario is paid to run the hospital and ensure that children get the services they need. The City Council of Frederica is responsible to provide services to elders within their means and capacity. And what is so special about government officials making it easy for people to organise a cleaning day in Helsinki? All these people are just doing their jobs, aren't they?

Nothing is further from the truth. Narratives about leading public transformation are magical – they reveal moments when actions tip the situation in a direction that will change the course of events for the better. They are unique and yet similar in so many ways. The role played by the people involved is irreplaceable; without them the change process would not have happened. In all cases, people leading the change process have challenged established ideas and practices and re-framed the issue from a broader perspective. They have articulated a public purpose worthy of support that made collaboration possible. They skilfully aligned authority and resources to uncover new ways to bridge the gaps between collective aspirations for a better future and the current reality. They built on the strength of others and made the initiative a collective effort. In the process, they transformed the relationship between government, users, beneficiaries and citizens. Initiatives like these are not ordinary; *they transform the world we live in.*

They may not make front page news. The initiators may not receive a Nobel Peace Prize, yet they play an essential role in building a better future and better society. They contribute to well-functioning societies able to invent solutions to public challenges. They create public institutions with the adaptive capacity to respond to changing needs and circumstances. They build the capacity of government to govern and get things done peacefully while exploring uncharted territories. They play an essential role in building the civic capacity and nurturing the public will for collective problem solving that make societies worth living in. This is the magic readers are invited to look for in reading the following appendices.

The people involved in these cases share a number of common characteristics. They are optimistic about the capacity to build a better future and believe in the transformative role of the State. They are committed and resilient. It takes endurance to stay the course and to stay focussed on the desired outcome. They are able to see the whole and are even willing to sacrifice the short-term interests of their organisation to make progress on a larger cause. In all cases, they are skilful relationship builders that encourage collaboration across organisations, sectors and systems.

Their stories provide an antidote to cynicism because they display the potential for seeing the factors at play in a different way and for discovering points of leverage to bring about change.

TOWARDS A SOCIETY WITHOUT RE-OFFENDING

By Lena Leong[1]
This case study was completed in November 2014. The author would like to thank Desmond Chin and Leonie Tan, as well as staff and ex-officers of SPS and SCORE for their assistance during the research and writing of this case study.

In 1998, the Singapore Prison Service (SPS) was confronted with two pressing issues – an overcrowded prison that was straining infrastructure and resources, and a shortage of manpower due to difficulties in staff retention and recruitment. The situation was compounded by poor public perception of the organisation and its work. Prison officers were overworked and had low morale. The situation became so bad that SPS had to ask its parent ministry, the Ministry of Home Affairs (MHA), to slow down law enforcement. SPS was also seriously contemplating overseas recruitment of prison officers to address the manpower shortage.

Towards the end of that year, Chua Chin Kiat was appointed Director of Prisons. Chua felt that a mere increase in staff headcount would not address SPS's problems and that they had to find new ways to reform the prison system. One of the first things he did was to create regular platforms for his leadership team to meet. Every officer two levels down from Deputy Director of SPS would meet together with Chua every Monday and Friday over breakfast. These were informal chats for the group to educate him on running of the prisons and for Chua to share with them his principles, values and aspirations for the Service. Wednesdays were set aside for more formal meetings to deliberate on issues raised at the breakfast meetings. Chua also set up a Research & Planning Branch to research, network with other research and correctional services, and coordinate organisation-wide initiatives. The branch, with a Head and two officers initially, scanned the literature on the practice of prison systems across the world. It tested and implemented many new ideas. Subsequently, the branch instituted three-year planning horizons and introduced an evidence-based orientation and approach to rehabilitation of inmates in SPS.

THE RIPPLE CONCEPT

SPS was a secure and safe institution with a zero-escape rate, but Chua questioned its value proposition if its focus was only on maintaining security and safety within the prisons. The recidivism rate then was high, at 44.4%, which meant that almost half the ex-offenders returned to prison within two years of release. How was SPS creating a safer society if it did not do anything to reduce repeat offences? Chua saw rehabilitation, and not incarceration, as the way forward.

Even though rehabilitation had always been one of SPS's guiding values, it remained a remote concept to prison officers, whose role was mainly custodial. Rehabilitation was considered the job of counsellors and volunteers. Efforts towards rehabilitation were fragmented and limited to work regimes, education and religious counselling. Prior to Chua's arrival at SPS, pockets of staff were already disturbed by trends that revealed inter-generational prisoners, which meant the children of inmates were becoming offenders. However, SPS's proposal to set up a Rehabilitation Division was rejected by MHA as the Ministry was concerned whether "the huge amount of resources requested would produce any results".[2] Given the lack of a vision for the future, SPS saw itself as a high security ship with no destination.[3]

> *"... before I formally took over, I had already resolved to do two things. One, I would look deeper into the possibility of introducing a formal structure to deliver programmes aimed at creating positive change in the prison inmates. In order to tackle the problem of overcrowding, I must stop the revolving door. Two, I would introduce a forward-looking element in the organisation of the service to take up research and planning, and ultimately to develop intellectual properties in the core competency areas of the Prison Service."*
>
> Chua Chin Kiat, Director, Singapore Prison Service (1999–2007)[4]

Ideas on the desired future of SPS were shared at its Work Plan Seminar in May 1999, where junior prison officers were invited to participate for the first time in SPS's history. The concept of a ripple, which came from one of the pre-seminar work groups, was used to symbolise and explain how organisational change could be achieved. Prison officers, at the centre of the ripple, must first be committed to the task of reforming inmates. They were the ones to set off the first wave. Inmates, who would respond to the actions of the prison officers, then set off the second ripple of change. To sustain the change in inmates, their families, the criminal justice system, and the community must be supportive. This ripple would then create a change in attitudes towards ex-offenders nationally and internationally.

As Chua believed SPS's vision had to be developed "by the staff for the staff" in order for it to outlast his tenure in SPS, he invited all prison officers to give their views at focus groups and over online chats after the seminar. Although most prison officers embraced the idea of rehabilitation, many also feared that "better" treatment would encourage defiance in inmates and compromise security. Of those who gave feedback, 250 prison officers who had the most interesting ideas were invited to a two-day visioning retreat, where many more divergent views surfaced. SPS senior management then pushed ahead to craft SPS's vision.

The initial vision proposals were met with scepticism by MHA. Security was MHA's paramount consideration and "ministry officials intimated that the bosses felt that the vision statement gave the impression that the Prison Service had gone soft".[5] Chua and his senior management team assured MHA that rehabilitation would be on top of what SPS was doing and they would test the idea as a pilot without additional resources. SPS's persistence paid off. After several rounds of refinement, including a re-visioning exercise with representatives from MHA, SPS was given the go-ahead to experiment with rehabilitation. Its new mission and vision statements were officially announced by the Home Affairs Minister at the ground-breaking ceremony of the new Changi Prison Complex in December 1999.

"I wanted the statement to be publicly unveiled to commit the Service and the Government to the cause. The families of inmates and community at large also needed to be enrolled into the vision for it to work ... I therefore needed not only to persuade my parent Ministry to approve the mission and vision statements but also the Minister to unveil it."

Chua Chin Kiat, Director, Singapore Prison Service (1999–2007)[6]

Mission
As a key partner in Criminal Justice, we protect society through the safe custody and rehabilitation of offenders, cooperating in prevention and after-care.

Vision
We aspire to be captains in the lives of offenders committed to our custody. We will be instrumental in steering them towards being responsible citizens with the help of their families and the community. We will thus build a secure and exemplary prison system.

The new mission and vision statements started a fundamental mindset shift in SPS – beyond security and safety to the rehabilitation and reintegration of offenders into society. They injected a sense of purpose and urgency and became instrumental in shaping many of SPS's subsequent strategies, including the Yellow Ribbon Project.

BECOMING CAPTAINS OF LIVES

Prison officers, at the heart of the ripple, were SPS's agents for change. The participative nature of the visioning exercise was a turning point in SPS's command and control organisational culture. A series of initiatives was further introduced to empower prison officers on the ground to voice their views, as well as encourage interactions and exchange of ideas across SPS in order to create a learning and more innovative work environment.

Even before the visioning exercise was completed, SPS had begun testing its ideas on rehabilitation. The Housing Unit Management System, a new approach to managing the prisons, was introduced in December 1999 to create a more inmate-centric management facility. Prison officers were used to keeping a distance from the inmates for fear that getting too close to them would heighten security risks. Periodic job rotations within SPS reinforced this divide. However, under the new system, prison officers were assigned to supervise a group of inmates, whom they had to know well enough to work out rehabilitation programmes based on the inmates' strengths, weaknesses and motivations. This went against prison officers' entrenched belief that their duty was to give inmates a hard time in order to deter re-offence. The SPS leadership team recognised that a fundamental change in mindset was needed and launched the system as a pilot. Six of the 15 institutions within SPS volunteered for the trial roll-out of the Housing Unit Management System. The pilot was fraught with challenges as prison officers were anxious over their expanded job scope, potential conflict of roles and fear of loss of control. However, over time, operational efficiency, intelligence gathering and job satisfaction improved, raising the level of security and discipline in the prisons. As positive outcomes emerged, confidence in and support for the system grew. Even so, it took SPS another three years after the launch of the new system to scale the initiative up to other prison institutions.

> "To begin with, it was difficult to change our own staff. The greatest enemy was ourselves – what if there was riot? We had to first change our officers to believe that something else was possible."
> Jason Wong, Deputy Director Singapore Prison Service (1988–2002)[7]

Another project, initiated before the launch of the new vision, was the Rehabilitation Framework. It was one of the first tasks assigned to the Research & Planning Branch when it was formed in 1998. The framework would optimise resource allocation and enable SPS to take systematic steps towards rehabilitating the 15,000 inmates under its charge. One of the key components of the framework was the Level of Service Inventory-Revised (LSI-R) instrument, an instrument used in correctional services in Canada, which SPS adapted for its needs. The LSI-R matched inmates to correctional programmes based on their criminogenic risks and rehabilitation needs. Using this instrument, prison officers could modify treatment plans, called Personal Route Maps, to cater to each inmate's progress throughout incarceration. Adapting the LSI-R was a gruelling process that included standardising it to the local profile, calibrating the system for use throughout incarceration and customising it for use by prison officers who were not psychometrically trained. Prison officers were unhappy about having to test and learn the instrument on top of their heavy workloads. In particular, older staff felt threatened by the new technology, which they feared would render their experience irrelevant. Nonetheless, the LSI-R was launched just in time for it to be used to assess and select inmates for admission into the new Prison School, launched in early 2000.

Providing inmates with an education was not new to SPS. Teachers from the Ministry of Education conducted lessons for inmates, but the curriculum did not include life or employability skills that would facilitate the inmates' reintegration into society. Lessons were conducted in makeshift classrooms scattered across the prison institutes and there was little interaction between teachers and prison officers. Inmates were reluctant learners who saw the lessons merely as a welcome relief from prison confinement. MHA was initially hesitant to invest resources into establishing a school, a domain which they felt belonged to the Ministry of Education. Nonetheless, SPS persisted and eventually obtained approval to proceed. With the opening of the Kaki Bukit Prison School in January 2000 – for the first time in SPS's history – the prison environment was converted into an educational institution with the operating philosophy of "School First, Prison Second".[8] A new curriculum tailored to the social development, employability and motivational needs of inmates was created. Inmates were addressed by name instead of number and they, themselves, were responsible for maintaining discipline in class. These innovations turned out to be powerful interventions in generating among the inmates a sense of ownership towards the school's goals. The enthusiasm of the inmates began to rub off on some of the prison officers in charge of the project, whose initial doubts faded as they observed the transformation in their wards.

These initiatives changed the way SPS operated. They stretched resources and were often perceived by some as contrary to the fundamental objectives of prison work and the professional identity of prison officers. An organisational climate survey in early 2000 revealed that many officers were unhappy. They felt that the SPS management did not fully understand the challenges they faced on the ground.

Nonetheless, the change champions pressed on to develop a three-year strategic framework from 2000 to 2002. The framework mapped SPS's stakeholder groups to primary functions and proposed 15 anchor projects, most of which were intended to improve SPS's internal efficiency, and aligned its functions to its vision. Two of the projects, the CARE Network and Family Involvement, became pivotal in transforming the way inmates were rehabilitated and reintegrated into society.

CHANGING PUBLIC PERCEPTIONS

SPS realised that its efforts at rehabilitating prisoners would come to naught, with the chances of re-offence remaining high, if the community refused to give an ex-offender a second chance. In fact, a public perception survey in 2000 revealed that the public knew and cared little about SPS and its work. SPS's past deterrent approaches to reduce re-offence had resulted in the public perceiving the prisons and inmates as scary. Besides, SPS's poor public image was hindering staff recruitment. SPS realised that it had to change the community's perception of SPS and ex-offenders in order to succeed in rehabilitation.

In 2002, when Chua was confident that SPS had created substantial systemic structures to help inmates reform and that the organisational culture had sufficiently shifted to support such an approach, he tasked SPS's Public Affairs Branch to launch a media campaign to rebrand the organisation. The exercise would not only boost the morale of serving prison officers, but also help SPS to attract recruits with values that were aligned to the organisation's vision.

The campaign, with the theme "Captains of Lives, Rehab, Renew, Restart", profiled SPS as an effective and forward-looking organisation with professional officers, who sought to protect society by keeping offenders in secure custody and rehabilitating.

Prison Is Not Just about Imprisonment
Singapore Prison Service has embarked on a bold, new commitment to place greater emphasis on rehabilitation. We are already committing funding, focus and expertise within SPS to enable inmates to renew and restart their lives. We need your help because it is our firm belief that this will eventually reduce the burden on the community of repeat offenders.

Secure Custody
Secure custody of inmates by SPS is our primary responsibility of keeping Singapore safe.

Rehabilitation
Rehabilitation is offered to inmates who are capable and willing. We have designed programmes to help them through in-care and after-care.

Recruitment
As Captains of Lives, we truly make a difference. We balance compassion with firmness, are well paid, have the opportunity for growth and can

be certain that the skills we acquire will be in demand wherever we go in life.

Community
Be bold with us. Be part of the move by Singapore to be number one by providing inmates with the opportunity to restart their lives and integrate into the community, thus reducing the burden of repeat crime rates on the community.

Everyone in SPS was involved in the media blitz. Superintendents briefed their staff on the concept, and senior management handpicked prison officers to be SPS's voice and face to the world, as well as to be role models to the staff. This helped to align internal and external messages. Three provocative television commercials with catchy taglines anchored the campaign.

With its new focus on working with families and communities, SPS was able to interest the media to run stories on reformed inmates in newspapers, over radio and television, and on billboards. Reporters were given tours of the prisons to help them understand and write about SPS's rehabilitation programme. Subsequent television commercials featured prison officers sharing their experiences in rehabilitation work.

At around the same time in 2002, Jason Wong, previously Deputy Director of SPS, was seconded to the Singapore Corporation of Rehabilitative Enterprises (SCORE) as its Chief Executive Officer. A self-funding statutory board under MHA, SCORE was in charge of prison industry, employment and skills training for inmates. Its concern with the availability of funding and business sustainability often ran into conflict with SPS's push for more attention to rehabilitation. SCORE embarked on its own transformation journey and adopted the following mission and vision statements.

Mission
We rehabilitate and help reintegrate offenders to become responsible and contributing members of society.

Vision
We build bridges of hope for offenders and their families. We contribute to a safe community by successfully reintegrating offenders. We exemplify and lead in creating a more compassionate society that offers second chances.

Wong, a firm believer in the power of storytelling, mooted the idea of producing a movie that would not only entertain but also spread the message of giving "second chances" to ex-offenders. Undeterred by the lack of funds, Wong broached the idea with a media company, which agreed to jointly produce a movie. In 2003, SCORE launched its first community movie, "Twilight Kitchen", which chronicled the journey of an ex-offender. The film was released in phases to different segments of the community to optimise the effects of each outreach exercise.

The combined media outreach efforts of SPS and SCORE were a success. SPS's advertisements became the talking point at public places. In 2002, SPS won the Singapore Creative Circle Award (Bronze) in the Television & Cinema category, as well as the Institute of Advertising Singapore award for Television Campaign of the Year. About 250 employers stepped forward to offer employment to ex-offenders. Qualified and highly motivated individuals who wanted to do their part for society applied to join the Prison Service. The external affirmation significantly lifted the spirits of SPS and SCORE officers. They felt proud to be part of the Prison Service, and internal support for SPS's rehabilitation and rehabilitation efforts surged.

The Yellow Ribbon Project

With an already strong focus on in-care for offenders, SPS realised that it had to strengthen the after-care support in order for its rehabilitation efforts to be effective. Earlier, in May 2000, SPS had officially set up the Community Action for the Rehabilitation of Ex-offenders (CARE) Network to optimise resources and integrate in-care and after-care support for ex-offenders. It comprised six other members in the after-care, social and security sectors.[9] The Network held annual retreats and met every quarter to set direction and co-ordinate efforts in the after-care sector.

In 2004, the CARE Network capitalised on the public's overwhelming response to SPS's and SCORE's publicity blitzes to launch the Yellow Ribbon Project (YRP) – a public education effort to raise awareness, generate acceptance and inspire action for the cause of giving ex-offenders a second chance at restarting their lives. The name was inspired by a 1970s song "Tie a Yellow Ribbon Round the Ole Oak Tree". It described an ex-offender's request to his wife to tie a yellow ribbon round an old oak tree as an indication of her forgiveness and acceptance. Every offender encounters two prisons – a physical prison, and a psychological and social prison. Offenders' families, friends, neighbours, employers, colleagues, and the community hold the keys to unlock the second prison.

The CARE Network had overall responsibility for the project. It was supported by YRP steering and sub-committees comprising mostly SPS and SCORE officers, who were responsible for the implementation of its programmes. Initially, SPS and SCORE funded YRP from their operating budget. The Tote Board later provided additional funding support, but only for the organising of subsequent campaigns. A separate Yellow Ribbon Fund (YRF), with Institution of Public Character status, was also set up to provide financial support for reintegration and family support programmes.

The initial aim of YRP was to change the public's perception of ex-offenders by publicising SPS's and SCORE's rehabilitation programme. The theme for its inaugural campaign in 2004 was "Help Unlock the Second Prison". The campaign comprised a series of activities anchored around a key event, a charity concert graced by then President S. R. Nathan and Mrs Nathan. Prison tours were organised to help policy makers and potential volunteers better understand life behind bars and the part they could play in supporting inmates' rehabilitation. About 200 employers attended a demonstration of inmates' skills at SCORE. 320,000 hand-made yellow ribbons were distributed to the public to raise awareness of the YRP cause.

The enthusiasm at the YRP launch surprised SPS and SCORE officers. The 7,000-strong audience at the concert broke into resounding applause when ex-offenders stood up to perform. Advocates wrote to the newspapers to support the YRP cause. Employers expressed interest in hiring ex-offenders. YRP's message of acceptance, renewal and hope was starting to shift society's view of inmates and ex-offenders. The success of the first YRP campaign gave the organisers confidence to embark on more ambitious programmes in succeeding years. The YRP became an annual event every September, spawning new activities with different themes that carried the same message – give ex-offenders a second chance (see Figure A(i)).

By the fourth year in 2007, 94% of respondents of a post-YRP survey indicated that they were aware of YRP's objectives. Regular networking forums involving both local and overseas professionals in correctional work, policy makers, the academia, community partners and employers emerged to discuss issues on the rehabilitation and reintegration of inmates. More professionals and corporate groups started to volunteer in the prisons to develop inmates' artistic, musical and culinary talents. Inmates and ex-offenders themselves began to participate in YRP events such as performing at roadshows and sharing their testimonies. The media gave extensive coverage of these events.

By the sixth year in 2009, YRP went beyond raising awareness to engaging the community to take action. Political leaders continued to participate in YRF fund-raising events. Community groups collaborated to run YRP-related events. Some even initiated their own projects. For example, SPS's Tattoo Removal Programme, a critical component of its zero-tolerance policy towards gang-related activities in the prisons, was made possible by GiGATT International Marketing Pte Ltd, a distributor of medical technologies. The company called the YRP hotline and donated laser equipment that enabled inmates to remove their tattoos and renounce their affiliations to gangs. The Board of Visiting Justices and Board of Inspection also initiated iCare, a matching dollar scheme that encouraged inmates to remit their prison work allowance to their families instead of spending it on food items in prisons. iCare enabled inmates to take responsibility for their families, and hence enhanced their self-esteem and resolve to change.

By 2013, the number of YRP volunteers had grown from 76 in 2004 to 2,625 in 2013. Together, they contributed resources and ideas that augmented SPS's rehabilitation and reintegration programmes.

Moving forward, SPS and SCORE hope to do less of organising YRP events but more of facilitating ground-up initiatives by creating networks and connecting like-minded individuals and organisations across the community sectors. They plan to increase the engagement of youths in tertiary institutions and secondary schools by seeking their views on reintegration issues. Besides raising awareness through talks in schools and organising learning journeys to prisons, they also plan to partner with community groups to facilitate youth-led volunteering projects and research. This would ensure that the community continues to embrace an inclusive society where ex-offenders have equal opportunities.

THE RIPPLE EFFECT OF YRP

What started off as the conviction of a group of SPS officers that inmates could be transformed grew with the support of their colleagues and society. YRP impacted staff and inmates, inmates' families, the criminal justice system, the community and beyond.

Staff

Reframing their work in the context of YRP goals gave SPS and SCORE officers a sense of shared purpose and focus. A lot of their work suddenly "made sense". Their view of the world was expanded and their aspirations were unleashed to do more for inmates. For example, they overcame employers' scepticism and doggedly grew a pool of employer advocates. They trained workplace supervisors and developed on-boarding programmes to ensure that employers were successful in inducting ex-offenders into their workforces. Without an additional budget, they sought partnerships with institutions and corporate groups such as the Singapore Workforce Development Agency (WDA) to build new training facilities, e.g. a fully equipped kitchen and computer laboratories. It also obtained funds from WDA to expand employability skills training – which used to be limited to electrical works and hair-dressing – to include generic work and supervisory skills, as well as progressive levels of trade certification in areas such as landscaping, laundry operations, culinary skills, food preparation, IT, and logistics. The number of inmates trained increased by 65%, from 3,567 in 2009 to 5,896 in 2013. Once the in-care infrastructure was in place, they worked on strengthening the after-care support for ex-offenders.

Inmates

Initially, the inmates themselves had no faith in the ability of the YRP to help them and cringed when approached to share their testimonies as YRP ambassadors. They did not realise they could paint, sing, compose songs and pass examinations. The YRP gave them hope, helped them channel their voices to the world, and restarted their lives. With the community more accepting of ex-offenders, more of them found employment and the recidivism rate dropped significantly, from 44.4% for the 1998 cohort to 27.4% for the 2011 cohort.

> *Darren's Story*
>
> *Darren Tan sat for his A-level examinations in the Prison School. He was accepted into university but was unable to leave the prison for the pre-admission interview. The university dean travelled to Changi Prison to interview him.*
>
> *A company then sponsored his university education. Darren eventually graduated with a law degree in 2013.*

Inmates' Families

The YRF also provided assistance to the families of inmates and ex-offenders. In 2006, the Yellow Ribbon Emergency Fund was set up under YRF to disburse cash within 48 hours to dependents of inmates to tide over urgent needs. The YRF-ISCOS Fairy Godparent programme was also started in 2006 to provide bursaries, tuition and mentoring to ex-offenders' children. In 2010, MHA initiated the Yellow Ribbon Community Outreach Project (YR-COP) as a pilot, where grassroots volunteers were assigned to families affected by incarceration to understand their needs and link them to community support avenues. By October 2014, 65 grassroots divisions were on YR-COP. More than 620 grassroots volunteers were trained to provide community support to assist needy families and about 2,100 inmates' families had been assisted.

Criminal Justice System

In 2005, the Government amended the Criminal Registration Act to strike out criminal records for minor offences, a move that gave a second chance to some types of offenders. With society more accepting of inmates and more open to giving ex-offenders a second chance at restarting their lives, SPS was able to implement community-based sentencing such as the Short Detention Order and the Day Reporting Order in 2011. Both were extensions of the Home Detention Scheme introduced in 2000, where offenders of minor crimes serve the tail-end of their sentences at home, tracked by electronic tagging devices. These amendments in legislation enabled such offenders to access community resources for their rehabilitation, minimising disruptions to inmates' families and employment opportunities while punishing them for their offence.

The Community and Beyond

The YRP helped to significantly reduce the stigmatisation of ex-offenders. Members of the public had gone beyond the act of wearing a yellow ribbon to providing funds, jobs and expertise to help inmates and ex-offenders. The number of employers in SCORE's job bank almost tripled from 1,381 in 2004 to 3,876 in 2013. More employers, as part of corporate social responsibility, were also prepared to mentor and develop ex-offenders and were proud to associate their companies with YRP.

More importantly, people at workplaces had become more accepting of ex-offenders as colleagues. The number of inmates securing jobs before they left prisons more than doubled from 951 in 2009 to 2,114 in 2013. More schools involved their students in activities with inmates and ex-offenders. In 2013, 15,000 students participated in YRP activities such as street sales, fund-raising and packing of YRP goodie packs. This number was an increase from 10,000 students in 2011. With societal acceptance, ex-offenders became more confident about confronting their past and sharing their journeys to encourage others, while inmates gained hope of a future beyond prisons and the motivation to change. The YRP crossed national boundaries and cultures – its concept of harnessing all of society to give ex-offenders a second chance served as an inspiration for the emergence of similar movements in Fiji, Nigeria, Mozambique, the USA, Australia and the Philippines.

SHIFTING FROM PRISON SERVICE
TO CORRECTIONAL SERVICE

SPS's framing of its mission in the context of societal goals enabled it to see new possibilities, identify new partners and create space for others to contribute. This improved the outcomes of SPS programmes and moved the results up the value chain. As talented recruits and community resources became available, SPS and SCORE were able to shift their focus towards new areas of work and building new capacity.

First, SPS strengthened its in-care strategy. In 2012, SPS implemented the Enhanced Supervision Scheme for Long Term Imprisonment for repeat drug offenders who would undergo regular urine tests, stricter monitoring, and intensified counselling with SPS's correctional rehabilitation specialists to reduce their chances of re-offence. SPS started the Pre-Release Centre, where inmates were put through more intensive rehabilitation programmes during the final 10 months of their sentences. These were intended to develop self-confidence and social skills and to prepare inmates for life upon release.

Second, SPS shifted more attention to close gaps in after-care. Internal research showed that re-offending rates significantly dropped when ex-offenders were able to stay in their jobs for the first six months. Hence, SCORE assigned career vocational officers to assess inmates' motivations to put them on the appropriate industry training track, and help them secure a job before they left prison. SCORE's employability case managers would then help newly released ex-offenders navigate the transition for the first six months upon their release, such as ensuring that they were on time for work, related well with their colleagues and settled into their new work routines. SPS further expanded its after-care role in January 2014 by amending the Prisons Act to subject inmates to conditional release, and to mandate inmates who were assessed to be at higher risk of re-offending to come under after-care programmes. These schemes aimed to support ex-offenders and deter them from re-offending.

> "We underestimate the difficulties ex-offenders face in transition. They can work three days a week as bookies and earn as much as S$3,000 a month. Loan-sharks pay them S$100 for splashing paint on one door. This is "easy money" compared to 10-hour shifts as cooks in a restaurant. The temptation to return to their former ways is very real and great."
> Patrick Lau, Chief Operating Officer Singapore Corporation of Rehabilitative Enterprises (2001-2013)[10]

Third, SPS expended efforts to build the capacity of its partners. In 2010, SPS introduced the Halfway House Service model to enhance the programmes and professionalism of halfway houses. More structured programmes were introduced to train volunteers in areas such as inmate subculture and counselling so that they could take on more complex work. More time was also invested into forging collaborations within CARE Network and with other partners to find joint solutions, identify opportunities and break the cycle of offending early. SPS's Rehabilitation and Reintegration Framework, which promoted an evidence-based and integrated approach to in-care and after-care, helped to create a shared language among stakeholders within and beyond SPS, and galvanised their efforts.[11]

SUSTAINING SOCIAL CHANGE

The YRP began as a clarion call for help – an appeal to everyone in society to give ex-offenders a second chance at restarting their lives. Each handmade yellow ribbon produced by an inmate symbolised his or her hope for acceptance. Out of nowhere, people came forward to support and give. What caused the shift?

"The most important achievement of all was not systemic or infrastructural, but cultural ... the critical mass of prison officers believed in rehabilitation and they put that belief into action."
Chua Chin Kiat, Director, Singapore Prison Service (1999-2007)[12]

The change started with a small group of SPS officers who believed that inmates could be transformed. They had big, audacious goals for rehabilitation and after-care, with families being strengthened and society playing its part. They intervened at multiple levels of leadership, organisational culture, mission and strategy, and concurrently attended to operational needs, shifting of mindsets and engaging vision. Often, they were learning on the go, sometimes setting off in directions different from their plans when experiments failed or when opportunities struck. Their journey was fraught with tensions, obstacles and setbacks. Empowering leadership gathered early adopters, tested and pushed through ideas, and generated quick wins. Once there was success, confidence and followers gradually gathered, and the change momentum grew.

Behind Every Inmate You See, There Is a Family
To strengthen family bonds and motivate change, the women prisons obtained special approval for the children of inmates to visit their mothers on Mother's Day. The sight of the children crying and hugging their mothers as they parted at the end of the day moved the prison officers and changed their view of rehabilitation. A video clip of the event went viral in SPS. Soon, prison officers in the male prisons also wanted to organise a similar event for Father's Day.

Most of the breakthroughs came only when SPS and SCORE officers were emotionally connected to the cause. Once they saw how repeated incarcerations detached offenders from society, destroyed families and put children at risk, and how their work could make a difference, they were motivated and began to perceive their relationships with inmates differently. The officers discovered new partners, created new structures and developed new capabilities that opened up opportunities beyond prisons. Many innovations were a result of officers on the ground seizing opportunities, taking risks and trying out new ideas. Change was facilitated by collective ownership of a compelling shared purpose.

Similarly, when inmates became emotionally connected with how the consequences of their offences affected their loved ones and the possibilities of a new future, they became motivated and learnt to make different life choices. Likewise, when stakeholders and members of the public connected with the stories of inmates and ex-offenders, and saw them as someone's parent or child – ordinary people who made mistakes and needed others to give them second chances – their perceptions of inmates and ex-offenders changed, and they offered help.

YRP was successful because most people believed in second chances, since people do make mistakes and would need others to believe in them again. SPS recognised this universal truth, branded it, and made it the galvanising force for its work. Change happened when people were moved by what they saw. It was sustained when mental models shifted and people began to choose to act differently and collectively commit to the cause.

Towards a Society without Re-offending

SPS embarked on its transformation journey 15 years ago. With a common cause in YRP, SPS's ties with SCORE have been strengthened through the sharing of resources such as space, manpower and budget. Setting early the conditions for internal culture shifts also helped to sustain organisational change. The Prison School has since doubled its student intake and moved to new premises with upgraded facilities. Its research team has also developed new tools to assess inmates and published papers in journals to share the SPS experience. SPS now has about 180 trained rehabilitation specialists attending to the in-care needs of inmates and after-care needs of ex-offenders.

In 2012, SPS won the Singapore Quality Award with Special Commendation for organisational excellence. More importantly, SPS has been able to attract the next generation of prison officers with values that are aligned to its vision of transforming the Prison Service into a respected profession. In an online survey that was part of its re-visioning exercise in October 2012, 90% of prison officers responded within two weeks. Of those who responded, 75% felt strongly that SPS should take on a leading role in the after-care of offenders and prevention of offending; 90% strongly felt that ensuring the safety and security of inmates was one of SPS's core roles; and 80% felt that facilitating the rehabilitation and reintegration of offenders was one of SPS's core roles.

SPS and SCORE are at a tipping point of transforming society. Through the YRP, they succeeded in creating societal awareness and cultivating advocates for rehabilitation. Nonetheless, as Teo Tze Fang, former CEO of SCORE, said: "It is for the Yellow Ribbon spirit – the spirit of giving second chances – to become spontaneously the spirit of Singapore within the next 10 years."[13]

At the SPS-SCORE Corporate Advance in 2013, SPS, under new Director of Prisons Soh Wai Wah, launched its new vision statement to further challenge staff to work towards a society without re-offending.

Vision
As Captains of Lives, we inspire everyone, at every chance, towards a society without re-offending.

Inmates can be a very difficult group of people to manage, and prison work can be very demoralising and demanding. The challenge for SPS and SCORE now is to build on the momentum, uphold the sense of purpose, pride and ownership in its officers, and keep sight of what matters. Their ultimate goal is for "the reintegration of ex-offenders to be initiated by the community rather than by any government agency or non-profit organisation".[14]

YEAR & THEME	KEY INITIATIVES
2004 Creating Awareness: Help Unlock the Second Prison	The Yellow Ribbon Project was launched: • The inaugural Yellow Ribbon Concert (2004, 2006 and 2008) was graced by then President of Singapore S. R. Nathan and attended by 7,000 people. • The movie "Coming Home", on three inmates preparing to reintegrate into society after serving their sentence, was launched. The movie premiere was attended by 6,500 people.
2005 Engaging the Community: Give Ex-offenders A Second Lease of Life	The YRP message of acceptance and support for ex-offenders was extended to a wider audience: • The inaugural Tie-A-Yellow Ribbon Walk (2005-2007) attracted 14,000 people. • The inaugural Yellow Ribbon Conference gathered partners in correctional work to share best practices and research. It became an annual event to develop better integrated rehabilitation and reintegration approaches. • The inaugural Yellow Ribbon Job Fair, co-organised with North East Community Development Council, offered 660 vacancies to pre-released inmates. • The movie "One More Chance", on the difficulties faced by three ex-offenders after their release from prison, was launched. It attracted 150,000 viewers.
2006 Engaging the Ex-Offenders: Widening the Reach, Deepening the Message	The YRP began to mobilise inmates and ex-offenders to contribute to society through community service: • The Yellow Ribbon Concert was broadcast over local television. • The inaugural Yellow Ribbon Creative Festival, comprising a poetry and song-writing competition, was held in Changi Prison to give inmates an opportunity to express their hopes and appreciation to those who had helped them. • The inaugural Celebrating Second Chances Award Ceremony (2006, 2008, 2011 and 2013) recognised 300 ex-offenders for remaining crime free. • MediaCorp produced and broadcast "Turning Point", which featured the struggles of four ex-offenders, on national television.

YEAR & THEME	KEY INITIATIVES
2007 Giving Back: Extending the Reach, Inspiring Action in Inmates and Ex-offenders	The YRP profiled inmates and ex-offenders as responsible members of society with gifts, talents, and acts of service: • Prime Minister Lee Hsien Loong was the guest of honour at the annual Tie-A-Yellow Ribbon Walk. • The Yellow Ribbon Community Service Project was introduced in prison. • The Inaugural Yellow Ribbon Community Art Exhibition (2007-2013) was launched, where works by inmates were sold to raise funds for YRF. • Other events organised included the Yellow Ribbon Culinary Competition, the Yellow Ribbon Appreciation Dinner, and the Yellow Ribbon Fund Charity Gala Dinner.
2009 Giving Back: Inmates and Ex- offenders Playing a Role to Give Back to Society	The YRP focused on encouraging inmates and ex-offenders to give back to society: • The inaugural Yellow Ribbon Prison Run (2009-2013) was flagged off by Deputy Prime Minister Teo Chee Hean. Among the participants were 80 ex-offenders. • The Tattoo Removal Programme, supporting SPS's zero tolerance policy towards gang-related activities in the prisons, was launched with the sponsorship of GiGATT International Marketing Pte Ltd.
2010 Coming Together, We Care: Engaging the Community for Action to Help Ex-offenders Reintegrate	The YRP focused on fostering partnerships with the community: • 11 ex-offenders and 250 community members, comprising ex-offenders' families and students, formed the YRP contingent at the Chingay Parade. • North East Community Council launched the Rekindle Programme that helped inmates from the Reformative Training Centre reconcile with their families.
2011 Little Gestures, Big Difference: Encourage Everyday Gestures that Signify Acceptance of Ex- offenders by the Community	The YRP encouraged small acts of kindness and support for inmates and ex-offenders: • ISCOS (Industrial & Services Co-operative Society Ltd) led ex-offenders and volunteers to serve lunch cooked by inmates to residents of a home for the aged. The event raised funds which were matched by the Southeast Community Development Council. • Marshall Cavendish Editions published the book *Yellow Ribbon*, depicting success stories of ex-offenders and their challenges in assimilating into society.

YEAR & THEME	KEY INITIATIVES
2012 Will: Inspire Inmates and Ex- offenders to Take Charge of their Own Rehabilitation and Contribute to the Society	The YRP encouraged inmates and ex-offenders and their families to work towards a better future with the support of the community: • An individual, 53-year-old Madam Jenae, ran 12 hours in a self-initiated Dusk till Dawn Challenge to raise more than S$130,000 for YRF in 2012. • The Yellow Ribbon mobile application was launched to update smartphone users on the latest YRP news.
2013 Celebrating 10 Years of Second Chances: The Road to Acceptance	The YRP celebrated its 10th anniversary with a stronger focus on empowering more Singaporeans with the opportunity to be part of the YRP movement: • Deputy Prime Minister Teo Chee Hean participated in the Yellow Ribbon Prison Run. • A record 1,230 participants formed a Giant Human Yellow Ribbon to commemorate YRP's 10th anniversary.

Figure A(i): A Broad Overview of Yellow Ribbon Campaigns

APPENDIX B
THE "CHAMPLAIN COMPLEX CARE PROGRAM" IN CANADA

By Michel Bilodeau
The author would like to thank Queena Li for writing assistance and Elke Loeffler for the use of graphic material.

Technological and clinical breakthroughs in life-extending treatments for children have improved the prognosis for many previously fatal conditions.[1] In many cases, children with chronic illnesses are able to live much longer lives through extensive treatment. However, one unfortunate consequence of these developments is that some infants, who would not have previously survived their illness at birth, now live as children with serious physical and neurologic disabilities.

These patients "represent the most technologically and medically complex cases" for the families, communities and care facilities that support them.[2] The children are considered "technology-dependent, [and] medically complex because of their diverse medical needs, and fragile because they [are] at high risk of a life-threatening episode".[3] Treatment regimens may include life-sustaining equipment, therapeutic services, regular paediatric care and at times consultations with up to 15 medical specialists.[4] The Provincial Council for Maternal and Child Health estimated that 3,700 children, or 0.1% of Ontario children, accounted for 50% of the province's paediatric in-patient costs in 2012.[5] The disproportionate financial costs of caring for technology-dependent, medically complex and fragile children are only exceeded by the tremendous social costs borne by their families and communities.

This was considered by all those involved as a situation where a single health agency, working on its own, would be unable to provide a comprehensive approach to the problem. The division of responsibilities within the Champlain Local Health Integration Network (LHIN) meant that one hospital was responsible for acute care, an agency funded by another Ministry was responsible for outpatient rehabilitation, another for home care and yet another one for social services. No organisation was funded to provide inter-agency coordination.

CHILDREN WITH COMPLEX CONDITIONS

In late fall 2008, the CEO of the Children's Hospital of Ontario (CHEO) attended one of his regular consultation meetings with the CHEO Family Forum, a group of parents with children using CHEO's services.[6] Some of these parents were caring for medically fragile children with complex conditions. He listened to the parents describe with resignation how they dedicated much of their lives to co-ordinating their children's complex care. As one parent explained, "when your child has a complex case involving multiple specialists with no standard cure, you enter a tangled web of medical coordination. Every clinic provides excellent outpatient services but as a group there is a complete lack of coordination, like a committee with no chairperson!"[7] The parents cited a lack of "coordination among service provider organisations, and between providers within CHEO" as a central source of their distress. Many of their children required visits to a regular paediatrician, numerous medical specialists, CHEO services and ongoing support from outpatient care facilities. The CEO learned about the amount of time and energy that parents dedicated to scheduling appointments with different specialists who were not in contact with each other.[8]

Although parents had effectively become case managers for their children, they did not always feel qualified to determine what information was medically pertinent to disclose. "We constantly questioned if we had done all we should have", one parent said, "Did we tell specialists important information, such as a recently-discovered drug allergy? Did each team member have a full picture of our son's needs and how his different conditions affect his overall health?"[9] Parents had to repeat "the same story over and over again" while ensuring all of the relevant care providers were up-to-date with the latest information about their child's condition. These challenges were worsened by the frustrations of being unable to co-ordinate appointments with various specialists on the same day, forcing parents to take more time off work and, in some cases, become full time caregivers.[10]

These parents, and others like them, desperately needed help, but they had long stopped believing that help would ever come.

These stories gave CHEO's CEO a family-centred perspective on the huge gaps in coordination across health care service providers in the Champlain region. These gaps in complex care placed enormous emotional and economic strain on the families of children with medically complex conditions. The CEO became committed to helping these families and others like them. He brought the issues to the members of CHEO's senior management to discuss ways to alleviate some of the challenges facing these children and their families.[11] The right solution was not immediately obvious. Some expressed concerns about the resources necessary to meaningfully tackle the problem while others "were unsure [of] whether this was part of CHEO's mandate".[12]

The discussion focussed on the role of CHEO. Was it limited to providing acute care? Participants soon agreed that the issue was much larger. First, as the only tertiary care centre for children in Eastern Ontario and Western Quebec, CHEO had to play a leadership role within the health system to promote children's health. Second, it was realised that addressing the issues required taking account of the social impact of these children's diseases on their family and on society as a whole.

After lengthy deliberation, CHEO's executives came to three important realisations:

Firstly, each family needed to have **one point of contact** that would harmonise and oversee the day-to-day requirements of their child's complex care. The case manager would have the chief responsibility to "know the child, be aware of the full case, coordinate appointments, and ensure there is a common chart for the patient".[13]

Secondly, the sheer number of physicians involved in a single complex case was the source of many coordination challenges for families. Children needed a **Most Responsible Physician** (MRP) to co-ordinate their medical care, not only to liaise with other physicians, but also to track the inevitable changes that occur throughout the stages of a child's development and medical condition.[14]

Lastly, CHEO's CEO and senior team realised that children with medically complex conditions tended to require services from **multiple organisations.**

Although CHEO was a world-class establishment in administering technologically advanced treatments and services, its patients also relied on other providers and community-based services. For example, the Champlain Community Care Access Centre (CCAC) provided children, many of them also CHEO patients, with "customized care plans in conjunction with school nurses, dietitians, occupational or speech therapists". In other instances, CHEO patients with "physical, developmental and behavioural issues" jointly relied on "rehabilitation services" provided by the Ottawa Children's Treatment Centre (OCTC).[15] Coordination within CHEO alone was not enough. Designing an effective and integrated family-centric approach to care-giving meant leveraging the contributions of partner organisations "in the broader context of system-wide and societal results".[16] With this realisation, CHEO sought to partner with several of Eastern Ontario's leading health care organisations. The partnership linked CHEO with the community-based services of CCAC, OCTC and Ottawa Children's Coordinated Access and Referral to Services (Coordinated Access). The Champlain LHIN provided oversight and approved the transfer of funding from CCAC to the project.[17] The result was an innovative pilot project for children with complex medical conditions called the Champlain Complex Care Program.

THE CHAMPLAIN COMPLEX CARE PROGRAM

The Champlain Complex Care Program aimed to improve the overall health of children living with medically complex conditions by supporting them to live at home and participate in their communities; "while, at the same time, standardising the processes and identifying efficiencies in the overtaxed system upon which they relied for their continuing care needs". The partner organisations embarked on an initial three-year pilot phase (2009-2012) with a view to scale up the partnership model to better serve "the approximately 500 children and young people who account for about 50% of the total 'paediatric-weighted' cases of this age group in the region".[18]

The Champlain Complex Care Program set out goals to:

- Provide a family-centred approach for technology-dependent, medically complex and fragile children and youth;
- Facilitate communication and collaboration among care providers;
- Coordinate needs across the system; and

- Relieve the burden on families of navigating the system alone, in order to aid in the overall objective of improving health status for those impacted.[19]

Getting Started

A review of how other hospitals have addressed the needs of their patients with medically complex conditions revealed that "a Patient-Centred Medical Home (focal point for a patient's healthcare information) could improve complex care coordination".[20] Among the different care models proposed by relevant research, one model suggested that "effective [...] care is delivered by a prepared provider team who engage productively with an activated, informed patient. Preparation means having the necessary expertise, information, time and resources to assure effective clinical management. Patients must also have the information and confidence to make best use of their involvement with their practice team".[21] These principles clarified some "key requirements for successful coordination" and began to shape the thinking of programme partners.[22]

The programme partners convened Family-Focussed Meetings with patients, families, clinical specialists, interdisciplinary medical teams and other health providers to assess each child's unique needs. The panel applied shared expertise and a common perspective to determine if co-ordinating care teams would be hospital, community-based or both. The final Programme Team comprised of a Project Manager, several nurse co-ordinators and a MRP, who together provided a comprehensive point of contact for patients. The Project Manager and MRP were based at CHEO while care co-ordinators were based in the partner organisation best suited to deliver the optimal response to patient needs. In turn, the organisations enlisted their allied networks of community services to provide the necessary respite care, coordination, education, palliative care and some other services.[23]

Next, the partners established an inclusive governance structure, which included a **Steering Committee** consisting of family representatives and senior executives from each partner organisation. The Programme Team and Steering Committee worked alongside an **"Advisory Committee** consisting of family members and middle management" representatives to explore various programme design options.[24] Involvement from differently situated practitioners in the health care community led to some inevitable disagreement over the path forward. Some participants had a tendency to find multiple reasons why it would not work (for example the absence of a common electronic medical chart). However, reporting these difficulties to the Steering Committee of Executives and families highlighted key issues, re-focussed attentions on the overall interest of the child and informed better guidance from the senior management group.[25]

Attending the Steering Committee's meetings, the CEO of CHEO recognised several important reasons for co-operation at the executive level. First, each executive was the steward of a partner organisation, each benefitting from enhanced coordination. The group could refer back to its clear objective when considering the Advisory Committee's input and the programme's goals. Secondly, the shared benefits of co-operation meant that CHEO did not seek to control the Steering Committee by itself; everyone at the table wanted the programme to succeed. Lastly, the already-familiar CEOs enjoyed "excellent working and personal relationships" with each other, allowing them to deliberate constructively.[26]

Robust linkages across partner organisations and departments in the governing structure ensured practical, "evidence-based decision making".[27] The programme's co-ordinated care structure not only created functional linkages between disciplines, but also across service providers. Under the **Care Coordination Model** (Figure B(i)), patient care dynamically reflected the order and modes of patient experience. As patient needs and conditions changed, so would the nature of their care.

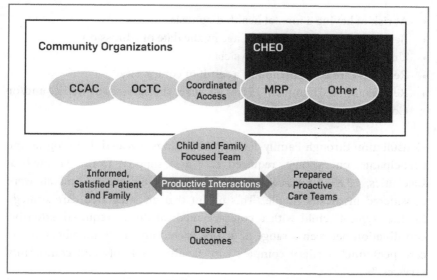

Figure B(i): Care Coordination Model[28]
(Adapted from Loeffler, Ridha and Cook-Major, *A partnership model for children with complex medical conditions*, Governance International, 2013).

Designing the Pilot Programme

In 2009, the partners began undertaking tasks to compile a "detailed pilot project proposal" and "investigate the feasibility of developing an EHR (electronic health record system); fund and appoint a MRP, a Coordinator and a Project Manager; set specific outcome goals and design a methodologically sound evaluation study to measure project outcomes; establish project inclusion criteria and identify patients meeting the criteria; agree on a process for selecting patients to participate in the pilot project; and develop a budget for the project, to start in March 2010".[29]

The pilot programme included 33 randomly selected participants and their families based on the following 'inclusion criteria':

- Multi-complex child
- Medically fragile
- Dependency on high intensity care/technological device
- Existing risk of an unexpected severe acute life-threatening event

- At risk of having a mental health diagnosis
- Between the 0 and 16 years of age by the date of admission
- Under the care of a family physician
- Requires care coordination as a result of complexity
- Resides in the Champlain LHIN and uses the services of CHEO and/or Community Programmes.[30]

Consultation through Family-Focussed Meetings revealed that programme participants, on average, required care and support from "11 medical specialties, 93.8% required specialised medical equipment and all were considered medically fragile". This meant that an integrated care strategy for the "typical" child with a complex medical illness required extensive coordination between a range of actors, including family members, home care personnel, tertiary complex care facilities, schools and community services.[31]

Preliminary inquiry revealed that establishing a sophisticated EHR system akin to what CHEO's Chief Information Officer (CIO) had conceived would not be feasible in the time available before the pilot was set to begin. "An interoperable EHR that could work with community partners was scheduled much further out, the CIO explained – no earlier than 2015".[32] The partner organisations were faced with identifying a paper-based alternative, which could still accurately convey each patient's complete health record.[33] Once again, "discussion[s] with the Family Forum yielded helpful feedback from parents. One described a notebook she created, containing a record of her child's visits, orders and procedures, and a short 'cheat sheet' of her child's 'key information', which she brought along to every appointment with a clinician, so as not to forget important details that the clinician would need to know about her child".[34] Programme partners recognised this idea as a simple, straightforward solution for capturing the details of "a child's condition and his/her current medical and psycho-social care providers and services" in one accessible document. The 'cheat sheet' idea was revised into a "simple paper form" called the Single Point of Care (SPOC), which was distributed to parents for bringing with them to appointments.[35]

One major success factor in designing and implementing this programme was parents' participation. Parents identified the problem, convinced those in charge that an improvement was needed, proposed solutions, worked with the professionals at every step of the way to design the programme and participated in its implementation. Without their effort, the programme would never have seen the light of day.

A Model of Service Delivery

Programme implementers formalised the structure of the Care Coordination Model to include a **Service Delivery Model** of three co-ordinated levels. The model determined a "best care provider" for each child based on his or her condition and required treatments, allowing patients to flow through the model to determine the right level and sites of care.[36] In this way, the Service Delivery Model's design reflects how patients navigate the health care system; patients with medically complex conditions can move back and forth across the model based on their fluctuating care needs (Figure B(ii)).

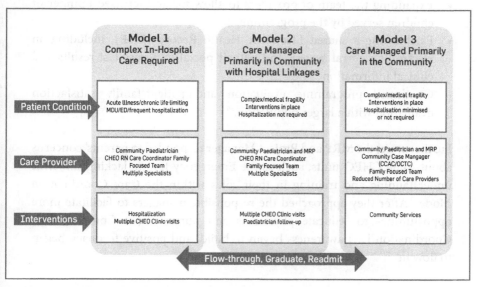

Figure B(ii): Service Delivery Model – Care Needs[37]
(Adapted from Loeffler, Ridha and Cook-Major, *A partnership model for children with complex medical conditions* Governance International, 2013).

The programme also introduced the addition of **Rapid Response Nurses** in November 2013. Research suggests that rapid response nurses help reduce the risk of a child's re-hospitalisation and preventable emergency room visits by "improving the quality of transition from acute care to home care".

Nurses visit patients in their homes in the first 24 hours after discharge from hospital to clarify any inquiries families may have about discharge instructions or medication as well as communicate with the child's primary care provider and arrange a follow-up appointment within seven days.[38]

The partnership also proposed extending the pilot's network of service providers to include additional community-based involvement by:

- Further extending the Partnership beyond healthcare to include education and community and youth services
- Establishing direct ties to other Ministries by inviting them to sit on Steering and Advisory Committees
- Partnering with primary care providers in the community
- Expanding the team of providers to allow for an increased number of children served by the programme
- Establishing a shared Electronic Health Record (EHR), including an electronic referral system and patient portal to access test results and clinical information
- Continued programme evaluation and patient/family satisfaction evaluation with a larger population.[39]

Furthermore, the MRP and Project Manager responded to parents' concerns about some CHEO units, such as the Emergency Room, lacking sufficient understanding and training in their roles within the Care Coordination Model. After they approached the responsible managers to facilitate more opportunities to "educate physicians and nurses about Complex Care Coordination [...] awareness began to build, and positive feedback began to flow in".[40]

Performance Indicators

Overall evaluations of the pilot phase suggest that the Champlain Complex Care Program provided patients and families with the "long awaited coordination of services" they once resigned themselves to living without. Participants subsequently experienced "improved access to care" and "increasing system throughput", which in turn generated a greater shift to community-based care across the healthcare system. Improved transition to community-based care represented the "potential to extend the service of a complex care programme to a larger population".[41]

To date, approximately 15% of participants have graduated from the programme. Each of the graduated participants today possesses an improved "ability and capacity to navigate the overall health and social care system, using tools and documentation which give them full access to services in the community", including support from a community care coordinator and primary care physician. Such enhancements make an important difference to an affected child's quality of life. They are improvements that give families caring for children with medically complex conditions an opportunity "to 'normalize' their households, return to work and lead a family life as close as possible to normal".[42]

Family survey results conveyed correspondingly "positive satisfaction from participating families", with responses emphasising the following benefits:

- No more need to answer the same question from a variety of providers
- A noticeable reduction in duplicate procedures/tests and referrals
- A single point of contact (care coordinator) whom they can call, eliminating unnecessary contacts with providers and unnecessary emergency department visits
- An individualised comprehensive Single Point of Care (SPOC) plan, developed uniquely for each patient/family.[43]

These survey insights demonstrate the programme's "ability to identify and reach the right population, provide services that impact on health care utilization and health outcomes, and provide an intervention with which children and families are satisfied".[44]

Other measures of success displayed similar results. The Child and Adolescent Needs and Strengths (CANS) assessment is a measurement of changes in strength and needs of children and young people. Studies commonly use CANS scores as an indicator of:

- Youth life domain functioning (e.g., sleep, recreation, school attendance and behaviour)
- Youth strengths (e.g., interpersonal, optimism, resiliency)

- Youth behavioural and emotional needs (e.g., depression, anxiety, anger control)
- Youth risk behaviours (e.g., suicide risk, danger to others, fire setting)
- Acculturation (e.g., language, identity, cultural stress)
- Caregiver strengths (e.g., supervision, mental health, safety).[45]

Programme participants were evaluated based on CANS and demonstrated increased strength and decreased healthcare needs, as shown by "reductions in the [associated] CANS score and sub-scores".

Costs and Savings

During the initial consultation phases of the pilot, the Steering Committee confronted the project's main impediment: funding. Near the end of the fiscal year, the CEO of the CCAC identified a small surplus of C$300,000, which regular CCAC operations could not expend before year end. The surplus funding would be returned to the Government of Ontario if not allocated to an initiative. Recognising the opportunity to overcome a major obstacle, CHEO and CCAC executives submitted a joint claim to the LHIN requesting a transfer of surplus funds to CHEO, which was then approved. For its part, CHEO's Department of Paediatrics provided for the MRP portion of the project. This means that, "there was now enough funding available to finance a one-year pilot project".[46] Since then, the pilot programme's annual operating budget has been on average C$350,000.[47]

In contrast to its relatively low initial costs, the programme has "generated savings for the health system of close to C$1 million per year, mainly due to the reduced number of hospital days needed by the participants".[48] Administrators observed that the number of hospitalised days decrease from an annual average of 20 days to 7 days.[49] The benefits of these outcomes "are distributed across the health sector" and many individual beneficiaries at a relatively low overall cost to society.[50]

However, the cost-benefit structure of initiatives such as the Champlain Complex Care Project also carries limitations. The problem, CHEO's CEO noted, is that "these savings [...] are not net savings" and "those who bear the direct cost [...] do not benefit from the results in a manner that translates into direct savings". For example, "reducing the number or duration of hospitalisation does not allow hospitals to reduce the number of beds or reduce staffing since others replace these patients".[51]

By the same token, small changes in the number of yearly patient visits to the emergency room have "negligible overall financial impact" because hospitals must generally continue to "maintain [the same level of] its 24/7 infrastructure (physician, nurses, lab, radiology, etc.)". In some ways, such reductions may even appear as a negative result on performance indicators "since a reduction in the number of visits increases the cost per visit and may make the hospital look less efficient".[52]

Most of the benefits do not accrue to those who bear the costs but rather to the families and society. Families could waste less time and energy visiting specialists, patients could receive better, more accessible care and the employers of their parents could enjoy "increased productivity and reduced absences from work".[53] In addition, some parents who had become full time providers could return to the workplace, improving their quality of life while generating tax revenues for the government.

Over three years, the programme's accumulated savings for the healthcare system totalled approximately C$1.65 million. A detailed breakdown reveals that cost reductions have taken the form of "decreases in number of in-patient days, equating to C$900K in annual savings [...]; decreases in emergency room visits, resulting in C$7K annual savings [...]; offset by increases in clinical visits in year one resulting in additional C$13K costs and then a decreased trend in year two, resulting in the equivalent savings".[54]

GOING FURTHER

The Champlain Complex Care Program has since evolved into a leading partnership model for co-ordinating health services to improve quality of care for children with complex medical conditions. It is, as defined by the Commission on the Reform of Ontario's Public Services, exemplary of the "ideal reformed system".[55]

A Steering Committee comprising of partner organisation CEOs (several positions having undergone turnovers), families and physicians continues to govern the direction of the Champlain Complex Care Program. An Advisory Committee and a Programme Team contribute their co-ordinated efforts to support ongoing operations. Each year, Partnership Agreements undergo a renewal process, which ensures key issues remain at the forefront of the Committee's shared concerns. Similarly, annual renewals allow partner organisations to "report their proposed financial and in-kind services for the upcoming year", keeping all those involved informed.[56]

The most important consequence of "providing the right care, at the right time, in the right place, by the right care provider" is giving more young people the chance to enjoy a better overall quality of life. Other groups of children who require frequent or multifaceted interaction with health care services may benefit from a "generalised" model that includes "all children with medically complex cases and ultimately all children with complex cases of any kind".[57]

"Public innovation takes shape at the crossroads of [...] reliance on [rules] that encourage predictability and standardization, and an applied process of experimentation to discover new and better ways of achieving results of value to society".[58] In designing the programme's pilot phase, administrators sought to achieve both components by applying expertise to reduce administrative redundancies and embracing user contributions to "explore what might work best in practice".[59] Those seeking to replicate the partnership model in other communities should also take care to note these characteristics of the Champlain Complex Care Program:

- Patient-centric and family-centred care
- Driven by coordination and navigation of services across providers (hospital, community, education) by inter-professional Patient Focused Teams
- Focused on complex chronic care of the small population of children and young people with technology-dependent and medically complex cases, which use the most resources
- Data collection, sharing and comparison between all providers
- Dedicated to reduced healthcare spending, by demonstrating rigorously the scope for diverting care out of hospital and into the community
- Quality assurance and supervision of the impact of the model of care on the system.[60]

Since these successes, CHEO and its community partners have received a C$2.4 million, five-year grant from the Canadian federal government towards scaling up their efforts to care for children with complex medical conditions.[61] This new project, called "the Navigator Programme", builds on lessons learned in the preceding pilot programme to better co-ordinate services across community partners and care providers, patients and their families.[62] Additionally, in November 2016, CHEO implemented a new electronic health record (EHR) for all patients that parents can access online 24 hours a day.[63]

In addition, the Government of Ontario has initiated the Health Links programme, which encourages health care providers in a specific region to pool expertise and resources to care for specific high cost populations.[64]

APPENDIX C

ELDER CARE IN FREDERICIA, DENMARK

By Public Governance International (PGI)
PGI is the home of the New Synthesis Initiative and is an organisation dedicated to building the capacity of public organisations to face the challenges of serving in the 21ˢᵗ century.

PGI would like to thank Christian Bason, Jesper Christiansen and Kristian Dahl for their review, and for contacting Karen Heebøll and Helene Bækmark whose helpful comments were much appreciated.

In the town of Fredericia, Denmark, an aging population was putting significant pressure on services and resources aimed at providing care to seniors.[1] Conventional approaches were generating undesirable results. The status quo was no longer working, and the growing costs of elder care in Fredericia would soon become unsustainable.

Several local and international drivers of change revealed a growing need for Fredericia's officials to re-think the approach to elder care. Like much of the highly industrialised world, Fredericia's population faced a rapidly surging 'age wave' of "increasing longevity and massive growth in the number of older people". Owing to modern "breakthroughs in [...] public health, sanitation, antibiotics, and anaesthesiology" more of Fredericia's citizens were living longer, but many also suffered from aging-associated diseases.[2]

The Municipality forecasted that at least 2,000 more residents, among its 55,000 inhabitants, would exceed the age of 65 by 2020.[3] Fredericia projected that the rapid demographic shift would double the current number of elder care beneficiaries. This would translate into an annual cost increase of at least DKK 45 million (approx. USD 6.7 million).[4] Fredericia's total annual budget of DKK 3.3 billion (approx. USD 400 million) could not absorb the growing costs of its already overburdened elder care system. In combination with the exacerbating effects of "recent international economic crises" on shrinking "local tax bases and income", rising elder care costs threatened to weaken the Municipality's overall ability to satisfy new and existing public needs.[5] In short, the future of Fredericia's elder care system, in its current projected state, called for additional resources that the Municipality did not have and could not use.

GETTING STARTED

In 2007, Fredericia's board of directors, representing the top executives of its municipal agencies, gathered to discuss the "welfare squeeze between heightened expectations and worsened finances". The board decided that it was not enough to simply accept "cutbacks and quality erosion" as an unavoidable sign of the times; instead they began looking for viable solutions to continue to provide high-quality elder care and "realized that they and the entire municipality needed to question the basic assumptions underlining current ways of organizing and performing".[6] The Director of Social Services envisioned Fredericia as "a municipality with active and resourceful elderly, who through prevention, rehabilitation, technology and social networking [...] maintain[ed] everyday life for as long as possible".[7] In keeping with this vision, the Municipality of Fredericia set out to develop and invest in a "comprehensive project model" for "ensuring that people can look after themselves [for] as long as possible".[8]

In November 2008, Fredericia's city council "appointed the [board of directors as a] steering committee" of a project to "fundamentally challenge basic assumptions about public service provision". Over the next year and a half, the steering committee conducted an extensive consultation process, including "meetings and a special innovation camp", to select "six target areas in which to promote" an overall agenda of 'radical innovation'.[9] The consultation process brought together "more people from inside the municipality", particularly professionals who interacted with elderly citizens in different public sectors, to engage their insights, contributions and involvement.[10] It became clear in the board's discussions that innovation in elder care was to become an important feature of the project. The consultation process proved to be a valuable exercise for generating a shared vision of how to effectively "assist senior citizens in mastering their own life – a daily life of greater enthusiasm and self-reliance".[11] The process aggregated multiple actors and interests into a shared sense of ownership over the common innovation dialogue and its consequences. The elected representatives of Fredericia's city council recognised the initiative as a 'top priority' and gave the board of directors "free rein to implement the initiative".[12]

Ambient Assisted Living

Fredericia's elected city council extended its support for the 'Ambient Assisted Living' initiative in fall 2009.[13] The goal of the project was to create "a triple win situation": to assist "empowered and [...] satisfied citizens" to live "more independent live[s]", increase "job satisfaction among staff due to working with satisfied elderly citizens" and raise "economic benefit for the municipality". Fredericia pursued these goals through re-imagining self-care for the elderly at a reduced cost for the Municipality. The five "sub-projects" of Ambient Assisted Living, particularly the 'Everyday Rehabilitation' and 'Home Help Training' programmes, reflected a "paradigm-shift" in conceptions of elder care as both a consideration of elderly needs and capabilities.[14] The project overturned "the idea of seniors as a burden, to [re-imagine] seniors as a source of strength in the community".[15]

Fredericia's process of discovery began with identifying patterns of passive care, which created dependencies and inefficiencies where elderly citizens could have otherwise contributed valuable knowledge, assets and capabilities. Engaging the contributions of citizens and their social networks towards strengthening problem areas was the key to extending Fredericia's elder care services beyond its untenable cost projections for 2020. Without an innovative solution, "traditional help and expensive compensatory initiatives" would become economically unviable at current projections, resulting in severe service reductions and public distress.[16]

Fredericia needed a new approach for conceiving the needs and capabilities of the elderly; it needed to explore the diverse ways in which seniors could remain in charge and active in their lives for as long as possible. Ambient Assisted Living became an "empowerment strategy", which concurrently upheld the Danish welfare state model and the responsibilities of the Municipality to care for its elderly citizens. In addition, the initiative enabled citizens to pursue their responsibilities and best interests in "tak[ing] care of themselves independently of public support for as long as possible".[17] The latter function addressed growing elder care costs on multiple fronts by proactively 'pushing' citizens to co-create competencies beyond self-identified dependence areas. On the preventative side, new elder care beneficiaries co-created rigorous training programmes to regain the ability to perform their chosen daily tasks. This early intervention targeted reductions in future costs by ensuring that seniors who have recently suffered a decline in health status do not become chronically dependent on Fredericia's elder care system. Ambient Assisted Living also engaged existing elder care users to co-produce a plan for reducing their dependence on long-term assistance. As seniors developed new and old skills to maximise self-care, the effect was a reversal of costs and movement out of an established group of beneficiaries. The multiple initiatives of Ambient Assisted Living converged on a new model of engagement between elderly citizens and the Municipality based on co-creation and co-production of sustainable, high-quality elder care services.

Everyday Rehabilitation and the 'Revolving Door' Problem

On February 1st 2010, Fredericia implemented the Everyday Rehabilitation project to empower elderly citizens who were seeking assistance from the Elderly Care Department for the first time.[18] Candidates for Everyday Rehabilitation were a distinct group of seniors that had previously been self-sufficient, but now required assistance following recent changes in health status. Early rehabilitative intervention was a crucial component of the Ambient Assisted Living programme; it was aimed at minimising the duration of new dependence on elder care resources to reduce costs over time. Fredericia's strategy enlisted seniors to help the Municipality investigate health conditions of seniors and co-create individual rehabilitation plans in keeping with the goal of self-sufficiency in their own homes. This process revealed a concerning health trend, which generated unsustainable costs and undesirable results for the Municipality's elder care services.

The steering committee was troubled to learn of 'revolving door' patterns of re-hospitalisation observed among Fredericia's seniors. Seniors over the age of 65 who were admitted for treatment by medical units often experienced "repeated cycles of recovery and improvement in hospital, followed by relapse upon discharge".[19] The syndrome suggested that existing formulations of long-term care and support services for transitioning from hospital to home lacked a crucial citizen perspective on the needs and preferences of older persons. When seniors in Fredericia experienced these kinds of 'shocks', such as hospitalisation or the loss of certain day-to-day competencies, they found few resources dedicated to helping them adapt to new circumstances or regain old capacities. The current allocation of resources did not correspond to the everyday experiences of the citizens who used them.

Everyday Rehabilitation filled these gaps by facilitating "close interdisciplinary collaboration between citizens/relatives, [public health] care, the Elderly Care Assessment Department, Rehabilitation Centre and the Assistive Technology Section" of the Municipality.[20] Everyday Rehabilitation shifted the focus of intervention to delivering physical "training in everyday activities [...] that a given elderly citizen desire[d] and [was] able to resume. The elderly citizens participate[d] in cooking, getting dressed, watering flowers, taking a bath, shopping, going to a leisure activity or socializing around town. Little by little, the elderly citizen gain[ed] confidence and physical capability, and start[ed] coping on their own and/or with less help from the Elderly Care Department".[21] Focussing on public results encouraged care providers to avoid approaching rehabilitation of seniors as a one-size-fits-all solution to "a well-defined problem".[22] Everyday Rehabilitation began with the "concrete situation of the citizen" and abandoned conventional ideas about old age as an essential mark of diminishing capacities. Personalised rehabilitation empowered elderly citizens to define their own measures of success based on "their own wishes and goals for a meaningful everyday life".[23]

Citizens actively participated in three interventions while undertaking the Everyday Rehabilitation process. Following an incident such as hospitalisation, elderly citizens underwent a "function assessment" in which "therapists and/or a nurse identif[ied], evaluate[d] and prepare[d] a single interdisciplinary rehabilitation plan in cooperation with the citizen" and "in dialogue with the rehabilitation team". The assessment emphasised the distinct strengths, capabilities and resources of the elderly, rather than their limitations.[24] "Instead of providing traditional methods of care to seniors who require[d] assistance, the municipality's social services department set up care teams who [met] with the seniors in their homes and ask[ed] a simple question, 'What would you like to be able to do again?'"[25] This question was important because it framed the conversation in the context of finding new ways to perform tasks and activities that seniors could perform in the past. Everyday Rehabilitation became a process to co-create and co-produce solutions from a citizen-centric perspective and to turn old capacities into new capacities.

Based on the reimagined assumption that senior citizens have much to offer in managing their own health and long-term care needs, the Everyday Rehabilitation approach set rehabilitative "activity targets" that not only encourage recovery, but enhance resilience.[26] Based on each citizen's personalised rehabilitation plan, daily training was "conducted by a team of home trainers [...] under the guidance of the rehabilitation team".[27] Seniors trained intensively in the first few weeks by performing daily tasks and activities they selected in earlier consultations, which were unique to them and their routines. Rehabilitation teams continued to "adjust [training exercises] on an ongoing basis [...] in cooperation with the citizen" to strengthen their motivations for independent living.[28] As citizens reached their co-created training targets and became more "self-reliant in [their] daily life", they received "less public assistance than originally requested or at least [maintained] the present capabilities".[29] As a result, many seniors became almost entirely self-sufficient again and no longer required assistance from the Municipality. Everyday Rehabilitation reduced the undesirable 'revolving door' patterns of re-hospitalisation among the elderly, which eroded natural capacities and generated a lower quality of life. While seniors who still required assistance following completion of their rehabilitation plan could continue to receive help through Home Help Training, emphasis on regaining capacities from the beginning reduced unnecessary inefficiencies and costs.[30] Over time, the Everyday Rehabilitation programme served as early prevention and offset some of the costs associated with projected increases in new elder care beneficiaries.

Home Help Training and Shifting from Dependency

The second sub-project, Home Help Training, assisted the 2,000 elderly citizens who already received help from Fredericia's Elderly Care Department.[31] Seniors eligible for Home Help Training were knowledgeable about Fredericia's elder care services, but many had become resigned to the unsatisfactory results of existing practices. Home Help Training provided an alternative to "long-term dependent relationships", which concealed true levels of competency and left elderly citizens unsatisfied with their quality of life.[32] In the past, there had been cases of "even fairly independent seniors [...] being shoehorned into institutions, because it was the only setting in which they could receive publicly funded services, equipment, and medication".[33] A significant portion of the elderly population became passive recipients of care services that no longer fit their needs. These excess costs were often attached to important long-running services, which Fredericia's resources could not indefinitely maintain. The experiences of elderly users of therapeutic support socks represented one example of a service that could be improved by training seniors to co-produce their own care.

"Support socks", also known as compression stockings, were a costly service to administer and receive in Fredericia. However, they were also life-saving devices for many seniors at risk of developing "deep vein clots that can result in pulmonary complications and death".[34] These specialised stockings, fitted around the calf to administer varying levels of compression, act as an artificial layer of muscle to tighten vein walls and aid circulation.[35] Effective compression therapy requires knowledge of the socks' therapeutic functions and their correct administering procedures. This expertise is not easily acquired without specialised training. A recent study of hospitalised postoperative compression therapy patients suggested that user error is fairly common among support sock users, with 29 percent of study participants not wearing the socks correctly and expressing confusion about their function.[36] To avoid these risks, caregivers in Fredericia had traditionally administered support socks by visiting the same elderly citizen's home twice in one day – once in the morning to put the socks on and once in the evening to remove them.[37]

From the provider's perspective, support socks became very costly in this situation because the Municipality bore the sole responsibility for administering the service. For the elderly citizen who received compression therapy, these compulsory visits were not only an inconvenience, they also fortified a sense of "dependency and [an] unwanted service relationship", which forced the "elderly citizen [...] to adapt their life to the schedule of the busy home [caregiver]".[38] Home Help Training transformed this experience from both the provider and citizen perspectives. It alleviated the pressure on Fredericia's resources as seniors who received training could reduce their dependency on the elder care system.

In initiating the Home Help Training programme, an "elderly care assessor" first visited elderly citizens who already received some measure of care. In collaboration with each elderly citizen, the care assessor set "objectives for the assistance based on a functional evaluation and the elderly citizen's wishes for an active and independent everyday life". This helped citizens exercise greater autonomy in co-designing the kinds of care they received. Seniors received at-home training from an interdisciplinary team of "visiting nurses, occupational therapists, physiotherapists and elderly care assessors".[39] Each team member's services were very "intensive in the beginning, with as many as 15 care trainers providing 31 days of intensive training, but gradually [tapered] off, and staff eventually [took] on a monitoring role. The ultimate goal [was] ensuring that seniors who wish[ed] to remain in their own home [were] physically capable of doing so".[40] Another function of the assessment and training process was to conduct a "systematic re-evaluation" in co-operation with the elderly citizen to determine whether they still desired the same level of assistance "that had been allocated to them in the first place". This kind of thinking challenged the perception that the health conditions of the elderly only alternated between "static and deteriorating", leaving open the possibility that "it might as well be improving".[41]

Likewise, the visiting caregivers, who often served as the first point of contact for the elderly, "changed their title into 'Independent Living Trainers'". This "deliberate change" reflected the revised training received by professionals throughout the Elderly Care Department in support of Fredericia's new approach to reducing dependencies among the elderly who live at home. The title change also highlighted "the importance that has been placed [by the Municipality] on the active collaboration, involvement, empowerment and engagement of the elderly citizens".[42] Engaging the elderly in co-creating and co-producing their own self-care allowed the Municipality to target the development of a citizen's most desired and latent capabilities. Home Help Training empowered seniors to "direct the system of care [towards greater independence at the very first opportunity] instead of being a passive recipient of care".[43] This tendency motivated independent living and accelerated reductions in the cost of assistance from Fredericia's Elderly Care Department over time.

RESULTS

The Ambient Assisted Living programme enabled elderly citizens to become "stronger in their own lives and express pride and experience [in their] improved life quality by regaining and maintaining their daily functions".[44]

Evaluations of the 778 citizens who participated in Everyday Rehabilitation since the project began in October 2008 indicate tremendous social benefits. Assessments found:

- 45.9% of the elderly citizens were able to re-gain or maintain a capacity for living independently
- 38.9% of the elderly citizens required less assistance or care than originally requested
- 84.8% of the elderly citizens expressed an increase in quality of life or a resumption of desired life activities.[45]

The employees of the Municipality have also enjoyed greater job satisfaction in their new relationships of engagement with the elderly. The group was able to see how their work developing competencies in the elderly had a significant and positive impact. This newfound confidence across the Elderly Care Department led to a "marked decrease in absenteeism among civil servants who, as a group, used to feel low esteem, experience open criticism in the press, and have both a high turnover and absenteeism".[46]

Lastly, Ambient Assisted Living has reduced the overall usage of services and resources aimed at providing care to seniors.[47] An external economic evaluation of the Ambient Assisted Living sub-projects showed that when compared to the usage of services before the project was initiated:

- The length of time an elderly citizen requires care or assistance was reduced
- The number of hours spent on practical housework assistance dropped by 5%
- The number of hours spent on personal care decreased by 23%
- In total, the reduction of practical housework assistance and care amounted to 26,828 hours, while the new training and rehabilitation approach required only an additional 4,450 hours. Overall, a significant reduction in hours
- And, a lower average cost of the home care module for elderly citizens after they have completed the project.[48]

These results suggest that, as Everyday Rehabilitation strengthened the competencies of the elderly, fewer seniors cycled through repeated hospitalisation and rehabilitative services following changes in health status. Likewise, the effectiveness of Everyday Rehabilitation often decreased the need for continued Home Help Training following the initial intensive training programme. In addition to garnering international awards and recognition, recent estimates suggest that, by the end of 2012, Ambient Assisted Living has saved the Municipality DKK 120 million (approx. USD 17 million).[49] While more time is still needed to observe the full economic benefits of the project, a senior who has regained self-sufficiency through the Ambient Assisted Living programme represents a savings of DKK 70,000 (approx. USD 10,000) every year for the Municipality.[50]

Following the success of Fredericia, many of the other 97 Danish municipalities were motivated by demographic and budgetary pressures to provide Everyday Rehabilitation services,[51] and in January of 2015, national legislation passed by the Danish Parliament required all municipalities to offer similar rehabilitation and training to the elderly.[52] While the ambitious expansion of a successful programme holds promise, it has its own risks. The Ambient Assisted Living programme was developed for the context of the Fredericia municipality, and applying it to new circumstances will require re-inventing the innovation to accommodate differences. As of now the expansion is an unknown story, but if it has an impact like that in Fredericia, it will lead to health and service improvements across Denmark.

APPENDIX D

CLEANING DAY IN HELSINKI, FINLAND

By Public Governance International (PGI)
PGI is the host of the New Synthesis Initiative and is an organization dedicated to building the capacity of public organisations to face the challenges of serving in the 21ˢᵗ century.

PGI would like to acknowledge the contributions of Rishanthi Pattiarachchi, Rachael Calleja, and Queena Li for their research and writing assistance in preparing both Appendix C and D.

On February 20, 2012, a resident of Helsinki, Finland, guided by the belief that "one man's trash is another man's treasure", wrote a post on a social media website with an idea to simplify urban recycling.[1] Pauliina Seppälä had observed that there was no Finnish equivalent to the annual citywide flea markets that residents of Amsterdam participated in to celebrate King's Day. The holiday had become the one day a year when citizens of Amsterdam were allowed to sell their second-hand items in the streets and parks without a formal permit.[2] In contrast, anyone wishing to sell goods in Helsinki's public areas was required to "apply for a time-consuming bureaucratic permission from the Public Works Department (PWD)".[3] This confusing process discouraged many citizens from trying to find "new purposes for [their] old objects, goods and clothes".[4] As a result, old items remained unused in storage or were discarded with the trash. Both outcomes generated unnecessary waste and stifled communities from taking responsibility for coming up with their own solutions.

The online post had identified these sentiments and proposed a community-organised event where people could simply "select a spot, act responsibly and cause no damage" rather than wait for the city to take charge.[5] The idea was that anyone could participate in a one-day flea market to sell, give away or exchange their used items in public spaces across Helsinki.[6]

Individual vendors could co-ordinate with each other to form larger flea market areas by marking their location on a searchable online map of the city. At the end of the day, individual sellers could take leftover items home with them or deposit the goods at temporary recycling centres.

The idea quickly generated an enthusiastic online response and sparked the formation of an online working group dedicated to organising the event. The group's collective action generated a platform of digital "tools, information, resources, [and] communication channels", which enabled the first ever Cleaning Day (Siivouspäivä) to be held in Helsinki on May 12, 2012.

Cleaning Day has since become an ongoing festival in Helsinki, held twice a year to local and national acclaim.[7] However, before it became a tradition, the idea for Cleaning Day was first a simple online post on a social media site. What began as one person's plan to declutter a closet, captured the interest of thousands of like-minded citizens. For this to happen, government and local authorities needed to come on board and support the initiative.

MOBILISATION

The post update received significant attention and comment from enthusiastic citizens connected through a shared social media network.[8] The solution appealed to many Helsinki-based users who wished to repurpose old items and reduce waste in their communities. After several commenters volunteered to assist with organising the event, the author of the original online post created a private social media group called Kirppispäivä (Flea market day) to facilitate further collaboration.[9] The private group helped to co-ordinate communication during the initial planning process and recruit other potential contributors. In addition to users who had publicly committed to helping with the event, the group creator also invited contacts who had expressed general interest.[10]

The online working group soon amassed a core group of active citizens with professional interests related to the "production and marketing of cultural/social" events who were well-suited to implementing a community flea market day. Some volunteers were freelance professionals with relevant skillsets looking to gain valuable experience. Others were employed in artistic or technical industries and were looking for a meaningful side-project to channel their creative energy. Each contributor recognised the creative benefits of helping to organise the event in addition to collectively giving back to their communities.

The accessibility of mainstream social media websites enabled the Cleaning Day organisers to unleash their collective problem-solving capacity despite their diverse backgrounds.[11] Contemporary social media was an accessible and user-friendly communication platform intended for a wide online audience. Many features translate familiar forms of everyday communication into a digital communication medium, including personal letters ('private messages'), and face-to-face meetings ('group discussions'), in addition to functionality similar to newspaper classifieds, event invitations and RSVPs. Modern social media does not require its users to learn complicated programming languages or syntax to navigate the environment or express themselves. This familiarity lowered the threshold for participation and opened the platform to citizens who were previously uncomfortable with online collaboration. This more inclusive audience expanded the capacity of the Cleaning Day working group to understand local problems and self-organise around solutions that served a larger range of citizen interests.

Following a period of deliberation, discussions on social media generated a name for the event: Siivouspäivä (Cleaning Day).[12] The working group created a corresponding publicly accessible social media page to engage the broader online community in Helsinki, inviting citizens to become vendors or reserve the date to attend as buyers. A popular digital magazine called *Nyt. fi* published an article covering the event, which directed a great deal of web traffic to the public page.[13] The social nature of online media in turn invited citizens to 'Like', comment and share content, which converted web traffic into a form of collective action. Social media transformed online browsing from a passive activity into an interaction, which invited participation and enabled self-organisation during the Cleaning Day planning process.

The rising online momentum generated an impressive response. Approximately 5,000 people 'Liked' the Cleaning Day page over the span of a few short days. Those looking for ways to tangibly contribute to organising the event were directed by others' comments to join the original private online group, Kirppispäivä.[14] These additions brought the total number of members in the core Kirppispäivä working group to a dozen active people, who self-divided themselves into smaller working groups to distribute duties. Each sub-group took the initiative to oversee certain areas of the event based on their respective skills and interests. The responsibilities included communicating with the media, co-ordinating with recycling and disposal firms, building a website and more.

Next, the core group embarked on building a website where vendors could mark their location on a searchable web map of the city.[15] For this, the group took stock of their collective knowledge of the Google Maps API (Application Programming Interface) and related programming skills.[16] In their online discussions, the group discovered that some of the volunteers could embed a digital "visualization of the selling and recycling spots in searchable locations" on the Cleaning Day website. Others could employ the 'Facebook login' API to "link easily and cheaply the selling spots to verifiable and contactable [Facebook] user profiles". These free digital tools, combined with the expertise of committed volunteers and their online social network, enabled ordinary citizens to self-organise a simple online system for collecting and communicating information across the city. The Cleaning Day website became a visual "database of the selling stands and [...] information repository of what is being sold and where".[17]

The First Cleaning Day: Taking Charge

The outcomes of successful self-organisation soon surpassed the digital beginnings of Cleaning Day. Provided with the opportunity and tools to implement the event, the citizens of Helsinki were more than willing to do the rest. During the first Cleaning Day, an estimated 3,000 vendors participated in the event across the city. 756 vendors marked their locations on the online map to communicate with potential buyers. By the end of the day, the national media was praising Cleaning Day for making recycling easier and facilitating the expression of a responsible urban culture.

Self-organised solutions generated similar results for dealing with leftover items after the event. The working group reflected on what they wanted for their communities and realised that Cleaning Day needed a system to discourage surplus items from becoming sidewalk litter or damaging property. The working group persuaded businesses and non-profit organisations to donate disposal containers for items that were difficult to recycle. Citizens volunteered to service the temporary recycling sites after sponsors could not afford to provide recycling attendants. For the first Cleaning Day, organisers were unable to persuade Helsinki officials to waive the mandatory rental fee for placing the disposal containers on public land. However, the working group decided, after careful consideration, that this was an important service for the community and pooled their individual resources to pay the fee.[18]

As a result of combined citizen efforts, the popularity of Helsinki's first Cleaning Day had very few negative consequences. Despite the considerable scale of the event, "no damage was made to the lawns or public spaces, and no trash was left behind".[19] This achievement was a testament to the desires of citizens to take ownership over the well-being of their communities and public spaces. The success of Cleaning Day, both in scale and in kind, spoke to the tremendous capacity of self-organised solutions to effectively serve community needs.

GAINING GOVERNMENT SUPPORT

Although the Cleaning Day organisers wanted to encourage as many people as possible to "just do it" rather than become discouraged by administrative requirements, they also had "no desire to break the law".[20] Improving coordination with the Helsinki PWD and other actors was an important priority for the event's organisers. The Cleaning Day website provided guidance to citizens about the procedures to acquire a PWD permit. This signalled to Helsinki's citizens and city officials that Cleaning Day was not about rule-breaking – it was about taking responsibility as citizens to solve the problems that impacted their local communities. The group's foresight became important following the success of the first Cleaning Day. In demonstrating their commitment to preserving the urban environment, the organisers built a strong working relationship with city officials based on mutual understanding and trust. An expanded view of the possible relationships between government and citizens opened up a space of possibilities for the effective removal of barriers to furthering community and collective action. The City of Helsinki took measures to empower citizens and their communities, to provide opportunities to invent solutions to common problems and to pursue a shared vision of the future.[21]

The success of the first Cleaning Day event encouraged collaboration among a number of actors, including government, private corporations such as recycling plants and the general public.[22] City officials supported the event's organisers by reducing the administrative barriers associated with providing and acquiring traditional permits for flea market activities.[23] On subsequent Cleaning Days, the PWD endorsed registration on the Cleaning Day web map as equivalent to acquiring a formal permit from the municipal government.[24] The partnership allowed the system to formalise and manage participation while reducing the potential for harm in affected communities.[25] The City of Helsinki also waived a number of service and rental fees for using public land to further support responsible disposal of leftover items after the event.[26] By encouraging community based self-organisation and citizen engagement, Helsinki officials were able to achieve several seemingly divergent goals. Cleaning Day simplified recycling across large urban communities, eliminated the discouraging effects of requiring citizens to obtain permits or employ private junk removal services. This reduced the amount of waste in the city.

Challenges

While social media enabled citizens to self-organise Cleaning Day more easily, digital platforms also carry their own unique set of challenges. During the initial planning stages of Cleaning Day, there were disagreements in the Kirppispäivä group over "how transparent to the larger community that process of organisation should be".[27] Some organisers supported eliminating all "distinctions between [...] organizer group and audience" and engaging in a "co-creative process" of consulting the public in decision making through social media. Others were more reluctant to transfer the organising authority to the larger community and preferred a "more controlled and centralized" structure. Social media provided an accessible outlet for both constituencies to express their preferences and arrive at a consensus. Those who preferred a "more creative and open community-based process" for self-organisation participated in digitally-supported discussions and polls. Those who favoured "a more controlled, and restricted way of working" were left "in charge of various areas" to demonstrate they could "work [...] independently" to produce results.[28] In the end, those who wanted a more centralised organisation outnumbered those who opposed it and many decisions were made by a core group of volunteers.

Results

Following the success of the first Cleaning Day in Helsinki, residents from dozens of other Finnish towns and cities have organised similar flea market events. After being lobbied by citizens to follow the Helsinki model of Cleaning Day, public authorities in many of these municipalities have also accepted self-reporting on an online map as functionally equivalent to acquiring a permit to sell goods in public spaces.[29]

On May 24, 2014, the residents of Kamakura, Japan, were inspired to organise the first Cleaning Day in Japan.[30] Since 2014, the event in Japan has become a national event with venues across the country co-ordinating community flea markets on the same day.[31]

In Helsinki, citizens have continued to organise Cleaning Days twice a year, drawing ever larger crowds of buyers and sellers from all over Europe. In 2015, there were more than 5,000 registered flea market locations marked on the official online map.[32] With multiple vendors often operating from the same location, record-setting estimates suggest that more than 10,000 vendors participated in Helsinki's 2015 Cleaning Day.[33]

ENDNOTES

Introduction

1   Jocelyne Bourgon with Peter Milley, *The New Frontiers of Public Administration: The New Synthesis Project* (Ottawa-Waterloo: Public Governance International and University of Waterloo, 2010), 6.

2   Thomas Homer-Dixon, *Complexity Science and Public Policy: IPAC New Directions Series* (Toronto: The Institute of Public Administration of Canada, December 2010), 7.

3   Jocelyne Bourgon, *A New Synthesis of Public Administration: Serving in the 21st Century* (Ottawa: McGill-Queens University Press, 2011).

4   Jocelyne Bourgon, "The First New Synthesis Laboratory for Master Practitioners," *Ethos* 13 (2014); June Gwee, ed., *Case Studies: Building Communities in Singapore* (Singapore: Civil Service College of Singapore, 2015).

5   The results of the lab held in Sarawak, Malaysia, were published in Jocelyne Bourgon et al., *Enforcement and Safety: A Retrospective of the Sarawak Civil Service High Performance Team (HPT) Retreat 2015* (Ottawa-Sarawak: Public Governance International and Government of Sarawak, 2015).

Chapter 1

1   Jocelyne Bourgon, *Distinctively Public Sector: The Case for the New Synthesis of Public Administration* (Ottawa: Public Governance International, 2015), 3.

2   Francis Fukuyama, *Political Order and Political Decay: From the Industrial Revolution to the Globalisation of Democracy* (New York: Farrar, Straus & Giroux, 2014), 37.

3   Ibid., 10.

4   Geoffrey M. Hodgson, "What are Institutions?", *Journal of Economic Issues* 40, no. 1 (2006): 2.

5   Max Weber, "Politics as a Vocation," in *From Max Weber: Essays in Sociology*, trans. H.H. Gerth and C. Wright Mills (New York: Oxford University Press, 1946), 77.

6   Woodrow Wilson, "The Study of Administration," *Political Science Quarterly* 2, no. 2 (1887): 198.

7   Derek Heater, *Citizenship: The Civic Ideal in World History, Politics and Education*, Third Edition (Manchester: Manchester University Press, 2004), 199.

8   Samuel P. Huntington, *Political Order in Changing Societies* (New Haven and London: Yale University Press, 1968), 12.

9   Thomas L. Friedman, "Order vs. Disorder, Part 3," *New York Times*, August 23, 2014.

10   Tim Stanley and Alexander Lee, "It's Still Not the End of History," *The Atlantic*, September 1, 2014.

11   Bourgon, *A New Synthesis of Public Administration*, 19.

12 Frances Westley, Brenda Zimmerman and Michael Patton, *Getting to Maybe: How the World is Changed* (Toronto: Random House Canada, 2006), 8-11.

13 Erik Brynjolfsson and Andrew Mcafee, *The Second Machine Age: Work, Progress, and Prosperity In A Time Of Brilliant Technologies* (New York: WW Norton & Company Inc., 2014), 4.

14 Ibid., 10.

15 Ian Morris, *Why the West Rules – For Now: The Patterns of History, and What They Reveal About the Future* (New York: Farrar, Straus and Giroux, 2010); Ian Morris, *Social Development* (Stanford: Self-Published, 2010), 89-92; K. Klein Goldewijk et al., "The HYDE 3.1 spatially explicit database of human induced land use change over the past 12,000 years," *Global Ecology and Biogeography* 20 (2011): 73-86.

16 Klaus Schwab, "The Fourth Industrial Revolution: what it means, how to respond," *World Economic Forum*, 14 January 2016, para 2.

17 Jordan Crook, "Instagram Crosses 130 Million Users, With 16 Billion Photos And Over 1 Billion Likes Per Day," *Techcrunch.com*, June 20, 2013; Josh Constine and Kim-Mai Cutler, "Facebook Buys Instagram For $1 Billion, Turns Budding Rival Into Its Standalone Photo App," Techcrunch.com, April 9, 2012.

18 Tom Goodwin, "The Battle Is For The Customer Interface," *Techcrunch.com*, March 3, 2015.

19 Brynjolfsson and McAfee, *The Second Machine Age*, 183.

20 Thomas L. Friedman, "Takin' It to the Street," *New York Times*, June 29, 2013.

21 Organisation for Economic Cooperation and Development (OECD), *Divided We Stand: Why Inequality Keeps Rising* (Paris: OECD Publishing, 2011), 1.

22 Brynjolfsson, and McAfee, *The Second Machine Age*, 160.

23 Joseph E. Stiglitz, "Inequality is not inevitable," *New York Times*, June 27, 2014.

24 Organisation for Economic Cooperation and Development (OECD), *Issues Paper on Corruption and Economic Growth* (Paris: OECD Publishing, 2013), 23.

25 Jocelyne Bourgon, *Technology and Governance* (Ottawa: Public Governance International, 2014), 9.

26 J. Painter, "What Kind of Citizenship for What Kind of Community?" *Political Geography* 26, no. 2 (2007): 221-224; Richard Yarwood, Citizenship (New York, NY: Routledge, 2014); Michael Saward, "Democracy and Citizenship: Expanding Domains," in *The Oxford Handbook of Political Theory*, ed. John Dryzek, Bonnie Honig and Anne Phillips, 400-419. (Oxford: Oxford University Press, 2006).

27 Jeffrey M. Berry and Sarah Sobieraj, *The Outrage Industry: Political Opinion Media and the New Incivility* (New York: Oxford University Press, 2014), 7 & 15.

28 Ibid., 6 & 24.

29 Friedman, "Order vs. Disorder, Part 3."

30 United Nations High Commissioner for Refugees (UNHCR), *World at War: UNHCR Global Trends – Global Forced Displacements* 2014 (Geneva, Switzerland: UNHCR, 2015), 2.

31 Ross Douthat, "ISIS in the 21st Century," *New York Times*, August 24, 2014.

32 Bourgon, *A New Synthesis of Public Administration*, 22-23.

33 Sean Patrick Bray, Gael Sirello and Olivier Sirello, "Democracy Beyond Nation-State: Fostering a European Civil Society And Common Identity," *The Huffington Post*, August 28, 2015.

34 Norman J. Ornstein and Thomas E. Mann, *The Permanent Campaign and its Future* (Washington D.C.: The American Enterprise Institute and The Brookings Institution, 2000), 219-223.

Chapter 2

1   Marjolijn Haasnoot et al., "Dynamic adaptive policy pathways: A method for crafting robust decisions for a deeply uncertain world," *Global Environmental Change* 23, no. 2 (2013): 485.

2   World Resources Report (WRR), *Decision Making in a Changing Climate* (Washington DC: World Resources Institute, 2011), quoted in Sreeja Nair and Michael P. Howlett, *Dealing with the Likelihood of Failure Over the Long-Term: Adaptive Policy Design Under Uncertainty* (Singapore: Lee Kuan Yew School of Public Policy, 2014), 4.

3   Jos C.N. Raadshelders, "A Coherent Framework for the Study of Public Administration," *Journal of Public Administration* 9, no. 2 (1999): 290.

4   Donald F. Kettl and James W. Fesler, *The Politics of the Administrative Process* (Washington, DC: CQ Press, 2011), 4.

5   Yilin Hou et al., "The Case for Public Administration with Global Perspective" (2011): i45, quoted in Jos C.N. Raadschelders, "The Future of the Study of Public Administration: Embedding Research Object and Methodology in Epistemology and Ontology," *Public Administration Review* 71, no. 6 (November/December 2011): 916-924, 922.

6   Donald F. Kettl, *The Transformation of Governance Public Administration for the Twenty-First Century*, Updated Edition (John Hopkins University Press, 2015), 24-28: 8.

7   For an example, see Donald F. Kettl, "Public Administration at the Millennium: The State of the Field," *Journal of Public Administration Research and Theory* 10, no. 1 (2000).

8   Alasdair Roberts, "Public Management: A Flawed Kind of Statecraft," in Brint Milward et al., "Roundtable – Is Public Management Neglecting the State?" *Governance: An International Journal of Policy, Administrations and Institutions*, 29, no. 3 (July 2016): 317.

9   Christopher Pollitt, "Envisioning Public Administration as a scholarly field in 2020," *Public Administration Review* 70 (2010): 292.

10   Christopher Pollitt, *New Perspectives on Public Services: Places and Technology* (Oxford: Oxford University Press, 2012); Gerrit Van der Waldt, "A Unified Public Administration? Prospects of constructing a grand, unifying theory for the field," paper presented at International Association of Schools and Institutions of Administration, Paris, July 6-10, 2015; Steven Kelman et al., "Dialogue on definition and evolution of the field of Public Management," *International Public Management Review* 4, no. 2 (2003): 1-19.

11   C.F. Abel, "Toward a Signature Pedagogy for Public Administration," *Journal of Public Affairs Education* 15, no. 2 (2009): 145-160.

12   Ian D. Clark et al., "Mapping the Topics and Learning Outcomes of a Core Curriculum for MPP and MPA Programs: A Paper for the Annual CAPPA Conference Glendon College, Toronto," May 25-26, 2015, 2 & 7; Ian Clark, B. Eisen and L. A. Pal, "What are the core curricular components of Master's-level public management education and how is learning within them assessed?", 201; Ian Clark and L. A. Pal, "Academic Respectability Meets Professional Utility: Canadian MPA/MPP Programs and Professional Competencies," 2011.

13   Christopher Pollitt and Liesbeth Op de Beeck, *Training Top Civil Servants: A Comparative Analysis* (KU Leuven, Public Governance Institute, 2010), 113-114.

14   Lester M. Salamon, *The Tools of Government: A Guide to the New Governance* (New York: Oxford University Press, 2002), 2.

15   Kettl, "Public Administration at the Millennium," 8.

16   H. Brinton Milward, "Beginning a Dialogue between Two Non-Intersecting Worlds," in Milward et al., "Roundtable – Is Public Management Neglecting the State?", 312.

17   Laura S. Jensen, "Three Neglected Concepts: State Capacity, Sovereignty, and Legitimacy," in Milward et al., "Roundtable – Is Public Management Neglecting the State?", 315.

18   Arjen Boin, "To Manage Major Crises, We Must Understand the State," in Milward et al., "Roundtable – Is Public Management Neglecting the State?", 323.

19   H.K. Colebatch, "The Need for Self-Awareness in Public Management Research," in Milward et al., "Roundtable – Is Public Management Neglecting the State?", 327.

20   Alasdair Roberts, "Public Management: A Flawed Kind of Statecraft," 318.

21   Bourgon, *A New Synthesis of Public Administration*, 7.

22   Ibid., 8.

Chapter 3

1   Donald F. Kettl, *The Transformation of Governance Public Administration for the Twenty-First Century*, Updated Edition (John Hopkins University Press, 2015), 17.

2   Bourgon, *A New Synthesis of Public Administration*, 31.

3   Bourgon with Milley, *The New Frontiers of Public Administration: The New Synthesis Project*, 6.

4   Bourgon, *A New Synthesis of Public Administration*, 37.

5   Bourgon, *Distinctively Public Sector*, 1.

6   Bourgon, *A New Synthesis of Public Administration*, 33.

7   Ibid., 36.

8   Ibid.

9   Ibid., 38.

10   Carmen Sirianni and Lewis Friedland, "Civic Innovation and American Democracy," *Change* 29, no.1(January/February 1997): 14-16.

11   John F. Helliwell, "Well-Being, Social Capital and Public Policy: What's New?" *NBER Working Paper Series w11807* (Cambridge, MA: The National Bureau of Economic Research, 2005).

12   Bourgon, *A New Synthesis of Public Administration*, 8.

13   Saward, "Democracy and Citizenship," 401-402.

14   Ibid.

15   Painter, "What kind of citizenship for what kind of community?", 76.

16   Elinor Ostrom, "Crowding Out Citizenship," *Scandinavian Political Studies* 23, no. 1(2000): 13.

17   Bourgon, *A New Synthesis of Public Administration*, 38-40.

18   David Halpern, *The Hidden Wealth of Nations* (UK: Polity Press, 2009).

19   Bourgon, *Distinctively Public Sector*, 10.

20   Xavier Mendoza and Alfred Vernis, "The Changing Role of Governments and the Emergence of the Relational State," *Corporate Governance* 8, no. 4 (2008): 390.

21   Bourgon, *A New Synthesis of Public Administration*, 45-47.

22   Heater, *Citizenship*, 199.

23   John Alford, *Engaging Public Sector Clients: From Service-Delivery to Co-Production* (Baskingstoke, UK: Palgrave Macmillan, 2009).

24   Geoff Mulgan, "Citizens and Responsibilities," in *Citizenship*, ed. Geoff Andrews (London: Lawrence & Wishart Limited, 1991), 37-49.

25   Bourgon, *A New Synthesis of Public Administration*, 35.

Chapter 4

1   Bourgon, *A New Synthesis of Public Administration*, 36-38.

2   Anne Stafford et al., *Child Protection Systems in the United Kingdom: A Comparative Analysis* (London; Philadelphia: Jessica Kingsley Publishers, 2012), 42-49.

3   Sonja Jütte et al., *How Safe Are Our Children?* (London: National Society for the Prevention of Cruelty to Children, 2014), 4-8.

4   Roar Solholm, John Kjøbli and Terje Christiansen, "Early Initiatives for Children at Risk – Development of a Program for the Prevention and Treatment of Behavior Problems in Primary Services," *Prevention Science* 14, no. 6 (2013): 535-544; Kathleen M. Moxley, Jane Squires and Lauren Lindstrom, "Early Intervention and Maltreated Children: A Current Look at the Child Abuse Prevention and Treatment Act and Part C," *Infants and Young Children* 25, no. 1 (2011): 3-18; Neil B. Guterman, "Early Prevention of Physical Child Abuse and Neglect: Existing Evidence and Future Directions," *Child Maltreatment* 2, no. 1 (1997): 12-34.

5   The Brunei Times, "More than 80% of Sarawak still covered by forest: Awang Tengah," *The Brunei Times*, March 28, 2013.

6   Bourgon et al., Enforcement and Safety, 41-44.

7   Ibid.

8   Jocelyne Bourgon, *A User's Guide for Practitioners* (Ottawa: Public Governance International, 2016).

Chapter 5

1   Bourgon, *A New Synthesis of Public Administration*, 155-163; Public Governance International, "HIV/AIDS in Brazil," NS World: Practice By Country-Brazil, *Public Governance International*.

2   Maria Goretti P. Fonseca and Francisco I. Bastos, "Twenty-Five Years of AIDS in Brazil: Principal Epidemiological Findings 1980-2005," *Cadernos de Saúde Pública* 27, sup. 3 (2007): S33.

3   Westley, Zimmerman and Patton, *Getting to Maybe*, 135-136.

4   Alan Berkman et al., "A Critical Analysis of the Brazilian Response to HIV/AIDS: Lessons Learned for Controlling and Mitigating the Epidemic in Developing Countries," *American Journal of Public Health* 95, no.7 (2005): 1162.

5   World Health Organisation, *The World Health Report 2004: Changing History* (Geneva: World Health Organisation, 2004), 23.

6   Joint United Nations Programme on HIV/AIDS (UNAIDS), *The Gap Report* (Geneva: UNAIDS, 2014), A7.

7   James W. Begun, Brenda Zimmerman and Kevin Dooley, "Health Care Organizations as Complex Adaptive Systems," in *Advances in Health Care Organization Theory*, ed. S. M. Mick and M. Wyttenbach (San Francisco: Jossey-Bass, 2003): 253-288; Fonseca and Bastos, "Twenty-Five Years of the AIDS Epidemic in Brazil"; Westley, Zimmerman and Patton, *Getting to Maybe*; Martha Ainsworth and A. Mead Over, *Confronting AIDS: public priorities in a global epidemic* (Washington D.C.: World Bank Research Report, 1997).

8   Elke Loeffler, Shaundra Ridha and Nathalie Cook-Major, *A partnership model for children with complex medical conditions: The Champlain Complex Care Programme in Canada* (Governance International, 2013). A full account of this case study is available in Appendix B.

9   Chris Feudtner et al., "Deaths attributed to pediatric complex chronic conditions: National trends and implications for supportive care services," *Pediatrics* 107, no. 6 (2001): E99.
10   Michel Bilodeau, *The Perspective of the CEO* (Ottawa: Public Governance International, 2015).
11   Ibid.
12   Bourgon et al., *Enforcement and Safety*, 41-103.
13   Full description is available in Bourgon et al., *Enforcement and Safety*, 101-103.
14   Mary Lydon et al., "Review of the National Road Safety Strategy," *Austroads*, 6 February 2015 (Sydney: Austroads Ltd., 2015), 53-69.

Chapter 6

1   Halpern, The Hidden Wealth of Nations, 173-174 & 251-252.
2   Dora Kostakopoulou, *The Future Governance of Citizenship* (Cambridge: Cambridge University Press, 2008), 15.
3   Ibid., 18.
4   Richard Bellamy, *Citizenship: A Very Short Introduction* (Oxford: Oxford University Press, 2008), 34.
5   Ostrom, "Crowding Out Citizenship," 13.
6   Mulgan, "Citizens and Responsibilities," 37-49.
7   Carmen Sirianni, "The Networks of Self-Governance," *Democracy: A Journal of Ideas*, no. 24 (Spring 2012), 21; Xavier de Souza Briggs, *Democracy as Problem Solving: Civic Capacity in Communities Across Globe* (Cambridge: The MIT Press, 2008), 8.
8   Helliwell, "Well-Being, Social Capital and Public Policy"; Halpern, *The Hidden Wealth of Nations*; Briggs, Democracy as Problem Solving.
9   Donald P. Moynihan, "The Response to Hurricane Katrina," in Report on *Risk Governance Deficits: An analysis and illustrate on of the most common deficits in risk governance* (Geneva: International Risk Governance Council, 2009).
10   Xavier de Souza Briggs, "Social Capital and the Cities: Advice to Change Agents," *The National Civic Review* 86, no. 2 (Summer 1997),113; Briggs, *Democracy as Problem Solving*.
11   Daniel Weinstock, "Citizenship and Pluralism," in *The Blackwell Guide to Social and Political Philosophy*, ed. Robert L. Simon, (Massachusetts, USA: Blackwell Publishers, 2002), 244.
12   Saward, "Democracy and Citizenship," 401-402; Painter, "What Kind of Citizenship for What Kind of Community?"; Yarwood, *Citizenship*.
13   Bourgon, *A New Synthesis of Public Administration*, 8.
14   Sirianni, "The Networks of Self-Governance," 22.
15   Bourgon, *A New Synthesis of Public Administration*, 46.
16   A full account of this case study is available in Appendix C.
17   Bourgon, *A New Synthesis of Public Administration*, 114-115.
18   Christian Bason, *Leading Public Sector Innovation: Co-creating for a Better Society* (Bristol, UK: Policy Press, 2010), 79.
19   Kurt Klaudi Klausen, "Still the century of government? No signs of governance yet!," *International Public Management Review* 15, no. 1 (2014), 41.
20   For more information on co-production see Elinor Ostrom, "Crossing the Great Divide: Co-production, Synergy, and Development," in *State-Society Synergy: Government and So-*

cial Capital in Development, ed. Peter Evans (Berkeley: University of California, 1997), 85-118; John Helliwell and Robert Putnam, "The Social Context of Well-Being," *Philosophical Transactions of the Royal Society of London* B 359 (2004): 1435-46; Ann Dale and Jenny Onyx, *A Dynamic Balance: Social Capital and Sustainable Community Development* (Vancouver: UBC Press, 2005).

21 V. Ostrom and E. Ostrom, "Public Goods and Public Choices," in *Alternatives for Delivering Public Services: Toward Improved Performance*, ed. E.S. Savas (Boulder, Colorado: Westview Press, 1977): 33-34, quoted in Alford, *Engaging Public Sector Clients*, 16.

22 Municipality of Fredericia, *Life Long Living – maintaining independent living as long as possible EY2012 Award*, 8-9.

23 Figure 6 was generated with participants in the context of NS labs to illustrate the diversity of choices open to government.

24 Alford, *Engaging Public Sector Clients; Bourgon, A New Synthesis of Public Administration*, 114.

25 Jörgen Tholstrup, "*Empowering Patients to Need Less Care and do better in Highland Hospital, South Sweden*," Good Practices–Case Studies, *Governance International*, March 30, 2010.

26 Ibid.

27 Ibid.

28 This includes government-linked companies that are established as limited companies under the Companies Act. Bourgon et al., *Enforcement and Safety*, 1.

29 Ibid.

30 Green New Deal, "Cleaning Day in Finland: sustainable consumption and a sense of community," *Green New Deal*, October 11, 2014.

31 iamsterdam, "King's Day street markets," *iamsterdam*.

32 Liisa Horelli et al., "When self-organization and urban governance intersect: Two cases from Helsinki," 292-293.

33 Visit Helsinki, "Cleaning Day 27.8," *Visit Helsinki*, May 31, 2016.

34 Horelli et al., "When self-organization and urban governance intersect," 294.

35 A full account of this case study is presented in Appendix D.

36 Public Governance International, "Technology Enabled Fishery Compliance in New Zealand," NS World: Practice by Country-New Zealand, *Public Governance International*.

37 Envision Charlotte, "About Envision Buildings," http://envisioncharlotte.com/about/envision-buildings/.

38 Envision Charlotte, *Envision Charlotte Project: 2016 Building Technologies Office Peer Review* (USA: Office of Energy Efficiency and Renewable Energy, Department of Energy, 2016).

39 Ibid.

40 Our Singapore Conversation Secretariat, *Reflections of Our Singapore Conversation: What future do we want? How do we get there?* (Singapore: Our Singapore Conversation Secretariat, 2013).

41 Ibid.

42 Welfare Policy Division, Seoul Metropolitan Government, *The Universal Welfare Standards enabled by and for the Citizens of Seoul – Seoul Welfare Standards* (United Nations Public Administration Network, 2012).

Chapter 7

1   Lena Leong, "Towards a Society without Re-offending," in *Case Studies: Building Communities in Singapore*, ed. June Gwee. (Singapore: Civil Service College, Singapore, 2015), 11-38.
2   Ibid., 29.
3   Ibid., 12.
4   Ibid.
5   Chin Kiat Chua, *The Making of Captains of Lives: Prison Reform in Singapore 1999 to 2007* (Singapore: World Scientific Publishing Co. Pte. Ltd., 2012), 28, quoted in Leong, "Towards a Society without Re-offending," 14.
6   Leong, "Towards a Society without Re-offending," 15.
7   Singapore Prison Service, "The Visioning Exercise," internal documentation, quoted in Leong, "Towards a Society without Re-offending," 17.
8   Leong, "Towards a Society without Re-offending," 21.
9   Ibid.
10 Ibid., 24.
11 Ibid., 25.
12 Ibid., 29-31.
13 Ibid., 32.
14 Ibid., 15.
15 Sandford Borins, *Governing Fables: Learning from Public Sector Narratives* (Charlotte, NC: Information Age Publishing Inc., 2011), 3.
16 John Hagel III, "Edge Perspectives with John Hagel: The Untapped Potential of Corporate Narratives," *Edge Perspectives with John Hagel*, October 7, 2013.
17 Bourgon, *A New Synthesis of Public Administration*, 71.
18 Leong, "Towards a Society without Re-offending," 15.
19 Marshall Ganz, "Public Narrative, Collective Action, and Power," in *Accountability through Public Opinion: From Inertia to Public Action*, ed. Marshal Ganz, Chapter 18 (Washington, DC: World Bank, May 2011), 282.
20 Hagel III, "Edge Perspectives with John Hagel."
21 Ibid.
22 Halpern, *The Hidden Wealth of Nations*, 5 &171.

Chapter 8

1   For examples, see Eva Sørensen and Jacob Torfing, "Enhancing Collaborative Innovation in the Public Sector," *Administration & Society* 43, no. 8 (2011): 842-868; P. Pierson, "Increasing Returns, Path Dependence, and the Study of Politics," *American Political Science Review* 94, no. 2: 251-267.
2   Christopher Pollitt, *Time, Policy, Management: Governing with the Past* (Oxford: Oxford University Press, 2008).
3   Steven Kelman, "The 'Kennedy School School' of Research on Innovation in Government," in I*nnovations in Government: Research, Recognition, and Replication*, ed. Sandford Borins (Washington, D.C.: Brookings Institute Press, 2008), 29 & 37.
4   OECD. Innovating the Public Sector: From Ideas to Impact. (Paris: OECD, 2014),19.
5   Pierson, "Increasing Returns" 251-267; Luc Bernier and Taïeb Hafsi, "The Changing Nature of Public Entrepreneurship," *Public Administration Review* 67, no.3 (2007): 488-503.

6   Jocelyne Bourgon, *Public Innovation and Public Purpose* (Ottawa: Public Governance International, 2015), 4.

7   Council for Science and Technology, *Improving Innovation in the Water Industry: 21st Century Challenges and Opportunities* (London: Council for Science and Technology, 2009); Christian Bason, "Design-Led Innovation in Government," *Stanford Social Innovation Review 10th Anniversary Essays*, Spring (2013), 15-17.

8   Bourgon, *Public Innovation and Public Purpose*, 6.

9   Ibid., 5.

10   Timothy Mitchell, "The Limits of the State: Beyond Statist Approach and their Critics," *The American Political Science Review* 85, no.1 (1991): 77-96.

11   Geoff Mulgan, *Innovation in the Public sector: How Can Public Organizations Better Create, Improve and Adapt* (UK: Nesta, 2014), 5.

12   Jesper Christiansen, *The Irrealities of Public Administration* (Denmark: Mindlab, 2013), 24; Geoff Mulgan, *The Art of Public Strategy: Mobilizing Power and Knowledge for the Common Good* (New York: Oxford University Press, 2009).

13   Directorate-General for Regional and Urban Policy, European Commission, *Guide to Social Innovation* (Brussels: European Commission, 2013), 5.

14   Bourgon, *Public Innovation and Public Purpose*, 6.

15   Ibid.

16   Ibid.

17   Christensen, *The Irrealities of Public Administration*, 34 & 58-71.

18   Ibid., 19.

19   Mulgan, *The Art of Public Strategy*, 1-7.

20   Bourgon, *Public Innovation and Public Purpose*, 6.

21   Tony Judt, *Ill Fares the Land* (New York: Penguin Books, 2011).

22   Mariana Mazzucato, *The Entrepreneurial State: Debunking Public vs. Private Sector Myths* (London: Anthem Press, 2014).

23   Alice H. Amsden, *Asia's Next Giant: South Korea and Late Industrialization* (New York: Oxford University Press, 1989), 78.

24   Mazzucato, *The Entrepreneurial State*, 19.

25   S. P. Vallas, Daniel L. Kleinman and Dina Biscotti, "Political Structures and the Making of U.S. Biotechnology," in *State of Innovation: The U.S. Government's Role in Technology Development*, ed. Fred Block and Matthew R. Keller (Boulder, Colorado: Paradigm, 2011), 71.

26   Richard M. Locke and Rachel Wellhausen ed., *A Preview of the MIT Production in the Innovation Economy Report* (Cambridge, Massachusetts: Massachusetts Institute of Technology, 2013), 25-27.

27   Mazzucato, *The Entrepreneurial State*, 19.

28   William Lazonick, "The US stock market and the governance of innovative enterprise," *Industrial and Corporate Change* 16, no. 6 (2007): 983-1035.

29   Harry M. Markowitz and Kenneth Blay, *Risk-Return Analysis: The Theory and Practice of Rational Investing* (New York: McGraw-Hill Education, 2013); William Lazonick and Mariana Mazzucato, "The Risk-Reward Nexus in the Innovation-Inequality Relationship," *Industrial and Corporate Change* 22, no. 4 (2013): 1096-1097.

30   Lazonick and Mazzucato, "The Risk-Reward Nexus in the Innovation-Inequality Relationship," 1093-1128.

31   Anthony B. Atkinson, Thomas Piketty and Emmanuel Saez, "Top Incomes in the Long Run of History," *Journal of Economic Literature* 49, no.1 (2011): 3–71.

32   Mazzucato, *The Entrepreneurial State*, 21.

33   Chris Freeman, "The 'National System of Innovation' in historical perspective," *Cambridge Journal of Economics* 19, no. 1 (1995): 5-24 & 6.

34   Ibid., 7.

35   Mazzucato, *The Entrepreneurial State*, 23-24.

36   OECD, *In It Together: Why Less Inequality Benefits All* (Paris: OECD Publishing, 2015).

Chapter 9

1   Brian O'Neil. *Reorganizing Government: New Approaches to Public Service Reform*, Back Ground Paper, Library of Parliament, January 1994, 11-15; Jocelyne Bourgon with Rachael Calleja, *The New Synthesis in Action: A Retrospective of the NS labs Conducted in 2013-14 Based on Singapore Experience* (Ottawa: Public Governance International, January 2015), 33.

2   Jocelyne Bourgon, "Leadership as an Integrated Process of Change," *Public Sector Digest* (Fall 2014):33-37.

3   Montgomery Van Wart, *Dynamics of Leadership in Public Service: Theory and Practice.* (New York: M.E. Sharp, 2011), 464.

4   Barbara Crosby and John Bryson, *Leadership for the Common Good: Tackling public problems in a shared-powered world*, 2nd edition (San Francisco: Jossey-Bass, 2005), 187-193; Paul 'T Hart, *Understanding Public Leadership* (London: Palgrave, 2014), 21-39; Ronald Heifetz, Alexander Grashow and Marty Linsky, *The Practice of Adaptive Leadership* (Cambridge: Harvard Business Press, 2009); Jeffrey S. Luke, *Catalytic Leadership: Strategies for an Interconnected World* (San Francisco: Jossey-Bass Inc., 1998); Ricardo S. Morse and Terry F. Buss, "The Transformation of Public Leadership," in *Transforming Public Leadership for the 21st Century*, ed. Ricardo S. Morse, Terry F. Buss, and C. Morgan Kinghorn (London: Routledge, 2007), 4-6; Van Wart, *Dynamics of Leadership in Public Service;* Montgomery Van Wart, "Lessons from Leadership Theory and the Contemporary Challenges of Leaders." *Public Administration Review*, 73, no. 4 (2013): 553–565.

5   Mary Uhl-Bien, Russ Marion and Bill McKelvey. "Complexity Leadership Theory: Shifting leadership from the industrial age to the Knowledge era," *The Leadership Quarterly* 18, no. 4 (2007): 302.

6   C.C. Manz et al., *"Emerging Paradoxes in Executive Leadership*: A Theoretical Interpretation of the Tensions Between Corruption and Virtuous Values," *Leadership Quarterly* 19, no. 3 (2008): 385-392; M.E. Palanski and F.J. Yammarino. "Integrity and Leadership: A Multi-Level Conceptual Framework." *Leadership Quarterly* 20, no. 3 (2009):405-420, quoted in Van Wart, *Dynamics of Leadership in Public Service.*

7   D.C. Menzel. *Ethics Management for Public Administrators: Building Organizations of Integrity* (Armonk, NY: M.E. Sharpe, 2007), quoted in Van Wart, *Dynamics of Leadership in Public Service: Theory and Practice.*

8   Donald F. Kettl. *The Global Public Management Revolution.* (Washington D.C.: Brookings Institution Press, 2006).

9   'T Hart, *Understanding Public Leadership*, 5.

10   Heifetz et al., *The Practice of Adaptive Leadership.*

11   Bourgon with Calleja, *The New Synthesis in Action*, 34.

12   Bourgon, *Leadership as an Integrated Process of Change.*

13   Luke, *Catalytic Leadership*, 25.

14   Ibid., 35.

15   Bourgon with Calleja, *The New Synthesis in Action*, 35.

16   Crosby and Bryson, *Leadership for the Common Good*; R.M. Linden, *Working across boundaries: Making collaboration work in government and non-profit organizations* (San Francisco: Jossey-Bass, 2002); Luke, *Catalytic leadership*, quoted in Ricardo S. Morse, "Integrative public leadership: catalysing collaboration to create public value," *The Leadership Quarterly* 21, no. 2 (2010): 231.

17   Bourgon with Calleja, *The New Synthesis in Action*, 35.

18   Patrick Gavan O'Shea et al., "Are the Best Leaders Both Transformational and Transactional? A Pattern Analysis," *Leadership* 5, no. 2 (2009): 237-259, quoted in Van Mart, *Dynamics of Leadership in Public Service: Theory and Practice*.

19   Bourgon, *A New Synthesis of Public Administration*, 55.

20   Steve Fraser, "Liberalism Is Under Attack From the Left and the Right," *The Nation*, June 2, 2016; Robert Kagan and Ivo Daalder, "The U.S. can't afford to end its global leadership role," *Brookings*, April 25, 2016.

21   Jocelyne Bourgon, "Et si le soleil se levait aussi à l'ouest : Le rôle de l'État/And if the sun also rose in the West: The role of the state," *Le Cercle des economistes, Recontres economiques d'Aix-en-Provence*, speech presented at the Economic Forum of Aix-en-Provence, France, 2012, 220.

22   Luke, *Catalytic Leadership*, xiii.

Chapter 10

1   Mary Parker Follett, *The New State: Group Organization – The Solution of Popular Government* (Pennysylvania: The Pennsylvania State University, 2009), 3-10.

2   Mariana Mazzucato and Michael Jacobs, ed., *Rethinking Capitalism: Economics and Policy for Sustainable and Inclusive Growth* (UK: Wiley-Blackwell, 2016); William Lazonick, *Sustainable Prosperity in the New Economy?: Business Organization and High-Tech Employment in the United States* (Michigan, USA: W E Upjohn Institute for Employment Research, 2009); Joseph E. Stiglitz, *The Great Divide: Unequal Societies And What We Can Do About Them* (New York: W.W. Norton & Company Inc., 2015); Joseph Heath, *Enlightenment 2.0* (Toronto: Harper Collins Publishers, 2014); Briggs, *Democracy as Problem Solving*; Bernard Crick, *In Defense of Politics* (London: Bloomsbury Publishing Plc, 2013).

3   Joseph E. Stiglitz, *The Euro: How a Common Currency Threatens the Future of Europe* (New York: W.W. Norton & Company Inc., 2016), xi.

4   Carmen M. Reinhart and Kenneth S. Rogoff, "This Time is Different: A Panoramic View of Eight Centuries of Financial Crises." Working Paper 13882, *National Bureau of Economic Research*, March 2008, 2.

5   Stiglitz, *The Euro*, 24.

6   OECD, *In It Together: Why Less Inequality Benefits All*, 20-21.

7   Ibid; Mazzucato & Jacobs, *Rethinking Capitalism*, 9.

8   OECD, *Divided We Stand: Why Inequality Keeps Rising*, 22.

9   Ibid, 26.

10   Friedman, "Takin' It to the Street."

11   Colin Crouch, *Post-Democracy* (UK: Polity, 2004); Wolfgang Merkel, "Is capitalism compatible with democracy?" *Z Vgl Polit Wiss/Comparative Governance and Politics* 8, no. 2 (July 2014): 109-128.

12   Ibid.

13 Stiglitz, *The Euro, xix.*
14 Robert Dahl, *Who Governs?: Democracy and Power in an American City* (New Haven: Yale University Press, 1961), quoted in Briggs, *Democracy as Problem Solving,* 7.
15 Archon Fung and Erik Olin Wright, *Deepening Democracy: Institutional Innovations in Empowered Participatory Governance* (London: Verso, 2003), quoted in Briggs, *Democracy as Problem Solving,* 7.
16 Briggs, *Democracy as problem solving,* 7.
17 Bourgon, *A New Synthesis,* 117-123.
18 Arch Puddington and Tyler Roylance, "Anxious Dictators, Wavering Democracies: Global Freedom under Pressure – Freedom in the World 2016," *Freedom House,* 2016, 3.
19 Ibid, 9.
20 Joshua Kurlantzick, *Democracy in Retreat: The Revolt of the Middle Class and the Worldwide Decline of Representative Government.* (New Haven: Yale University Press, 2013), 1-11.
21 Samuel P. Huntington, "Will More Countries Become Democratic?" *Political Science Quarterly* 99, no. 2 (Summer, 1984): 243-244; Seymour Martin Lipset, "Some Social Requisites Of Democracy: Economic Development and Political Legitimacy," *American Political Science Review* 53, no. 1 (1959): 75.
22 Puddington and Roylance, "Anxious Dictators, Wavering Democracies," 3.
23 Heath, *Enlightenment 2.0.*
24 "A Look Back: 2006 Podcast Interview with the San Francisco Chronicle." Stephen T. Colbert's Interview on January 16, 2006.
25 Shawn Lawrence Otto, *The War on Science: Who's Waging It, Why It Matters, What We Can Do About It* (Minnesota: Milkweed Editions, 2016), 23 & 160-161.
26 Berry and Sobieraj, *The Outrage Industry: Political Opinion Media and the New Incivility.*
27 Crick, *In Defense of Politics,* 4.

Conclusion
1 Bourgon, "The Future of Public Service," 390-404.
2 "MDG 1: Eradicate Extreme Poverty and Hunger." *MGD Monitor.*
3 Jacob Poushter, *Smartphone Ownership and Internet Usage Continues to Climb in Emerging Economies* (Washington D.C.: Pew Research Centre, 2016), 16-20.
4 Zanny Minton Beddoes, "Planet Trump." *The Economist: The World in 2017,* November 10, 2016.
5 Milward et al., "Is Public Management Neglecting the State?" 312.
6 Milward et al., 314.
7 Milward et al., 313.
8 Robert B. Denhardt and Janet Vinzant Denhardt, "The New Public Service: Serving Rather than Steering." Public Administration Review 60, no. 6 (2000): 549.

Appendix A
1 A more extensive version was published by Lena Leong, "Towards a Society without Re-offending." In Case *Studies: Building Communities in Singapore,* edited by June Gwee, 11-38 (Singapore: Civil Service College, Singapore, 2015).
2 Chua, *The Making of Captains of Lives.*
3 Singapore Prison Service, "The Visioning Exercise", internal documentation.
4 Chua, *The Making of Captains of Lives.*

5   Ibid.

6   Chua, *The Making of Captains of Lives.*

7   Civil Service College of Singapore Class Sharing, 2013.

8   Singapore Prison Service, "School First, Prison Second. Kaki Bukit Centre Prison School", internal documentation.

9   The six representatives from the social and security sectors were: Ministry of Home Affairs, Ministry of Social and Family Development, Industrial & Services Co-operative Society Ltd (ISCOS), National Council of Social Service, Singapore After-Care Association and Singapore Anti-Narcotics Association.

10 Interview conducted by Lena Leong, 2014.

11 Singapore Prison Service, *The Courage to Believe: Unlocking Life's Second Chances* (Singapore: Singapore Prison Service, 2013).

12 Chua, *The Making of Captains of Lives*, 2012.

13 Ibid.

14 Ibid.

Appendix B

1   Feudtner et al., "Deaths attributed to pediatric complex chronic conditions," E99.

2   Loeffler, Ridha and Cook-Major, *A partnership model for children with complex medical conditions.*

3   Marco Marabelli, Sue Newell and Janis Gogan, "Pilot-testing a pediatric complex care coordination service," *Journal of Information Technology Teaching Cases* 6, no. 1 (2016): 2.

4   Bilodeau, *The Perspective of the CEO*, 1.

5   Loeffler, Ridha and Cook-Major, *A partnership model for children with complex medical conditions*; KPMG LLP, *SickKids Socio-Economic Impact Study* (Amstelveen: KPMG LLP, 2012), 1-148.

6   Bilodeau, *The Perspective of the CEO*, 1.

7   Marabelli, Newell and Gogan, "Pilot-testing a pediatric complex care coordination service," 5.

8   Bilodeau, *The Perspective of the CEO*, 1.

9   Marabelli, Newell and Gogan, "Pilot-testing a pediatric complex care coordination service," 5.

10 Bilodeau, *The Perspective of the CEO*, 1.

11 Loeffler, Ridha and Cook-Major, *A partnership model for children with complex medical conditions.*

12 Bilodeau, *The Perspective of the CEO*, 1.

13 Ibid., 2.

14 Loeffler, Ridha and Cook-Major, *A partnership model for children with complex medical conditions.*

15 Ibid.

16 Bourgon, *Distinctively Public Sector*, 3.

17 Loeffler, Ridha and Cook-Major, *A partnership model for children with complex medical conditions.*

18 Ibid.

19 Ibid.

20 Marabelli, Newell and Gogan, "Pilot-testing a pediatric complex care coordination service," 6.

21 E.H.Wagner et al., "A Survey of Leading Chronic Disease Management Programs: Are They Consistent with the Literature?," *Managed Care Quarterly* 7, no. 3 (1999): 58.

22 Marabelli, Newell and Gogan, "Pilot-testing a pediatric complex care coordination service," 6.

23 Loeffler, Ridha and Cook-Major, *A partnership model for children with complex medical conditions*.

24 Ibid.

25 Bilodeau, *The Perspective of the CEO*, 2.

26 Ibid.

27 Loeffler, Ridha and Cook-Major, *A partnership model for children with complex medical conditions*.

28 Ibid.

29 Marabelli, Newell and Gogan, "Pilot-testing a pediatric complex care coordination service," 6.

30 Loeffler, Ridha and Cook-Major, *A partnership model for children with complex medical conditions*.

31 Ibid.

32 Marabelli, Newell and Gogan, "Pilot-testing a pediatric complex care coordination service," 6.

33 Ibid., 2.

34 Ibid., 6.

35 Ibid., 2.

36 Ibid.

37 Loeffler, Ridha and Cook-Major, *A partnership model for children with complex medical conditions*.

38 Ibid.

39 Ibid.

40 Marabelli, Newell and Gogan, "Pilot-testing a pediatric complex care coordination service," 9.

41 Loeffler, Ridha and Cook-Major, *A partnership model for children with complex medical conditions*.

42 Ibid.

43 Ibid.

44 Ibid.

45 Ibid.

46 Bilodeau, *The Perspective of the CEO*, 3.

47 Loeffler, Ridha and Cook-Major, *A partnership model for children with complex medical conditions*.

48 Bilodeau, *The Perspective of the CEO*, 4.

49 Champlain Complex Care Program, "Champlain Complex Care Newsletter," *Champlain Complex Care Program*, Winter, 2014/2015.

50 Bilodeau, *The Perspective of the CEO*, 4.

51 Ibid.

52 Ibid.

53 Ibid.

54 Loeffler, Ridha and Cook-Major, *A partnership model for children with complex medical conditions*.

55 Commission on the Reform of Ontario's Public Services, *Public Services for Ontarians: A Path to Sustainability and Excellence* (Ontario: Queen's Printer for Ontario, 2012), 167.

56 Loeffler, Ridha and Cook-Major, *A partnership model for children with complex medical conditions.*

57 Ibid.

58 Bourgon, *Public Innovation and Public Purpose*, 6.

59 Bourgon, *Distinctively Public Sector*, 6.

60 Loeffler, Ridha and Cook-Major, *A partnership model for children with complex medical conditions.*

61 Children's Hospital of Eastern Ontario. "*Unique pilot program to help families of kids with most complex medical needs*," Newsroom, CHEO. July 17, 2015.

62 Ibid.

63 Children's Hospital of Eastern Ontario. "CHEO gives patients online access to their hospital records – anytime, anywhere," Newsroom, *CHEO*. November 28, 2016.

64 More information about Health Links can be found at: http://www.health.gov.on.ca/en/pro/programs/transformation/community.aspx.

Appendix C

1 Kurt Klaudi Klausen, "Ambient Assisted Living: How Fredericia Municipality Reinvented Itself and Became Innovative," in *Public Management in the Twenty-First Century*, ed. Tor Busch et al., Chapter 10 (Olso: Universitetsforlaget AS, 2013), 129.

2 Ken Dychtwald, "Maturity Reimagined," speech, American Society on Aging's 2015 Annual Conference, Los Angeles, CA, March 23, 2015.

3 Klausen, "Ambient Assisted Living," 129.

4 Lorna Campbell and Lis Wagner, "As long as possible in one's own life – sub-project: Home-rehabilitation," Why was this example implemented?, *INTERLINKS*.

5 Klausen, "Ambient Assisted Living," 129.

6 Ibid.

7 Karen Heebøll, *Life Long Living Maintaining Everyday Life as Long as Possible*, PowerPoint presented at the Opening Conference for the European Year for Active Aging and Solidarity between Generations 2012: Staying Active – What does it Take?, 1.

8 Municipality of Fredericia, Denmark, "Name of project: Life Long Living – maintaining independent living as long as possible," 6-7.

9 Klausen, "Ambient Assisted Living," 130.

10 Ibid., 131.

11 Municipality of Fredericia, Denmark, "Name of project: Life Long Living," 3-4.

12 Klausen, "Still the century of government?," 41.

13 Klausen, "Ambient Assisted Living," 129.

14 Municipality of Fredericia, Denmark, "Name of project: Life Long Living," 1-2.

15 Lindsay McGinn, *Don't Move Me There! Promoting Autonomy in the Provision of Long-term Care for Seniors in Canada* (Ottawa: University of Ottawa, 2015), 42.

16 Municipality of Fredericia, Denmark, "Name of project: Life Long Living," 1.

17 Klausen, "Ambient Assisted Living," 133.

18 Municipality of Fredericia, Denmark, "Name of project: Life Long Living," 5.

19 John Harris and Vicky White, *A Dictionary of Social Work and Social Care* (Oxford: Oxford University Press, 2013).

20 Klausen, "Ambient Assisted Living," 132.

21 Municipality of Fredericia, Denmark, "Name of project: Life Long Living," 5.

22 Jesper Christiansen and Laura Bunt, *Innovation in policy: allowing for creativity, social complexity and uncertainty in public governance* (London: MindLab, 2012), 13.
23 Municipality of Fredericia, Denmark, "Name of project: Life Long Living," 5.
24 Ibid.
25 McGinn, *Don't Move Me There!*, 42.
26 Municipality of Fredericia, Denmark, "Name of project: Life Long Living," 6-7.
27 Klausen, "Ambient Assisted Living," 132.
28 Ibid.
29 Municipality of Fredericia, Denmark, "Name of project: Life Long Living," 5.
30 McGinn, *Don't Move Me There!*, 42-45.
31 Municipality of Fredericia, Denmark, "Name of project: Life Long Living," 6-7.
32 Ibid, 4.
33 Stunden, Shannon Bower and David Campanella, *From Bad to Worse: Residential Elder Care in Alberta* (Edmonton: Parkland Institute, 2013), 23.
34 American Journal of Nursing, "Compression Stockings Incorrectly Used In 29 Percent Of Patients," Science News, *ScienceDaily*, August 23, 2008: 1.
35 SIGVARIS, "What is compression therapy?," *SIGVARIS*, 2015.
36 American Journal of Nursing, "Compression Stockings Incorrectly Used In 29 Percent Of Patients," 1.
37 Christiansen and Bunt, *Innovation in policy*, 12.
38 Ibid.
39 Municipality of Fredericia, Denmark, "Name of project: Life Long Living," 6-7.
40 McGinn, *Don't Move Me There!*, 42-45.
41 Klausen, "Still the century of government?," 41.
42 Municipality of Fredericia, Denmark, "Name of project: Life Long Living," 6-7.
43 Klausen, "Still the century of government?," 41.
44 Klausen, "Ambient Assisted Living," 134.
45 Municipality of Fredericia, Denmark, "Name of project: Life Long Living," 8-9.
46 Klausen, "Ambient Assisted Living," 134.
47 Ibid.
48 Municipality of Fredericia, Denmark, "Name of project: Life Long Living," 8-9.
49 Ibid.
50 McGinn, *Don't Move Me There!*, 42-45.
51 European Commission, *Powering European Public Sector Innovation: Towards A New Architecture. Report of the Expert Group on Public Sector Innovation* (Luxembourg: Publications Office of the European Union, 2013), 34.
52 European Commission, 2015 *Strategic Social Reporting Questionnaire – Denmark* (Luxembourg: Publications Office of the European Union, 2015), 5.

Appendix D

1 Green New Deal, "Cleaning Day in Finland."
2 iamsterdam, "King's Day street markets."
3 Horelli et al., "When Self-Organization Intersects with Urban Planning: Two Cases from Helsinki," *Planning Practice & Research* 30, no. 3 (2015): 293.
4 Green New Deal, "Cleaning Day in Finland."
5 Horelli et al., "When Self-Organization Intersects," 293.

6   Ibid., 292-293.
7   Visit Helsinki, "Cleaning Day 27.8," Visit Helsinki, May 31, 2016.
8   Horelli et al., "When Self-Organization and urban governance intersect," 292-293.
9   Pauliina Seppälä, "Tiny Social Movements: Experiences of Social Media Based Co-Creation," in *Towards Peer Production in Public Services: Cases from Finland*, ed. Andrea Botero, Andrew Gryf Paterson and Joanna Saad-Sulonen (Helsinki: Aalto University, 2012), 67.
10 Seppälä, "Tiny Social Movements," 67.
11 Ibid., 72.
12 Ibid., 68.
13 Ibid., 67.
14 Ibid.
15 Cleaning Day, "Cleaning Day," *Siivouspäivä*.
16 Horelli et al., "When self-organization and urban governance intersect," 292.
17 Ibid.
18 Ibid., 294.
19 Ibid.
20 Ibid.
21 Jocelyne Bourgon, "The history and future of nation-building? Building capacity for public results," *International Review of Administrative Sciences* 76, no. 2 (2010): 197–218.
22 Horelli et al., "When self-organization and urban governance intersect," 294.
23 Andrea Botero, Andrew Gryf Paterson and Joanna Saad-Sulonen, "Introduction," in *Towards Peer Production in Public Services: Cases from Finland*, ed. Andrea Botero, Andrew Gryf Paterson and Joanna Saad-Sulonen, (Helsinki: Alto University, 2012), 7.
24 Public Works Department, Customer Services, "Restaurant Day and Cleaning Day," *City of Helsinki Public Works Department*, October 20, 2015.
25 Botero and Saad-Sulonen, "Peer-Production in Public Services," 7.
26 Horelli et al., "When self-organization and urban governance intersect," 294.
27 Seppälä, "Tiny Social Movements," 68.
28 Ibid.
29 Cleaning Day, "Basics of Cleaning Day," How Can I Join, *Cleaning Day*.
30 Cleaning Day Japan, "Cleaning Day Japan," *Facebook*, June 2, 2016.
31 Ibid.
32 Cleaning Day, "Cleaning Day changes the whole Finland into a huge flea market on Saturday 28th of May," Press Release, *Cleaning Day*. May 3, 2016.
33 Ibid.

BIBLIOGRAPHY

Abel, C.F. "Toward a Signature Pedagogy for Public Administration." *Journal of Public Affairs Education* 15, no. 2 (2009): 145-160.

Ainsworth, Martha and A. Mead Over. *Confronting AIDS: public priorities in a global epidemic*. Washington, D.C.: World Bank, 1997.

Alford, John. *Engaging Public Sector Clients: From Service-Delivery to Co-Production*. Baskingstoke, UK: Palgrave Macmillan, 2009.

"A Look Back: 2006 Podcast Interview with the San Francisco Chronicle." Stephen T. Colbert's Interview on January 16, 2006. *Colbert News Hub*. February 24, 2013. http://www.colbertnewshub.com/2013/02/24/back-2006-podcast-interview-san-francisco-chronicle/ (accessed September 8, 2016).

American Journal of Nursing. "Compression Stockings Incorrectly Used In 29 Percent Of Patients." Science News, *ScienceDaily*. August 23, 2008. https://www.sciencedaily.com/releases/2008/08/080820163107.htm (accessed June 6, 2016).

Amsden, Alice H. *Asia's Next Giant: South Korea and Late Industrialization*. New York: Oxford University Press, 1989.

Atkinson, Anthony B., Thomas Piketty and Emmanuel Saez. "Top Incomes in the Long Run of History." Journal of Economic Literature 49, no. 1 (2011): 3–71.

Bason, Christian. "Design-Led Innovation in Government." *Stanford Social Innovation Review 10th Anniversary Essays*, Spring (2013): 15-17.

––. *Leading Public Sector Innovation: Co-creating for a Better Society*. Bristol, UK: Policy Press, 2010.

Beddoes, Zanny Minton. "Planet Trump." *The Economist: The World in 2017*. November 10, 2016.

Begun, James, W. Brenda Zimmerman and Kevin Dooley. "Health Care Organizations as Complex Adaptive Systems." In *Advances in Health*

Care Organization Theory, edited by S. M. Mick and M. Wyttenbach, 253-288. San Francisco: Jossey-Bass, 2003.

Bellamy, Richard. *Citizenship: A Very Short Introduction*. Oxford: Oxford University Press, 2008.

Berkman, Alan, Jonathan Garcia, Miguel Muñoz-Laboy, Vera Paiva and Richard Parker. "A Critical Analysis of the Brazilian Response to HIV/ AIDS: Lessons Learned for Controlling and Mitigating the Epidemic in Developing Countries." *American Journal of Public Health* 95, no. 7 (2005): 1162-1172.

Bernier, Luc and T. Hafsi. "The Changing Nature of Public Entrepreneurship." *Public Administration Review* 67, no. 3 (2007): 488-503.

Berry, Jeffrey M. and Sarah Sobieraj. *The Outrage Industry: Political Opinion Media and the New Incivility*. New York: Oxford University Press, 2014.

Bilodeau, Michel. *The Perspective of the CEO*. Ottawa: Public Governance International, 2015.

Borins, Sandford. *Governing Fables: Learning from Public Sector Narratives*. Charlotte, NC: Information Age Publishing Inc., 2011.

Bourgon, Jocelyne. *A User's Guide for Practitioners*. Ottawa: Public Governance International, 2016.

––. *Public Innovation and Public Purpose*. Ottawa: Public Governance International, 2015.

–––. *Distinctively Public Sector: The Case for the New Synthesis of Public Administration*. Ottawa: Public Governance International, 2015.

–––. "Leadership as an Integrated Process of Change." *Public Sector Digest*, Fall (2014): 33-37.

–––. "The First New Synthesis Laboratory for Master Practitioners." *Ethos* 13 (2014): 90-97.

–––. *Technology and Governance*. Ottawa: Public Governance International, 2014.

–––. "Et si le soleil se levait aussi à l'ouest : Le rôle de l'État/And if the sun also rose in the West: The role of the state." Speech presented at the Economic Forum of Aix-en-Provence, France, *Le Cercle des economistes, Recontres economiques d'Aix-en-Provence* (2012): 217-220.

–––. *A New Synthesis of Public Administration: Serving in the 21st Century*. Ottawa: McGill-Queens University Press, 2011.

–––. "The history and future of nation-building? Building capacity for public results." *International Review of Administrative Sciences* 76, no. 2 (2010): 197–218.

–––. "The Future of Public Service: A Search for a New Balance." *Australian Journal of Public Administration* 67, no. 4. (2008): 390-404.

Bourgon, Jocelyne with Rachael Calleja, Rishanthi Pattiarachchi and Queena Li. Enforcement and Safety: A Retrospective of the Sarawak Civil Service High Performance Team (HPT) Retreat 2015. Ottawa-Sarawak: Public Governance International and Government of Sarawak, 2015.

Bourgon, Jocelyne with Rachael Calleja. The New Synthesis in Action: A Retrospective of the NS labs Conducted in 2013-14 Based on Singapore Experience. Ottawa: Public Governance International, January 2015.

Bourgon, Jocelyne with Peter Milley. *The New Frontiers of Public Administration: The New Synthesis Project.* Ottawa-Waterloo: Public Governance International and University of Waterloo, 2010.

Botero, Andrea, Andrew Gryf Paterson and Joanna Saad-Sulonen. "Introduction." In *Towards Peer Production in Public Services: Cases from Finland*, edited by Andrea Botero, Andrew Gryf Paterson and Joanna Saad-Sulonen, 6-12. Helsinki: Aalto University, 2012.

Bray, Sean Patrick, Gael Sirello and Olivier Sirello. "Democracy Beyond Nation-State: Fostering a European Civil Society And Common Identity." *The Huffington Post*. August 28, 2015. http://www.huffingtonpost.com/european-horizons/democracy-beyond-nationst_b_8052108.html (accessed July 10, 2016).

Briggs, Xavier de Souza. *Democracy as Problem Solving: Civic Capacity in Communities Across the Globe.* Cambridge, MA: MIT Press, 2008.

–––. "Social Capital and the Cities: Advice to Change Agents." *The National Civic Review* 86, no. 2 (Summer 1997):111-117.

Brynjolfsson, Erik and Andrew Mcafee. *The Second Machine Age: Work, Progress, and Prosperity in a Time of Brilliant Technologies.* New York: WW Norton & Company Inc., 2014.

Campbell, Lorna and Lis Wagner. "As long as possible in one's own life – sub-project: Home-rehabilitation." Why was this example implemented?, *INTERLINKS*, http://interlinks.euro.centre.org/model/example/AsLong AsPossibleInOnesOwnLife_SubProjectHomeRehabilitation (accessed June 6, 2016).

Champlain Complex Care Program. "Champlain Complex Care Newsletter Winter 2014/15." *Champlain Complex Care Program.* December, 2014. http://www.cheo.on.ca/en/Champlain-complex-care (accessed August 12, 2016).

Children's Hospital of Eastern Ontario (CHEO). "CHEO gives patients online access to their hospital records – anytime, anywhere." Newsroom, *CHEO.* November 28, 2016. http://www.cheo.on.ca/en/newsroom?newsid=693 (accessed November 30, 2016).

–––. "Unique pilot program to help families of kids with most complex medical needs." Newsroom, *CHEO.* July 17, 2015. http://www.cheo. on.ca/en/news-room?newsid=593 (accessed August 12, 2016).

Christiansen, Jesper. *The Irrealities of Public Administration.* Denmark: Mindlab, 2013.

Christiansen, Jesper and Laura Bunt. *Innovation in policy: allowing for creativity, social complexity and uncertainty in public governance.* London: MindLab, 2012.

Chua, Chin Kiat. *The Making of Captains of Lives: Prison Reform in Singapore 1999 to 2007.* Singapore: World Scientific Publishing Co. Pte. Ltd, 2012.

Clark, Ian D., Ben Eisen, Mary Catharine Lennon and Leslie A. Pal. "Mapping the Topics and Learning Outcomes of a Core Curriculum for MPP and MPA Programs." A Paper for the Annual CAPPA Conference Glendon College, Toronto, May 25-26, 2015. http://www.glendon.yorku. ca/cappa2015/wp-content/uploads/sites/22/Mapping_the_Topics_ aPresentation-Clark-eisen-Lennon-Pal-NEW-27may.pdf (accessed August 11, 2016).

Clark, I. D., B. Eisen and L.A. Pal. "What are the core curricular components of Master's-level public management education and how is learning within them assessed?" Paper presented at the 3rd Annual CAPPA Research Conference, Kingston, Canada, May 21-22, 2014. http://portal. publicpolicy.utoronto.ca/en/BestPractices/Documents/What_Are_ Core_Cur ricular_Components_21May2014.pdf (accessed August 11, 2016).

Clark, I. D. and L. A. Pal. "Academic Respectability Meets Professional Utility: Canadian MPA/MPP Programs and Professional Competencies." A report originally commissioned by the Canadian Association of Programs in Public Administration, 2011. https://portal.publicpolicy.

utoronto.ca/en/BestPractices/Documents/AcademicRespectability MeetsProfessionalUtility21Nov2011.pdf. (accessed August 11, 2016).

Cleaning Day. "Basics of Cleaning Day." How Can I Join, *Cleaning Day.* http://siivouspaiva.com/en/info/basics-of-cleaning-day (accessed June 6, 2016).

Cleaning Day. "Cleaning Day changes the whole Finland into a huge flea market on Saturday 28th of May." Press Release, *Cleaning Day.* May 3, 2016. http://siivouspaiva.s3.amazonaws.com/2016/05/03/08/59/04/380/ pressrelease_28.5docx.docx (accessed May 16, 2016).

Cleaning Day Japan. "Cleaning Day Japan." Cleaning Day Japan, *Facebook.* June 2, 2016. https://www.facebook.com/cleaningdayjp (accessed June 7, 2016).

Cleaning Day. "Cleaning Day." *Siivouspäivä.* http://siivouspaiva.com/en (accessed June 6, 2016).

Commission on the Reform of Ontario's Public Services. *Public Services for Ontarians: A Path to Sustainability and Excellence.* Ontario: Queen's Printer for Ontario, 2012.

Constine, Josh and Kim-Mai Cutler. "Facebook Buys Instagram For $1 Billion, Turns Budding Rival Into Its Standalone Photo App." *Techcrunch. com.* April 9, 2012. http://techcrunch.com/2012/04/09/facebook-to-acquire-instagram-for-1-billion/ (accessed April 5, 2016).

Council for Science and Technology. *Improving Innovation in the Water Industry: 21st Century Challenges and Opportunities.* London: Council for Science and Technology, 2009.

Cricks, Bernard. *In Defense of Politics.* London: Bloomsbury Publishing Plc, 2013.

Crook, Jordan. "Instagram Crosses 130 Million Users, With 16 Billion Photos and Over 1 Billion Likes Per Day." *Techcrunch.com.* June 20, 2013. http://techcrunch.com/2013/06/20/instagram-crosses-130-million-users-with-16-billion-photos-and-over-1-billion-likes-per-day/ (accessed April 5, 2016).

Crosby, B.C. and J.M. Bryson. *Leadership for the Common Good: Tackling Public Problems in a Shared-powered World.* Second Edition. San Francisco: Jossey-Bass, 2005.

Crouch, Colin. *Post-Democracy.* UK: Polity, 2004.

Dahl, Robert. *Who Governs?: Democracy and Power in an American City.* New Haven: Yale University Press, 1961.

Dale, Ann and Jenny Onyx. *A Dynamic Balance: Social Capital and Sustainable Community Development*. Vancouver: UBC Press, 2005.

Denhardt, Robert B., and Janet Vinzant Denhardt. "The New Public Service: Serving Rather than Steering." *Public Administration Review* 60, no. 6 (2000): 549-559.

Directorate-General for Regional and Urban Policy, European Commission. *Guide to Social Innovation*. Brussels: European Commission, 2013.

Douthat, Ross. "ISIS in the 21st Century." *New York Times*. August 24, 2014. http://www.nytimes.com/2014/08/24/opinion/sunday/ross-douthat-isis-in-the-21st-century/ (accessed April 6, 2016).

Dychtwald, Ken. "Maturity Reimagined." Speech at the 2015 Annual Conference of the American Society on Aging, Los Angeles, CA. March 23, 2015.

Envision Charlotte. "About Envision Buildings." *Envision: Charlotte*. http://envisioncharlotte.com/about/envision-buildings/(accessed August 12, 2015).

———. *Envision Charlotte Project: 2016 Building Technologies Office Peer Review*. USA: Office of Energy Efficiency and Renewable Energy – Department of Energy, 2016.

European Commission. *2015 Strategic Social Reporting Questionnaire – Denmark*. Luxembourg: Publications Office of the European Union, 2015.

———. *Powering European Public Sector Innovation: Towards A New Architecture Report of the Expert Group on Public Sector Innovation*. Luxembourg: Publications Office of the European Union, 2013.

Feudtner, Chris, Ross M. Hays, Gerri Haynes, J. Russell Geyer, John M. Neff and Thomas D. Koepsell. "Deaths attributed to pediatric complex chronic conditions: National trends and implications for supportive care services." *Pediatrics* 107, no. 6 (2001): E99.

Follett, Mary Parker. *The New State: Group Organization – The Solution of Popular Government*. Pennysylvania: The Pennsylvania State University, 2009.

Fonseca, Maria Goretti P. and Francisco I. Bastos. "Twenty-five years of the AIDS epidemic in Brazil: principal epidemiological findings, 1980-2005." *Cadernos de Saúde Pública* 27, sup 3 (2007): S333-S344.

Fraser, Steve. "Liberalism Is Under Attack From the Left and the Right." *The Nation*. June 2, 2016. https://www.thenation.com/article/liberalism-is-under-attack-from-the-left-and-the-right/ (accessed August 5, 2016).

Freeman, Chris. "The 'National System of Innovation' in historical perspective." *Cambridge Journal of Economics* 19, no. 1 (1995): 5-24.

Friedman, Thomas L. "Order vs. Disorder, Part 3." *New York Times*. August 23, 2014. http://www.nytimes.com/2014/08/24/opinion/sunday/thomas-l-friedman-order-vs-disorder-part-3.html?_r=0 (accessed April 5, 2016).

–––. "Takin' It to the Street." *New York Times*. June 29, 2013. http://www.nytimes.com/2013/06/30/opinion/sunday/takin-it-to-the-streets.html (accessed April 5, 2016).

Fukuyama, Francis. *Political Order and Political Decay: From the Industrial Revolution to the Globalisation of Democracy*. New York: Farrar, Straus & Giroux, 2014.

Fung, Archon and Erik Olin Wright. *Deepening Democracy: Institutional Innovations in Empowered Participatory Governance*. London: Verso, 2003.

Ganz, Marshall. "Public Narrative, Collective Action, and Power." In *Accountability through Public Opinion: From Inertia to Public Action*, edited by Marshal Ganz, Chapter 18: 273-289. Washington, DC: World Bank, May 2011.

Goldewijk, Klein, K., A. Beusen, M. de Vos and G. van Drecht. "The HYDE 3.1 spatially explicit database of human induced land use change over the past 12,000 years." *Global Ecology and Biogeography* 20, no. 1 (2011): 73-86.

Goodwin, Tom. "The Battle Is For The Customer Interface." *Techcrunch.com*. March 3, 2015. http://techcrunch.com/2015/03/03/in-the-age-of-disintermediation-the-battle-is-all-for-the-customer-interface/ (accessed April 5, 2016).

Green New Deal. "Cleaning Day in Finland: sustainable consumption and a sense of community." *Green New Deal*. October 11, 2014. http://greennewdeal.eu/jobs-and-society/successes/cleaning-day-in-finland-sustainable-consumption-and-a-sense-of-community.html (accessed June 7, 2016).

Guterman, Neil B. "Early Prevention of Physical Child Abuse and Neglect: Existing Evidence and Future Directions." *Child Maltreatment* 2, no. 1 (1997): 12-34.

Gwee, June, ed. *Case Studies: Building Communities in Singapore*. Singapore: Civil Service College of Singapore, 2015.

Haasnoot, Marjolijn, Jan H. Kwakkel, Warren E. Walker and Judith ter Maat. "Dynamic adaptive policy pathways: A method for crafting robust decisions for a deeply uncertain world." *Global Environmental Change* 23, no. 2 (2013): 485–498.

Hagel III, John. "Edge Perspectives with John Hagel: The Untapped Potential of Corporate Narratives." *Edge Perspectives with John Hagel*. October 7, 2013. http://edgeperspectives.typepad.com/edge_perspectives/2013/10/the-untapped-potential-of-corporate-narratives.html (accessed November 25, 2015).

Halpern, David. *The Hidden Wealth of Nations*. United Kingdom: Polity Press, 2009.

Harris, John and Vicky White. *A Dictionary of Social Work and Social Care*. Oxford: Oxford University Press, 2013.

Heater, Derek. *Citizenship: The Civic Ideal in World History, Politics and Education*. Third Edition. Manchester: Manchester University Press, 2004.

Heath, Joseph. *Enlightenment 2.0*. Toronto: Harper Collins Publishers, 2014.

Heebøll, Karen. *Life Long Living Maintaining Everyday Life as Long as Possible*. PowerPoint presented at the Opening Conference for the European Year for Active Aging and Solidarity between Generations 2012: Staying Active – What does it Take?. http://www.slideserve.com/quito/life-long-living-maintaining-everyday-life-as-long-as-possible (accessed May 11, 2016).

Heifetz, Ronald, Alexander Grashow and Marty Linsky. *The Practice of Adaptive Leadership*. Cambridge: Harvard Business Press, 2009.

Helliwell, John F. "Well-Being, Social Capital and Public Policy: What's New?" *NBER Working Paper series w11807*. Cambridge, MA: The National Bureau of Economic Research, 2005.

Helliwell, John and Robert Putnam. "The Social Context of Well-Being." *Philosophical Transactions of the Royal Society of London* B 359, no. 1449 (2004): 1435-46.

Horelli, Liisa, Joanna Saad-Sulonen, Sirkku Wallin and Andrea Botero. "When Self-Organization Intersects with Urban Planning: Two Cases from Helsinki." *Planning Practice & Research* 30, no. 3, 16 pages (2015).

Hodgson, Geoffrey M. "What are Institutions?" *Journal of Economic Issues* 40, no. 1 (2006): 1-25.

Homer-Dixion, Thomas. *Complexity Science and Public Policy: IPAC New Directions Series.* Toronto: The Institute of Public Administration of Canada, 2010.

Hou, Yilin, Anna Ya Ni, Ora-orn Poocharoen, Kaifeng Yang and Zhirong J. Zhao. "The Case for Public Administration with Global Perspective." Special issue, *Journal of Public Administration Research and Theory* 21, supplement 1(2011): i45-51.

Huntington, Samuel P. "Will More Countries Become Democratic?" *Political Science Quarterly* 131, no. 2 (2016):237-266.

--. *Political Order in Changing Societies.* New Haven and London: Yale University Press, 1968.

iamsterdam. "King's Day street markets." *iamsterdam.* http://www.iamsterdam.com/en/visiting/whats-on/kings-day/whats-on/kings-day-street-markets (accessed June 7, 2016).

Joint United Nations Programme on HIV/AIDS (UNAIDS). *The Gap Report.* Geneva: UNAIDS, 2014.

Judt, Tony. *Ill Fares the Land.* New York: Penguin Books, 2011.

Jütte, Sonja, Holly Bentley, Pam Miller and Natasha Jetha. *How Safe Are Our Children?* London: National Society for the Prevention of Cruelty to Children, 2014. https://www.nspcc.org.uk/globalassets/documents/research-reports/how-safe-children-2014-report.pdf (accessed February 12, 2016).

Kagan, Robert and Ivo Daalder. "The U.S. can't afford to end its global leadership role." *Brookings.* April 25, 2016. https://www.brookings.edu/2016/04/25/the-u-s-cant-afford-to-end-its-global-leadership-role/ (accessed August 5, 2016).

Kelman, Steven. "The 'Kennedy School School' of Research on Innovation in Government." In *Innovations in Government: Research, Recognition, and Replication,* edited by Sandford Borins, 28-51. Washington, D.C.: Brookings Institute Press, 2008.

Kelman, S., F. Thompson, L.R. Jones and K. Schedler. "Dialogue on definition and evolution of the field of Public Management." *International Public Management Review* 4, no. 2 (2003):1-19.

Kettl, Donald F. and James W. Fesler. *The Politics of the Administrative Process*. Washington, DC: CQ Press, 2011.

Kettl, Donald F. *The Transformation of Governance: Public Administration for the Twenty-First Century*, Updated Hopkins University Press, 2015.

———. *The Transformation of Governance: Public Administration for Twenty-First Century America*. Baltimore: John Hopkins University Press, 2002.

———. "Public Administration at the Millennium: The State of the Field." *Journal of Public Administration Research and Theory* 10, no. 1 (2000): 7-34.

Klausen, Kurt Klaudi. "Still the century of government? No signs of governance yet!" *International Public Management Review* 15, no. 1 (2014): 1-16.

———. "Ambient Assisted Living: How Fredericia Municipality Reinvented Itself and Became Innovative." In *Public Management in the Twenty-First Century*, edited by Tor Busch, Alexander Heichlinger, Erik Johnsen, Kurt Klaudi Klausen, Alex Murdock and Jan Ole Vanebo, Chapter 10: 128-134. Olso: Universitetsforlaget AS, 2013.

Kostakopoulou, Dora. *The Future Governance of Citizenship*. Cambridge: Cambridge University Press, 2008.

KPMG LLP. *SickKids Socio-Economic Impact Study*. Amstelveen: KPMG LLP, 2012: 1-148. https://www.sickkids.ca/pdfs/About-SickKids/51294-Project%20Impact%20-%20Final%20Report%20-%20Sept%207%20 2012.pdf (accessed August 17, 2016).

Kurlantzick, Joshua. *Democracy in Retreat: The Revolt of the Middle Class and the Worldwide Decline of Representative Government*. New Haven: Yale University Press, 2013.

Lazonick, William. *Sustainable Prosperity in the New Economy?: Business Organization and High-Tech Employment in the United States*. Michigan: W E Upjohn Institute for Employment Research, 2009.

———. "The US stock market and the governance of innovative enterprise." *Industrial and Corporate Change* 16, no. 6 (2007): 983-1035.

Lazonick, William and Mariana Mazzucato. "The Risk-Reward Nexus in the Innovation-Inequality Relationship." *Industrial and Corporate Change* 22, no. 4 (2013): 1093-1128.

Leong, Lena. "Towards a Society without Re-offending." In *Case Studies: Building Communities in Singapore*, edited by June Gwee, 11-38. Singapore: Civil Service College, Singapore, 2015.

Linden, R.M. *Working across boundaries: Making collaboration work in government and non-profit organizations*. San Francisco: Jossey-Bass, 2002.

Lipset, Seymour Martin. "Some Social Requisites of Democracy: Economic Development and Political Legitimacy." *American Political Science Review* 53, no. 1 (1959):69-105.

Locke, Richard M. and Rachel Wellhausen, *ed. A Preview of the MIT Production in the Innovation Economy Report*. Cambridge, Massachusetts: Massachusetts Institute of Technology, 2013.

Loeffler, Elke, Shaundra Ridha and Nathalie Cook-Major. "A partnership model for children with complex medical conditions: The Champlain Complex Care Programme in Canada." *Governance International*. December 3, 2013. http://www.govint.org/good-practice/case-studies/a-partnership-model-for-children-with-complex-medical-conditions (accessed July 2, 2016).

Luke, Jeffrey S. *Catalytic Leadership: Strategies for an Interconnected World*. San Francisco: Jossey-Bass Inc., 1998.

Lydon, Mary, Jeremy Woolley, Martin Small, James Harrison, Trevor Bailey and Daniel Searson. "Review of the National Road Safety Strategy." *Austroads*. Sydney: Austroads Ltd., 2015.

Manz, C.C., V. Anand, M. Joshi and K.P. Manz. "Emerging Paradoxes in Executive Leadership: A Theoretical Interpretation of the Tensions Between Corruption and Virtuous Values." *Leadership Quarterly* 19, no.3 (2008):385-392.

Marabelli, Marco, Sue Newell and Janis Gogan. "Pilot-testing a pediatric complex care coordination service." *Journal of Information Technology Teaching Cases* 6, no. 1 (2016): 45-55.

Markowitz, Harry M. and Kenneth Blay. *Risk-Return Analysis: The Theory and Practice of Rational Investing*. New York: McGraw-Hill Education, 2013.

Mazzucato, Mariana and Michael Jacobs, ed. *Rethinking Capitalism: Economics and Policy for Sustainable and Inclusive Growth*. UK: Wiley-Blackwell, 2016.

Mazzucato, Mariana. *The Entrepreneurial State: Debunking Public vs. Private Sector Myths.* London: Anthem Press, 2014.

McGinn, Lindsay. *Don't Move Me There! Promoting Autonomy in the Provision of Long-term Care for Seniors in Canada.* Ottawa: University of Ottawa, 2015.

MDG Monitor. "MDG 1: Eradicate Extreme Poverty and Hunger."*MDG Monitor.* September 14, 2016. http://www.mdgmonitor.org/mdg-1-eradicate-poverty-hunger/ (accessed August 18, 2016).

Mendoza, Xavier and Alfred Vernis. "The Changing Role of Governments and the Emergence of the Relational State." *Corporate Governance* 8, no. 4 (2008): 389-396.

Merkel, Wolfgang. "Is capitalism compatible with democracy?" Z Vgl *Polit Wiss/Comparative Governance and Politics 8, no. 2* (July 2014):109-128. https://www.researchgate.net/publication/267318219_Is_capitalism_compatible_with_democracy (accessed September 8, 2016).

Menzel. D.C., *Ethics Management for Public Administrators: Building Organizations of Integrity.* Armonk, NY: M.E.Sharpe, 2007.

Milward, Brint, Laura Jensen, Alasdair Roberts, Mauricio I. Dussauge-Laguna, Veronica Junjan, René Torenvlied, Arjen Bion, H.K. Colebatch, Donald Kettl and Robert Durant. "Roundtable – Is Public Management Neglecting the State?" *Governance: An International Journal of Policy, Administrations and Institutions* 29, no. 3 (July 2016): 311-334.

Mitchell, Timothy. "The Limits of the State: Beyond Statist Approach and their Critics." *The American Political Science Review* 85, no. 1 (1991): 77-96.

Morris, Ian. *Why the West Rules – For Now: The Patterns of History, and What They Reveal About the Future.* New York: Farrar, Straus and Giroux, 2010.

––––. *Social Development.* Stanford: Self-Published, 2010.

Morse, Ricardo S. "Integrative public leadership: catalysing collaboration to create public value." *The Leadership Quarterly* 21, no. 2 (2010):231-245.

Morse, Ricardo S. and Terry F. Buss. "The Transformation of Public Leadership." In

Transforming Public Leadership for the 21st Century, edited by Ricardo S. Morse, Terry F. Buss, and C. Morgan Kinghorn, 3-20. London: Routledge, 2007.

Moynihan, Donald P. "The Response to Hurricane Katrina." In *Report on Risk Governance Deficits: An analysis and illustration of the most common deficits in risk governance*, 68-70. Geneva: International Risk Governance Council, 2009.

Moxley, Kathleen M., Jane Squires and Lauren Lindstrom. "Early Intervention and Maltreated Children: A Current Look at the Child Abuse Prevention and Treatment Act and Part C." *Infants and Young Children* 25, no. 1 (2011): 3-18.

Mulgan, Geoff. *Innovation in the Public Sector: How Can Public Organizations Better Create, Improve and Adapt*. UK: Nesta, 2014.

–––. *The Art of Public Strategy: Mobilizing Power and Knowledge for the Common Good*. New York: Oxford University Press, 2009.

–––. "Citizens and Responsibilities." In *Citizenship*, edited by Geoff Andrews, 37-49. London: Lawrence & Wishart Limited, 1991.

Municipality of Fredericia. "Life Long Living – maintaining independent living as long as possible EY2012 Award, 8-9." *Municipality of Fredericia*. https://www.fredericia.dk/LMIEL/presserum/Documents (accessed July 2, 2016).

–––. "Name of project: Life Long Living – maintaining independent living as long as possible." *Municipality of Fredericia*. https://www.fredericia. dk/LMIEL/presserum/Documents/Life%20Long%20Living%20 Fredericia%20dk%20EY2012%20award_16%2009%2012.pdf (accessed August 12, 2016).

Nair, Sreeja and Howlett, Michael P. *Dealing with the Likelihood of Failure Over the Long-Term: Adaptive Policy Design Under Uncertainty*. Singapore: Lee Kuan Yew School of Public Policy, 2014.

O'Neil, Brian. "Reorganizing Government: New Approaches to Public Service Reform." Back Ground Paper, *Library of Parliament*. January 1994. http://publications.gc.ca/Collection-R/LoPBdP/BP/bp375-e.htm (accessed AUGUST 16, 2016).

O'Shea, Patrick Gavan, Roseanne J. Foti, Neil M. A. Hauenstein and Peter Bycio. "Are the Best Leaders Both Transformational and Transactional? A Pattern Analysis." *Leadership* 5, no. 2 (2009): 237-259.

Organisation for Economic Co-operation and Development (OECD). *In It Together: Why Less Inequality Benefits All*. Paris: OECD, 2015.

–––. *Innovating the Public Sector: From Ideas to Impact*. Paris: OECD, 2014.

–––. Issues Paper on Corruption and Economic Growth. Paris: OECD, 2013.

———. *Divided We Stand: Why Inequality Keeps Rising*. Paris: OECD Publishing, 2011.

Ornstein, Norman J. and Thomas E. Mann. *The Permanent Campaign and its Future*. Washington D.C.: The American Enterpise Institute and The Brookings Institution, 2000.

Ostrom, Elinor. *"Crowding Out Citizenship."* Scandinavian Political Studies 23, no. 1 (2000): 3-16.

———. "Crossing the Great Divide: Co-production, Synergy, and Development." In State-Society *Synergy: Government and Social Capital in Development*, edited by Peter Evans, 85-118. Berkeley: University of California, 1997.

Ostrom V. and E. Ostrom. "Public Goods and Public Choices." In *Alternatives for Delivering Public Services: Toward Improved Performance*, edited by E.S. Savas, 7-49. Boulder, Colorado: Westview Press, 1977.

Otto, Shawn Lawrence. *The War on Science: Who's Waging It, Why It Matters, What We Can Do About It*. Minnesota: Milkweed Editions, 2016.

Our Singapore Conversation Secretariat. *Reflections of Our Singapore Conversation: What future do we want? How do we get there?* Singapore: Our Singapore Conversation Secretariat, 2013. https://www.reach.gov.sg/oursgconversation (accessed February 4, 2015).

Painter, J. "What Kind of Citizenship for What Kind of Community?" *Political Geography* 26, no. 2 (2007):221-24.

Palanski, M.E. and F.J. Yammarino. "Integrity and Leadership: A Multi-level Conceptual Framework." *Leadership Quarterly* 20, no.3 (2009):405-420.

Pierson, P. "Increasing Returns, Path Dependence, and the Study of Politics." *American Political Science Review* 94, no. 2 (2000): 251-267.

Pollitt, Christopher. *New Perspectives on Public Services: Places and Technology*. Oxford: Oxford University Press, 2012.

———. "Envisioning Public Administration as a Scholarly Field in 2020." *Public Administration Review* 70, s. 1 (2010): 292-294.

———. *Time, Policy, Management: Governing with the Past*. Oxford: Oxford University Press, 2008.

Pollitt, Christopher and Liesbeth Op de Beeck. *Training Top Civil Servants: A Comparative Analysis*. KU Leuven, Belgium: Public Governance Institute, 2010.

Poushter, Jacob. *Smartphone Ownership and Internet Usage Continues to Climb in Emerging*

Economies. Washington D.C.: Pew Research Centre, 2016.

Public Governance International. "HIV/AIDS in Brazil." NS World: Practice by Country-Brazil, *Public Governance International*. http://www.pgionline.com/hivaids-in-brazil/ (accessed July 5, 2016).

———. "Technology Enabled Fishery Compliance in New Zealand." NS World: Practice by Country-New Zealand, *Public Governance International*. http://www.pgionline.com/technology-enabled-fishery-compliance-in-new-zealand/ (accessed July 5, 2016).

Public Works Department – Customer Services. "Restaurant Day and Cleaning Day." *City of Helsinki Public Works Department*. October 20, 2015. http://www.hel.fi/www/hkr/en/permits/events_promotions/restaurant_day (accessed July 4, 2016).

Puddington, Arch and Tyler Roylance. "Anxious Dictators, Wavering Democracies: Global Freedom under Pressure – Freedom in the World 2016." *Freedom House*, 2016. https://freedomhouse.org/sites/default/files/FH_FITW_Report_2016.pdf (accessed September 8, 2016.

Raadschelders, Jos C.N. "The Future of the Study of Public Administration: Embedding Research Object and Methodology in Epistemology and Ontology." *Public Administration Review* 71, no. 6 (November/December 2011): 916-924.

———. "A Coherent Framework for the Study of Public Administration." *Journal of Public Administration Research and Theory* 9, no. 2 (1999): 281-303.

Reinhart, Carmen M. and Kenneth S. Rogoff. "This Time is Different: A Panoramic View of Eight Centuries of Financial Crises." *National Bureau of Economic Research Working Paper 13882* (March 2008). http://www.nber.org/papers/w13882.pdf (accessed September 8, 2016).

Salamon, Lester M. *The Tools of Government: A Guide to the New Governance*. New York: Oxford University Press, 2002.

Saward, Michael. "Democracy and Citizenship: Expanding Domains." In *The Oxford Handbook of Political Theory*, edited by John Dryzek, Bonnie Honig and Anne Phillips, 400-419. Oxford: Oxford University Press, 2006.

Schwab, Klaus. "The Fourth Industrial Revolution: what it means, how to respond." *World Economic Forum*. January 14, 2016. https://www.weforum.org/agenda/2016/01/the-fourth-industrial-revolution-what-it-means-and-how-to-respond/(accessed August 10, 2016).

Seppälä, Pauliina. "Tiny Social Movements: Experiences of Social Media Based Co-Creation." In *Towards Peer Production in Public Services: Cases from Finland,* edited by Andrea Botero, Andrew Gryf Paterson and Joanna Saad-Sulonen, 62-75. Helsinki: Aalto University, 2012.

SIGVARIS. "What is compression therapy?" *SIGVARIS.* 2015. http://www.sigvaris.com/ca/en-ca/knowledge (accessed June 6, 2016).

Singapore Prison Service. "School First, Prison Second. Kaki Bukit Centre Prison School." Internal documentation.

———. "The Visioning Exercise." Internal documentation.

———. *The Courage to Believe: Unlocking Life's Second Chances.* Singapore: Singapore Prison Service, 2013.

Sirianni, Carmen. "The Networks of Self-Governance." *Democracy: A Journal of Ideas.* Spring 2012, no. 24. http://democracyjournal.org/magazine/24/the-networks-of-self-governance/(accessed July 20, 2016).

Sirianni, Carmen and Lewis Friedland. "Civic Innovation and American Democracy." *Change* 29, no. 1(January/February 1997):14-23.

Solholm, Roar, John Kjøbli and Terje Christiansen. "Early Initiatives for Children at Risk —Development of a Program for the Prevention and Treatment of Behavior Problems in Primary Services." *Prevention Science* 14, no. 6 (2013): 535-544.

Sørensen, Eva and Jacob Torfing. "Enhancing Collaborative Innovation in the Public Sector." *Administration & Society* 43, no. 8 (2011): 842-868.

Stafford, Anne, Nigel Parton, Sharon Vincent and Connie Smith. *Child Protection Systems in the United Kingdom: A Comparative Analysis.* London: Jessica Kingsley Publishers, 2012.

Stanley, Tim and Alexander Lee. "Its Still Not the End of History." *The Atlantic.* September 1, 2014. http://www.theatlantic.com/politics/archive/2014/09/its-still-not-the-end-of-history-francis-fukuyama/379394/ (accessed September 9, 2016).

Stiglitz, Joseph E. *The Euro: How a Common Currency Threatens the Future of Europe.* New York: W.W. Norton & Company Inc., 2016.

———.*The Great Divide: Unequal Societies And What We Can Do About Them.* New York: W.W. Norton & Company Inc., 2015.

———. "Inequality is not inevitable." *New York Times.* June 27, 2014. http://opinionator.blogs.nytimes.com/2014/06/27/inequality-is-not-inevitable/ (accessed April 5, 2016).

Stunden, Shannon Bower and David Campanella. *From Bad to Worse: Residential Elder Care in Alberta*. Edmonton: Parkland Institute, 2013.

'T Hart, Paul. *Understanding Public Leadership*. London: Palgrave, 2014.

The Brunei Times. "More than 80% of Sarawak still covered by forest: Awang Tengah." *The Brunei Times*. March 28, 2013. http://www.bt.com.bn/2013/03/28/more-80-sarawak-still-covered-forest-awang-tengah (accessed April 5, 2016).

Tholstrup, Jörgen. "Empowering Patients to Need Less Care and do better in Highland Hospital, South Sweden." Good Practices Case Studies, *Governance International*. March 30, 2010. http://www.govint.org/good-practice/case-studies/empowering-patients-to-need-less-care-and-do-better-in-highland-hospital-south-sweden/ (accessed March 25, 2015).

Uhl-Bien, Mary, Russ Marion and Bill McKelvey. "Complexity Leadership Theory: Shifting leadership from the industrial age to the knowledge era." *The Leadership Quarterly* 18, no. 4 (2007): 298-318.

United Nations High Commissioner for Refugees (UNHCR). *World at War: UNHCR Global Trends – Global Forced Displacements 2014*. Geneva, Switzerland: UNHCR, 2015.

Vallas, S. P., Daniel L. Kleinman and Dina Biscotti. "Political Structures and the Making of U.S. Biotechnology." In *State of Innovation: The U.S. Government's Role in Technology Development*, edited by Fred Block and Matthew R. Keller, Chapter 3: 57-76. Boulder, Colorado: Paradigm, 2011.

Van der Waldt, Gerrit. "A Unified Public Administration? Prospects of constructing a grand, unifying theory for the field." Paper Presented at the International Association of Schools and Institutions of Administration (IASIA) Conference from 6-10 July 2015, Paris, France.

Van Wart, Montgomery. "Lessons from Leadership Theory and the Contemporary Challenges of Leaders." *Public Administration Review* 73, no. 4 (2013): 553–565.

–––. *Dynamics of Leadership in Public Service: Theory and Practice*. New York: M.E. Sharp, 2011.

Visit Helsinki. "Cleaning Day 27.8." *Visit Helsinki*. May 31, 2016. http://www.visithelsinki.fi/en/whats-on/events-in-helsinki/cleaning-day-278 (accessed June 7, 2016).

Wagner, E. H., C. Davis, J. Schaefer, M. Von Korff and B. Austin. "A Survey of Leading Chronic Disease Management Programs: Are They Consistent with the Literature?" *Managed Care Quarterly* 7, no. 3 (1999):56-66.

Weber, Max. "Politics as a Vocation." In *From Max Weber: Essays in Sociology*, translated by H.H. Gerth and C. Wright Mills, 77-128. New York: Oxford University Press, 1946.

Weinstock, Daniel. "Citizenship and Pluralism." In *The Blackwell Guide to Social and Political Philosophy*, edited by Robert L. Simon, Chapter 11: 239-270. Massachusetts, USA: Blackwell Publishers, 2002.

Welfare Policy Division, Seoul Metropolitan Government. "The Universal Welfare Standards enabled by and for the Citizens of Seoul (Seoul Welfare Standards)." *United Nations Public Administration Network*. 2012. http://unpan3.un.org/unpsa/Public_NominationProfile.aspx?id=1962 (accessed September 18, 2014).

Westley, Frances, Brenda Zimmerman and Michael Patton. *Getting to Maybe: How the World is Changed*. Toronto: Random House Canada, 2006.

Wilson, Woodrow. "The Study of Administration." *Political Science Quarterly* 2, no. 2 (1887): 197-222.

World Health Organisation. *The World Health Report 2004: Changing History*. Geneva:

World Health Organisation, 2004.

World Resources Report (WRR). *Decision Making in a Changing Climate*. Washington DC: World Resources Institute, 2011.

Yarwood, Richard. *Citizenship*. New York: Routledge, 2014.

INDEX

ABOUT THE AUTHOR

Jocelyn Bourgon – President of Public Governance International (PGI) and project leader of the New Synthesis Initiative; an international collaborative research effort aimed at exploring the new frontiers of public administration. Former Clerk of the Privy Council and Secretary to the Cabinet of Canada, she served as Deputy Minister of several major departments including Transport, the Canadian International Development Agency and Consumer and Corporate Affairs. Jocelyne Bourgon has also served as President of a UN Committee of Experts in Public Administration and governance, president of the Commonwealth Association for Public Administration and Management (CAPAM) and Canada's Ambassador to the Organisation for Economic Co-operation and Development (OECD). She is the author of *A New Synthesis of Public Administration: Serving in the 21st Century* (2011).